— ★ 职场红人系列 ★ —

警官实用英语口语

李桂芝/编著 （美）Lucky Lin/英文审校

PRACTICAL
Oral English for Police Officers

机械工业出版社
CHINA MACHINE PRESS

本书内容丰富，共分二十个单元，既有以公安工作为背景的介绍与寒暄、指路与问路、救助、报失与招领、电话交流等迎来送往服务性英语口语，又有社区警务、各种涉外案件、事件处理等执法用英语口语。每篇课文分为生词与词组、常用句型、情景对话和创造性练习四个部分，以朗读、视译、创造性练习为训练顺序。

本书贴近涉外警务实践；形式新颖，练习的安排易于操作，是公安院校在校学生和一线警察必备的警务英语工具书。

图书在版编目（CIP）数据

警官实用英语口语 / 李桂芝编著. —北京：机械工业出版社，2020.12
ISBN 978－7－111－67226－5

Ⅰ.①警… Ⅱ.①李… Ⅲ.①公安工作-英语-口语 Ⅳ.①D631

中国版本图书馆 CIP 数据核字（2021）第 002326 号

机械工业出版社（北京市百万庄大街 22 号　邮政编码 100037）
策划编辑：孙铁军　　　　　　责任编辑：孙铁军　张晓娟
责任校对：苏筛琴　　　　　　责任印制：李　昂
北京联兴盛业印刷股份有限公司印刷

2021 年 8 月第 1 版·第 1 次印刷
169mm×239mm·18.25 印张·320 千字
标准书号：ISBN 978－7－111－67226－5
定价：49.80 元

电话服务　　　　　　　　　网络服务
客服电话：010-88361066　　机　工　官　网：www.cmpbook.com
　　　　　010-88379833　　机　工　官　博：weibo.com/cmp1952
　　　　　010-68326294　　金　书　网：www.golden-book.com
封底无防伪标均为盗版　　　机工教育服务网：www.cmpedu.com

前言

随着世界经济全球化、社会信息化的深度发展，特别是中国对外开放程度越来越深入，参与国际交往越来越多，中国已成为国际交往的重要舞台。在华外国人数量越来越多，从而要求我国警察不断创新外国人入出境管理的方法和手段、提升对在华外国人的管理与服务水平、提高涉外案（事）件处置能力、丰富国际警务交流合作的形式，这些势必对公安民警的英语水平提出更高要求。根据我国法律规定，公安机关处理涉外案件时应当使用我国通用的语言文字，但应当为不通晓我国语言文字的外国人提供翻译。从一线警务工作的实践经验可知，公安机关处理日常警务不可能时刻配备英文翻译，虽然在询问、讯问外国人等重要涉外警务工作中聘请了翻译，但有时翻译人员无法及时到达办案现场，有时翻译不熟悉法律、警务方面知识，这些都会影响涉外案件的办理效率和对涉外人员询问或讯问的预期效果，因此，我国公安工作急需大量既熟悉警务专业知识，又能熟练运用外语特别是英语的国际化警务执法人才。为了满足这一需求，帮助我国警察提升警务英语口语能力，《警官实用英语口语》应运而生。

本书根据当今涉外警务工作特点和实际需要编写而成，共有二十个单元，每个单元均有生词与词组、常用句型、情景对话、创造性练习等四个部分。本书选择的涉外警务场景丰富多样，既有介绍寒暄、电话交流、救助、社区警务、外国人入出境管理等服务和管理中的日常用语，又有处置"三非"案件、涉外治安案件、涉外交通违法案件、涉外毒品案件、涉外网络案件等警务执法用语。本书贴近实际、实用性强，以最新的法律法规为办案依据，选用贴近真实涉外警务的语言情景，帮助学习者在语言技能训练的同时，提高警务执法实践能力，能够做到学用结合、以学促用。本书可以作为公安院校警务英语口语课堂教材，也可以作为公安民警在职培训或自学教材，还可以作为公安院校在校学员和一线民警的英语口语学习参考书。

在本书编写过程中，编者借鉴了中国人民公安大学刘振江教授编写同类书籍的架构设计和编写思路，并得到了中国人民公安大学陈素媛教授和袁家韵老师的热心帮助和指导支持，特别是美国伊利诺伊中心学院（ICC）教授 Lucky Lin 对本书英文做了认真的校对修改，从而保证了英语的准确地道，在此表示衷心的感谢。中国人民公安大学张惠德教授、山东警察学院亓伟伟老师、南京市公安局交警支队葛道风警官、南京市公安局江宁分局交警大队圣钱生警官、中山市公安局东区分局刑侦大队周立明警官、上海市公安局刑事侦查总队夏格警官等均从公安业务角度给予了具体指导，机械工业出版社孙铁军编辑提供了鼎力帮助，在此一并表示真诚的谢意！此外，编者还广泛搜集网络资料，并借鉴了国内同行的相关研究成果。

由于编者水平有限，书中疏漏之处在所难免，恳请同行专家和广大读者批评指正。

编者
2021 年 8 月

目 录

前言

| Unit 1 | Introductions and Greetings
介绍与寒暄 ·· 001

| Unit 2 | Telephone Calls
电话交流 ·· 010

| Unit 3 | Giving and Asking for Directions
指路与问路 ·· 019

| Unit 4 | Rescue Operations
救助 ·· 026

| Unit 5 | Handling Reports
接警 ·· 038

| Unit 6 | Lost and Found
受理报失与失物招领 ·· 045

| Unit 7 | Security Inspection
安全检查 ·· 056

| Unit 8 | Police Patrol and Traffic Stops
巡逻与盘查 ·· 065

| Unit 9 | Traffic Directions and Control
道路交通秩序管理 ··· 074

| Unit 10 | Community Policing Management Involving Foreigners
涉外社区警务管理·· 082

| Unit 11 | Administration of the Foreigner's Entry and Exit
外国人入出境管理·· 094

| Unit 12 | Handling Cases of Illegal Immigration
外国人"三非"案件处置·· 102

| Unit 13 | Handling Public Security Cases Involving Foreigners
涉外治安案件查处·· 113

| Unit 14 | Dealing with Traffic Violations and Accidents Involving Foreigners
涉外道路交通违法行为和交通事故处理························ 132

| Unit 15 | Handling Other Administrative Cases Involving Foreigners
其他涉外行政案件查处·· 142

| Unit 16 | Handling Drug-related Crime Cases Involving Foreigners
涉外毒品案件查处·· 148

| Unit 17 | Handling Cyber Crimes Involving Foreigners
涉外网络犯罪案件查处·· 164

| Unit 18 | Handling Other Criminal Cases Involving Foreigners
其他涉外刑事案件处理·· 185

| Unit 19 | Handling Terrorist Attack
应对恐怖袭击·· 199

| Unit 20 | International Police Exchange and Cooperation
国际警务交流与合作·· 210

创造性练习参考答案·· 219
附录 I　常用警务英语词汇··· 242
附录 II　公安机关各级领导职务英文名称······························ 265

附录 III	涉外机构名称	266
附录 IV	服务设施名称	268
附录 V	中国警衔名称	269
附录 VI	应急电话	270
附录 VII	证件名称	271
附录 VIII	常用涉外法律法规名称	273
附录 IX	常见涉外处罚名称	275
附录 X	各国警察常用武器装备	276
附录 XI	国际刑警组织通报	279
参考文献		281

Unit 1
Introductions and Greetings
介绍与寒暄

Nowadays, Chinese police officers need to have the ability to introduce themselves and others in English appropriately and politely.

When we introduce ourselves on formal occasions, "May I introduce myself. My name is…", while on informal occasions, "Hello, I'm …" is good enough.

When being introduced to each other, usually the host (or the hostess), the man, the junior or the younger is introduced to the guest, the woman, the superior or the senior. When a couple is introduced, the husband is introduced before his wife.

When introducing Chinese colleagues or leaders to foreigners, the police officer should pay attention to the following. Firstly, such English titles as secretary, director, engineer, manager, master can't be used before the family name. For example, "This is Mr. Zhang, director of the municipality's public security bureau." is preferred. Secondly, in English speaking countries, married ladies usually use their husbands' family names, so when the wife of professor Deng is introduced, the correct way is to say "This is Mrs. Deng, wife of professor Deng." or "This is Ms/Ma'am Li, wife of Professor Deng."

When greeting each other after being introduced, people normally address each other Mr. (Mrs., Miss or Ms.) followed by their family names (Brown, Smith); it is considered too early to call the person by his or her given name only if you have first met. You may address a person only by his or her given name when you have become familiar with each other or you have got the person's permission.

当前，对于我国警察来说，能够用英语得体地自我介绍或介绍他人日显重要。

在正式场合下做自我介绍时，应该说："May I introduce myself. My name is..."，而在非正式场合下，通常用"Hello, I'm..."。

用英语为别人做相互介绍时，通常应首先将男主人（或女主人）、男子、地位低、年纪轻的介绍给客人、女子、地位高、年长者。如果介绍一对夫妇，先介绍丈夫，后介绍妻子。

此外，向外国朋友介绍中国同事或上级时，有两点值得注意：

1. 有些名称词在英语用法上不能直接用于姓氏前，如：secretary, director, engineer, manager, master 等，所以，如介绍说"这位是省厅张厅长"要说："This is Mr Zhang, director of the municipality's public security bureau."

2. 介绍已婚女士时，要考虑到西方人的习俗：女士婚后改用其丈夫姓，而我国女士婚后仍保持娘家姓氏。如介绍说："这位是邓教授的夫人。"可用"This is Mrs Deng, wife of Professor Deng."或"This is Ms/Ma'am Li, wife of Professor Deng."。

经过介绍彼此认识后相互寒暄时，应该用 Mr.（Mrs., Miss or Ms.）再加上姓（Brown, Smith）来称呼对方。初次见面直呼其名（John, Mary）会被认为太随便，更不能用 Mr.（Mrs., Miss or Ms.）加上名字（Mr. John, Mrs. Mary）称呼对方。熟识之后或者经对方允许后，才能直呼其名（John, Mary）。

Part I　New Words and Useful Expressions
生词与词组

comfortable　　　　英[ˈkʌmftəbl] 美[ˈkʌmfərtəbl] *adj.* 舒适的，舒服的

Commissioner　　　英[kəˈmɪʃənə(r)] 美[kəˈmɪʃənər] 警监

Commissioner Third Class 三级警监

Unit 1 Introductions and Greetings
介绍与寒暄

technician	英[tekˈnɪʃn] 美[tekˈnɪʃn]	n. 技术人员
conference	英[ˈkɒnfərəns] 美[ˈkɑːnfərəns]	n. 会议
scenic	英[ˈsiːnɪk] 美[ˈsinɪk]	adj. 风景优美的 n. 风景胜地

scenic spot 景点

delicious   英[dɪˈlɪʃəs] 美[dɪˈlɪʃəs] adj. 美味的，可口的

delegation 英[ˌdelɪˈɡeɪʃn] 美[ˌdelɪˈɡeɪʃn] n. 代表团

Provincial Public Security Department 省公安厅

on behalf of 代表

the Municipal Public Security Bureau 市公安局

deputy director of the bureau 公安局副局长

CUNY-John Jay College of Criminal Justice 纽约城市大学约翰杰刑事司法学院

a welcome board 接机牌

Part II Useful Sentence Patterns
常用句型

- Hello, Mr. Brown. I'm Ma Dong, an officer from Shaanxi Provincial Public Security Department.

  您好，布朗先生。我是陕西省公安厅民警，叫马东。

- I'm here to meet you on behalf of the department.

  我是代表省厅来接您的。

- Mr. France, this is Mr. Zhang, deputy director of the bureau.

  弗朗斯先生，这位是张先生，本市公安局副局长。

- Good morning, Mr. Franklin. Let me introduce Mr. Wang, general director of the Municipal Public Security Bureau, Commissioner Third Class.

  早上好，弗兰克林先生，我来介绍一下，这是王先生，本市公安局局长，三级警监。

- Excuse me, but are you, Mr. Black, from John Jay College of Criminal Justice?

  对不起，打扰一下，请问您是约翰杰刑事司法学院的布莱克先生吧？

Part III　Situational Dialogues
情景对话

|情景 1|　Self-Introduction at the Airport
在机场自我介绍

(P stands for Chinese police, F stands for foreigner)

F: Hello, I'm Edgar Brown from America.

P: Hello, Mr. Brown. I'm Ma Dong, an officer from Shaanxi Provincial Public Security Department. Nice to meet you.

F: Nice to meet you too.

P: I'm here to meet you on behalf of the department.

F: It's very kind of you.

P: Let's go and the car is waiting outside.

F: OK.

外：你好，我是从美国来的埃德加·布朗。

马：您好，布朗先生。我是陕西省公安厅民警，叫马东。很高兴见到你。

外：见到你我也很高兴。

马：我是代表省厅来接您的。

外：太好了。

马：我们走吧，车子就在外面等着。

外：好的。

|情景 2|　Introducing First Oneself and Then Another to a Foreign Guest at the Airport
在机场向外国客人首先自我介绍，然后介绍另一位

France: Hello, I'm Jim France from Canada.

Lu: Hello, Mr. France. I'm Lu Nan, an officer from Xiamen Municipal Public Security Bureau. Nice to meet you.

France: Nice to meet you too, Mr. Lu.

Unit 1

Introductions and Greetings
介绍与寒暄

Lu: Mr. France, this is Mr. Zhang, deputy director of the bureau. He is here to meet you.

France: How do you do, Mr. Zhang?

Lu (To Zhang): This is Mr. France from Canada.

Zhang: How do you do, Mr. France? Welcome to Xiamen.

France: It's very kind of you to come and meet me.

Zhang: Did you have a pleasant journey?

France: Yes, I had a very comfortable and pleasant journey.

Zhang: I'm glad to hear that.

Lu: Let's go.

France: OK, let's go.

弗朗斯：您好，我是加拿大来的吉姆·弗朗斯。

陆：您好，弗朗斯先生。我叫陆南，厦门市公安局民警。很高兴见到您。

弗朗斯：您好，陆先生，见到您我也很高兴。

陆：弗朗斯先生，这位是张先生，本市公安局副局长。他是来接您的。

弗朗斯：您好，张先生。

陆（对张）：这位是加拿大来的弗朗斯先生。

张：您好，弗朗斯先生。欢迎您到厦门来。

弗朗斯：感谢您来接我。

张：旅途愉快吧？

弗朗斯：是的，既舒服又愉快。

张：那太好了。

陆：我们走吧。

弗朗斯：好的。

| 情景 3 | Introducing General Director of a Municipal Public Security Bureau to a Foreigner
把市公安局局长介绍给外国人

Interpreter: Good morning, Mr. Franklin. Let me introduce Mr. Wang, general director of the Municipal Public Security Bureau, Commissioner Third Class. (To Mr. Wang) Mr. Wang, this is Mr. Franklin, a bomb technician from America.

Wang: Nice to see you, Mr. Franklin.

Franklin: Nice to see you, too, Mr. Wang.

Wang: Welcome to Urumqi. This is my business card.

Franklin: Thank you. This is mine.

Wang: We're very glad you agreed to come to this conference.

Franklin: The pleasure is all mine. I'd like to take this opportunity to learn from your experiences.

翻译：早上好，弗兰克林先生。我来介绍一下，这是王先生，本市公安局局长，三级警监。王先生，这位是美国来的排爆专家弗兰克林先生。

王：您好。见到您很高兴。

弗兰克林：您好。见到您我也很高兴。

王：欢迎您到乌鲁木齐来。这是我的名片。

弗兰克林：谢谢，这是我的名片。

王：很高兴您能来参加这次会议。

弗兰克林：感到荣幸的应该是我。我希望借此机会学习你们的经验。

|情景 4| Informal Self-Introduction at the Table
用餐时非正式的自我介绍

Liu: Hello, I'm Liu Tao, a police officer from Yantai.

Hodgens: Nice to see you. I'm Fred Hodgens.

Liu: Nice to see you, too. There are so many people here tonight. We missed getting introduced. Is this your first visit to Qingdao?

Hodgens: Yes. Qingdao is so beautiful!

Liu: And it has a lot of scenic spots, too. An ideal city for sightseeing. Here, have some of this seafood, please.

Hodgens: Oh, it's so delicious!

Unit 1

Introductions and Greetings
介绍与寒暄

Liu: I'm glad you like it. Please have some more.

刘：你好，我叫刘涛，来自烟台的一名警察。

霍金斯：见到你很高兴。我叫弗莱德·霍金斯。

刘：见到你我也很高兴。今天晚上这儿人真多。我们没得到被介绍的机会。你是第一次来青岛吗？

霍金斯：是的。青岛真美！

刘：而且有许多景点。理想的观光城市。请尝尝这道海鲜吧。

霍金斯：味道真美！

刘：你喜欢就好！再吃一点。

情景 5 Received at a Foreign Airport
在国外机场受到接待

Situation: Chinese police officers go to CUNY-John Jay College of Criminal Justice to attend a forum on preventing crimes. They are met at the airport by Mr. Black from John Jay College, who is holding a welcome board.

(B stands for Mr. Black and Y stands for one Chinese police officer Yang Hua, L stands for another officer Liu Yang.)

Y: Excuse me, but are you, Mr. Black, from John Jay College of Criminal Justice?

B: Yes, I'm Tom Black. You must be an officer from China.

Y: Yes, I'm Yang Hua from Shanghai Municipal Public Security Bureau. Nice to meet you.

B: Nice to meet you too, Mr. Yang.

Y: Mr. Black, this is Mr. Liu Yang from Beijing Municipal Public Security Bureau, head of this delegation. Mr. Liu, this is Mr. Black from John Jay College of Criminal Justice.

B: Nice to meet you, Mr. Liu.

L: Nice to meet you too, Mr. Black.

B: I'm here to meet all of you, welcome.

L: That's very kind of you. Thank you.

B: You're welcome. Let's go. You must be tired after the long journey.

L: OK.

场景介绍： 中国警察去纽约城市大学约翰杰刑事司法学院参加预防犯罪论坛。在机场举着欢迎牌迎接他们的是该学院的布莱克先生。

(B代表布莱克先生，Y代表中国警官杨华，L代表另一名警官刘洋。)

杨华：对不起，打扰一下，请问您是约翰杰刑事司法学院的布莱克先生吧?

布莱克：是的，我是汤姆·布莱克。您一定是来自中国的警官吧?

杨华：是的，我是上海市公安局的杨华，很高兴见到您。

布莱克：杨先生，见到您我也很高心。

杨华：布莱克先生，这位是北京市公安局的刘洋先生，我们代表团团长。刘警官，这位是约翰杰刑事司法学院的布莱克先生。

布莱克：很高兴见到您，刘先生。

刘洋：很高兴见到您，布莱克先生。

布莱克：我是来接你们的。欢迎大家!

刘洋：太好了!谢谢您。

布莱克：不客气，我们走吧，你们一定累了吧。

刘洋：好的。

Part IV　Creative Work
创造性练习

把外国客人引荐给领导

Situation：

美国洛杉矶县警察局警长布莱恩·穆勒和约翰·塞特菲尔德来北京参加市公安局举办的国际警务战术论坛，北京市公安局孙局长于当天下午接见了他们。宾主互致问候，孙局长邀请客人当晚共进晚餐，以示欢迎。

Unit 1　Introductions and Greetings
介绍与寒暄

> 听录音，请在听到提示音后开始口译。

翻译：下午好，塞特菲尔德先生和穆勒先生。我来介绍一下，孙先生，北京市公安局局长。孙先生，这位是约翰·塞特菲尔德警长，这位是布莱恩·穆勒警长。他们来自美国洛杉矶县警察局。

孙局长：你们好！

外宾：您好！

孙：欢迎你们来北京。你们的参加，会使本次论坛更加成功。

外：谢谢。我们很高兴有机会来贵单位访问。

孙：这次论坛为我们提供了分享经验的机会。

外：确实如此。

孙：希望你们在这里过得愉快！

外：谢谢。肯定会的。

孙：今晚我们想请你们共进晚餐。

外：噢，十分感激。

孙：这么远的旅程，你们一定累了。好好休息一下吧。晚上见。

外：再见。

Unit 2
Telephone Calls
电话交流

Etiquettes in telephone calls are also somewhat different from culture to culture. When calling an English-speaking foreigner (John Smith, for example), one usually begins with "Hello!" followed by "Is that you, Mr. Smith?" or "Is Mr. Smith in?" or "May I speak to Mr. Smith, Please?" It is not proper to say "Are you Mr. Smith?" or "Who are you?" or "I'm looking for Mr. Smith," which are word-for-word translations of what Chinese people say when they make telephone calls in Chinese.

When answering a phone call from an English-speaking foreigner, you should greet "Hello!" first, then tell the caller who you are and what agency you are from, such as "This is Officer Chen from Evergreen Police Station." After that, ask "Can I help you?" or "Who is it calling?" or "Who is it speaking, please?" The answer is "This is Smith speaking," rather than "I'm Smith", which is also Chinese English.

When answering a phone for somebody else, it's better to say "What name shall I give?" or "Who shall I say is calling?" If the person wanted on the phone is not nearby, a polite response can be "Hold the line, please. I'll get him/her for you." or "Hold on for a moment." If the person wanted happens to be close, you can hand the receiver to him/her and say "It's for you." or "For you." If the person wanted isn't in, you may say "Sorry, he/she isn't in." or "I'm afraid he/she is out." and ask the caller if he/she wants to leave a message by saying "May I take a message for you?" or "Can I take a

Unit 2 Telephone Calls 电话交流

message?" or "Would you like to leave a message?"

If you need to leave a message, you may choose "Could you take a message for me?" or "Please tell him /her that…" or "Will you please tell him/her to call me back later?"

When answering a phone, if the caller dials the wrong number, it's polite to respond like "Sorry, you've dialed the wrong number." If you realize you have dialed the wrong number, remember to apologize like "Sorry, I've dialed the wrong number."

Whatever you say on the phone should be brief, clear and to the point. Say "Good-bye" politely before hanging up.

给外国人（以约翰·史密斯为例）打电话时，通常以 hello 开始，然后用下列表达法之一问对方：

Is that you, Mr. Smith? 您是史密斯先生吗？
Is Mr. …in？某某先生在吗？
May I speak to…？我可以和某某讲话吗？

应避免按汉语习惯用下列表达法问对方：

×Who are you? 哪一位？
×Are you…? 你是某某某吗？
×I'm looking for…我找某某某。

接听外国人打来的电话时，通常也以 hello 开始，然后往往先向对方通报自己的姓名或单位，如：

This is Officer Chen from Evergreen Police Station. 这是常青派出所陈警官。

接下来接电话者用下列表达法之一问：

Can I help you? 请问您需要什么帮助？
Who is that calling? 请问您是哪位？
Who is that speaking, please? 请问您是哪位？

打电话的人应回答说：

This is Smith speaking. 我是史密斯。

不要按中文的习惯回答：

× I'm Smith.

代人接电话，最好说：What name shall I give? /Who shall I say is calling? 若要离开去叫人，须跟对方说：Hold the line, please. I'll get him/her to phone.（别挂断，我就去找他/她听电话。）或 Hold on for a moment.（请等一会儿。）反之，若电话要找的人在身边，代接电话的人可说"It's for you."或"For you."（你的电话。）如果打电话要找的人不在，代接电话的人可说"Sorry, he/she isn't in."或"I'm afraid he/she is out."（他/她不在。）如果问对方是否要留话，可说：May I take a message for you? /Can I take a message? /Would you like to leave a message?

打电话者若要拜托接电话人转告要找的人某事时，可问：Could you take a message for me? /Please tell him (her) that (sth.) …/Please tell him (her) I called. /Will you please tell him (her) to call me back later?

若对方打错电话，接电话者可说：Sorry, you've dialed the wrong number. 打电话人发现拨错号码，应说：Sorry, I've dialed the wrong number.

至于通话内容，要简明扼要。通话结束时应礼貌地道别。

Part I　New Words and Useful expressions
生词与词组

etiquette　　　英 ['etɪkət; 'etɪket] 美 ['etɪkət, 'etɪket] n. 礼节，礼仪

apologize　　　英 [ə'pɒlədʒaɪz] 美 [ə'pɑːlədʒaɪz] vi. 道歉

corporation　　英 [ˌkɔːpə'reɪʃn] 美 [ˌkɔːrpə'reɪʃn] n. 公司

provide　　　英 [prə'vaɪd] 美 [prə'vaɪd] vt. 提供

convenient　　英 [kən'viːniənt] 美 [kən'viːniənt] adj. 方便的

lobby　　　　英 ['lɒbi] 美 ['lɑːbi] n. 大厅；休息室

Unit 2 Telephone Calls 电话交流

cancel 英 [ˈkænsl] 美 [ˈkænsl] vt. 取消
appointment 英 [əˈpɔɪntmənt] 美 [əˈpɔɪntmənt] n. 约定
institution 英 [ˌɪnstɪˈtjuːʃn] 美 [ˌɪnstɪˈtuːʃn] n. 机构
interpreter 英 [ɪnˈtɜːprətə(r)] 美 [ɪnˈtɜːrprətər] n. 口译者
exchange 英 [ɪksˈtʃeɪndʒ] 美 [ɪksˈtʃeɪndʒ] n. 交换；交流
cooperation 英 [kəʊˌɒpəˈreɪʃn] 美 [koʊˌɑːpəˈreɪʃn] n. 合作，协作
Vancouver 英 [vænˈkuːvə(r)] 美 [vænˈkuːvər] n. 温哥华（加拿大主要城市）

hang up 挂断电话

can't make it 无法履约（双方都知道约会是什么的情况下，一方不能履约）

keep the appointment 赴约

look forward to sth. 期望，盼望

Part II Useful Sentence Patterns 常用句型

■ May I speak to Mr. Steiner, please?
请问斯坦纳先生在吗？

■ Who shall I say is calling?
请问您是哪一位？

■ Our station has decided to call on foreign companies in our neighborhood to gather some suggestions on our work.
我们派出所决定收集辖区内外资企业对我们工作的意见和建议。

■ Hello, is that you, Mr. Aretino?
喂，您好，请问是阿瑞提诺先生吗？

■ Who is it speaking?
请问您是哪一位？

■ Hold the line, please. (To Mr. Liu) Mr. Phillips wants to speak to you.
请稍等。（对刘警官）菲利普斯先生找您。

- I'm afraid I can't make it this evening.

  我今晚恐怕不能去赴约了。(双方都知道约会是什么的情况下,一方不能履约)

- Hope you'll be feeling better soon.

  祝您早日康复。

- This is Robins Williams speaking. Who is it calling?

  我是罗宾斯·威廉姆斯。请问您是哪位?

- We are looking forward to meeting you all.

  我们盼望着早日见到你们。

Part III Situational Dialogues
情景对话

情景 1 Making an Appointment
约定会面

Secretary: Hello. Electronic Products Corporation.

P: Hello. May I speak to Mr. Steiner, please?

Secretary: Who shall I say is calling?

P: Officer Li of Sunshine Police Sub-Station.

S: Just a moment, please, Officer Li. (To Steiner) Officer Li of Sunshine Police Substation wants to speak to you.

Steiner (On phone): Hello. This is Steiner speaking.

P: Good morning, Mr. Steiner. In order to provide better service, our station has decided to call on foreign companies in our neighborhood to gather some suggestions on our work. When will be convenient for you?

Steiner: I've had an appointment this afternoon. How about nine o'clock tomorrow morning?

P: OK. See you at nine tomorrow morning then. Bye-bye.

Steiner: Bye-bye.

Unit 2 Telephone Calls
电话交流

秘书：喂，您好。这里是电子产品公司。

警：您好。请问斯坦纳先生在吗？

秘书：您是哪一位？

警：向阳派出所李警官。

秘书：请稍等，李警官。（对斯坦纳）向阳派出所李警官请您接电话。

斯坦纳：您好。我是斯坦纳。

警：早上好，斯坦纳先生。为了更好地服务大家，我们派出所决定收集辖区内外资企业对我们工作的意见和建议，您看什么时间方便？

斯坦纳：今天下午我已经有安排了。明天上午九点可以吗？

警：好的。明天上午九点见。

斯坦纳：再见。

情景 2 A Phone Call to Invite Some Foreign Guests to Dinner
电话邀请外宾赴宴

P: Hello, is that you, Mr. Aretino?

F: Yes. Who is it speaking?

P: This is Guo Liang, a police officer of Qingdao municipal Public Security Bureau. The director of the bureau would like to invite your delegation to dinner at six tomorrow evening. Will you come?

F: Thank you for your invitation. We certainly will.

P: Excellent. We'll send a minibus to pick you up at five thirty.

F: OK. We'll be waiting in the lobby of the hotel.

P: See you tomorrow evening.

F: See you.

警：喂，您好，请问是阿瑞提诺先生吗？

外：是我。您是哪一位？

警：我是青岛市公安局的郭亮。明天晚上6点我们局长想请你们代表团共进晚餐。请问你们能来吗？

外：谢谢邀请。我们一定参加。

警：明晚5点半我们会派一辆面包车去接你们。

外：好的。到时我们在宾馆大厅等候。

警：明晚见。

外：明晚见。

情景 3 A Phone Call to Cancel an Appointment
电话取消赴约

P: (Answering the phone) Hello. Beijing Municipal Public Security Bureau. Can I help you?

F: Hello. This is John Phillips speaking. May I speak to Mr. Liu?

P: Hold the line, please. (To Mr. Liu) Mr. Phillips wants to speak to you.

Mr. Liu: Hello, Mr. Phillips. This is Liu Hua.

F: Good afternoon, Mr. Liu. I'm afraid I can't make it this evening. I have a headache and a fever. I have to stay in bed.

D: Sorry to hear that. Is it serious? You'd better go and see a doctor.

F: It's not so serious. I've taken some medicine. I'm so sorry for not being able to keep the appointment.

D: It doesn't matter. Take good care of yourself. Hope you'll be feeling better soon.

F: Thank you. Bye-bye.

D: Bye-bye.

警：(接电话) 喂，您好。这里是北京市公安局。请问有什么能帮您的？

外：您好，我是约翰·菲利普斯。请问刘警官在吗？

警：请稍等。(对刘警官) 菲利普斯先生找您。

刘警官：您好，菲利普斯先生，我是刘华。

外：您好，刘警官。今晚我恐怕不能前去赴约了。我头痛，有点儿发烧，需要休息一下。

刘警官：哦，很遗憾。严重吗？您最好去医院看看。

外：没那么严重。我已经吃了些药。不能赴约，我深感抱歉。

Unit 2 Telephone Calls 电话交流

刘警官：没关系。多多保重，祝您早日康复。

外：谢谢，再见。

刘警官：再见。

| 情景 4 | A Long-distance Call to Notify a Foreign Institution of the Arrival of the Chinese Delegation
长途电话通知外国机构中国代表团将要抵达

P: Hello! May I speak to Mr. Robins Williams, please?

F: Hello! This is Robins Williams speaking. Who is it calling?

P: This is Yang Ming, interpreter of the Policing Exchange and Cooperation Delegation from China. The delegation will take Flight Number 585 to Vancouver the day after tomorrow, that is, November the sixth. We'll arrive at Vancouver Airport at 4 in the afternoon of the same day.

F: OK. I'll send two police officers to meet you. They'll hold a signboard with the name of your delegation printed on it.

P: Thank you very much.

F: Have a pleasant journey. We are looking forward to meeting you all. Bye-bye.

P: Bye-bye.

警：喂，您好！请问罗宾斯·威廉姆斯先生在吗？

外：喂，您好！我是罗宾斯·威廉姆斯。请问您是哪位？

警：我叫杨明，是中国警务交流与合作代表团的译员。我代表团将乘585号航班于后天，也就是11月6日，前往温哥华，到达温哥华机场的时间是当天下午4点。

外：好的，我会派两名警官去接你们的。他们手里会拿一个牌子，上面印着贵代表团的名字。

警：非常感谢。

外：祝你们旅途愉快。希望早日见到你们。再见。

警：再见。

Part IV　　Creative Work
创造性练习

> 听录音，请在听到提示音后开始口译。

外：喂，您好。

警：喂，您好，请问是史密斯先生吗?

外：是的，请问您是哪位?

警：您好，史密斯先生，我是月坛派出所的李杨警官。

外：您好，李警官。

警：史密斯先生，为了更好地服务大家，我们派出所决定做个问卷调查，收集辖区内外国居民对我们工作的意见和建议，您看什么时间方便?

外：今天我已经有安排了。明天下午两点可以吗?

警：好的。明天下午两点见。

外：明天见。

Unit 3
Giving and Asking for Directions
指路与问路

When foreigners ask for directions, police officers must be especially patient and considerate and do their utmost to give correct and clear instructions. It is better to use traffic lights or signs and outstanding buildings as references when they show the way to consulters. If the place asked about is too far away it will be very helpful to tell them how to take a bus, taxi, or subway and when to make a change if needed.

If you ask the way in a foreign country, please don't forget to say "Hello" or "Hi" or "Excuse me" before and "Thanks" after it.

The words, expressions and sentence patterns below are often used to show and ask for directions. It is important and necessary for Chinese officers to get familiar with them.

遇到外国人问路时，我国民警应该耐心、体贴，尽力给出准确、清晰的解答。给外国人指路时，民警最好借助一些交通标志、典型建筑物等参照物指明方位。如果问路者要去的地方比较远，需要乘坐公共汽车、出租车、地铁等交通工具时，需要告诉他们如何乘车、如何换乘等。

如果我国警方工作人员在境外问路，要先说"Hello""Hi"或"Excuse me"，礼貌地打招呼，问路后要说"Thanks"来道谢。

我国警察在指路、问路时经常需要使用本单元的词语和句型，应熟记于心。

Part I New Words and Useful Expressions
生词与词组

utmost   英[ˈʌtməʊst] 美[ˈʌtmoʊst] n. 极限；最大可能
patient   英[ˈpeɪʃnt] 美[ˈpeɪʃnt] adj. 有耐心的
considerate   英[kənˈsɪdərət] 美[kənˈsɪdərət] adj. 体贴的
instruction   英[ɪnˈstrʌkʃn] 美[ɪnˈstrʌkʃn] n. 说明
reference   英[ˈrefrəns] 美[ˈrefrəns] n. 参照物
consulter   英[kənˈsʌltə] 美[kənˈsʌltər] n. 咨询者
intersection   英[ˌɪntəˈsekʃn] 美[ˌɪntərˈsekʃn] n. 交叉；十字路口
opposite   英[ˈɒpəzɪt; ˈɒpəsɪt] 美[ˈɑpəzɪt; ˈɑpəsɪt] adj. 相反的；对面的
souvenir   英[ˌsuːvəˈnɪə(r)] 美[ˌsuːvəˈnɪr, ˈsuːvənɪr] n. 纪念品；礼物
shuttle   英[ˈʃʌtl] 美[ˈʃʌtl] n. 公共汽车

get familiar with 熟悉
sound pretty easy 听起来很简单
go straight ahead 直走

Part II Useful Sentence Patterns
常用句型

- Excuse me, sir. Could you tell me where the nearest post office is?

  不好意思，打扰一下，警官，请问您能告诉我离这里最近的邮局在哪吗？

- See the tall building over there? There is a post office just behind it.

  看见那边那座高楼了吗？楼后面就有一个邮局。

- Excuse me, I wonder if you can show me how to get to Jinling Hotel?

  打扰一下，请问您能告诉我去金陵宾馆怎么走吗？

- Just go along this road until you come to the next intersection. Turn left and walk about 300 meters.

  沿着这条路一直往前走，走到下一个十字路口时左转，然后继续走大约300米。

Unit 3 Giving and Asking for Directions
指路与问路

- Could you tell me how to get to Xidan shopping mall?
  您能告诉我到西单商场怎么走吗？

- There is a bus stop just across the street. 在马路对面就有一个公交车站。

- It's about a 30-minute ride. 坐公交车大约半个小时。

- Excuse me. Could you tell me where I can buy some souvenirs?
  您好！您能告诉我哪里能买到旅游纪念品吗？

- Take the shuttle bus. It leaves for downtown every 2 hours.
  乘班车去吧。每两小时发一辆到市中心。

- It returns from the same place as it arrives downtown. There is a return bus every 2 hours.
  班车在市中心的终点就是它返程的起点。返程班车也是每两小时一辆。

Part III Situational Dialogues
情景对话

|情景 1| Showing the Way to the Nearest Post Office
指去往最近邮局的路

F: Excuse me, sir. Could you tell me where the nearest post office is?

P: See the tall building over there? There is a post office just behind it. Go straight ahead. It's only a 10-minute walk.

F: Thank you.

P: Not at all.

外：不好意思，打扰一下，警官，请问您能告诉我离这里最近的邮局在哪吗？

警：看见那边那座高楼了吗？楼后面就有一个邮局。一直往前走，10 分钟就能走到。

外：谢谢。

警：不用客气。

| 情景 2 | Showing the Way to Jinling Hotel
　　　　　指去往金陵宾馆的路

F: Excuse me, I wonder if you can show me how to get to Jinling Hotel?

P: Sure. Just go along this road until you come to the next intersection. Turn left and walk about 300 meters. You will see a white building on your right side. Jinling Hotel is just opposite it and there is a big sign that says "Jinling Hotel".

F: Sounds pretty easy. Thank you.

P: You're welcome.

外：打扰一下，请问您能告诉我去金陵宾馆怎么走吗？

警：当然可以。沿着这条路一直往前走，走到下一个十字路口时左转，然后继续走大约300米，在右手边就会看到一栋白色的大楼，对面就是金陵宾馆，门口挂着牌子，上面写着"金陵宾馆"。

外：感觉不难找，谢谢。

警：别客气。

| 情景 3 | Showing the Way to Xidan Shopping Mall
　　　　　指去往西单商场的路

F: Excuse me, officer.

P: Can I help you?

F: Could you tell me how to get to Xidan shopping mall?

P: Sure. It's quite far from here. You'd better take a taxi or a bus.

F: Which bus should I take?

P: Bus Number 1.

F: Where can I take it?

P: There is a bus stop just across the street.

F: How long does it take to get to Xidan?

Unit 3 Giving and Asking for Directions
指路与问路

P: It's about a 30-minute ride.

F: Thank you.

P: Don't mention it.

外：不好意思，打扰一下，警官。

警：有事吗？

外：您能告诉我到西单商场怎么走吗？

警：当然可以。这里离西单商场比较远，您最好搭出租车或乘公交车去。

外：坐哪一路公交车呢？

警：1路。

外：在哪儿坐呢？

警：在马路对面就有一个公交车站。

外：到那里需要多长时间呢？

警：坐公交车大约半个小时。

外：谢谢。

警：别客气。

| 情景 4 | Asking the Way to a Souvenir Shop in a Foreign Country
在国外问去往旅游纪念品商店的路

Chinese: Excuse me. Could you tell me where I can buy some souvenirs?

Foreigner: You can do it right here in this hotel. See the counters beside the gate? You can buy some souvenirs there.

C: I've looked around there, but I didn't find what I like.

F: Why not go downtown?

C: But how can I get there?

F: Take the shuttle bus. It leaves for downtown every 2 hours.

C: When will the next one leave?

F: In ten minutes.

C: Where do I take the bus?

F: Just outside the gate.

C: How to get back?

F: Take the same shuttle bus. It returns from the same place as it arrives downtown. There is a return bus every 2 hours.

C: Thank you very much.

F: You're welcome.

中国人：您好！您能告诉我哪里能买到旅游纪念品吗？

外国人：在本旅馆里就能买到。看到大门旁的柜台了吗？那儿就能买到一些纪念品。

中：我去看过，但没有我想买的那种。

外：为什么不到闹市区去看看？

中：怎么才能到闹市区呢？

外：乘班车去吧。每两小时发一辆到闹市区。

中：下一辆什么时候发车？

外：10分钟后。

中：在哪儿上车？

外：就在门外。

中：回来乘什么车？

外：回来也乘班车。班车在闹市区的终点就是它返程的起点。返程班车也是每两小时一辆。

中：多谢了。

外：不用客气。

Part IV Creative Work
创造性练习

Situations：

1. Showing the Way to Quanjude Restaurant（指去往全聚德烤鸭店的路）

Unit 3　Giving and Asking for Directions
指路与问路

> 听录音，请在听到提示音后开始口译。🎧

外国人：您好，警官。您能告诉我去全聚德前门店怎么走吗？

中国警察：没问题。不过这里离前门店有点远，您最好搭出租车或乘公交车去。

外：请问搭出租车去的话，需要多少钱呢？

警：大约需要40元人民币吧。

外：我知道了，谢谢。如果乘公交车的话，需要坐哪一路车呢？

警：1路。

外：在哪儿坐呢？

警：在马路对面就有一个公交车站。

外：到那里需要多长时间呢？

警：坐公交车大约30分钟。

外：谢谢。

警：不客气。

2. Asking the Way to Blue Ash Campus（询问如何去往蓝灰校区）

Situation：王晶是在美国辛辛那提大学做访问学者的中国警察，在该大学的主校区向一名外国学生打听如何去往蓝灰校区。

王：不好意思，打扰一下，请问您能告诉我如何去蓝灰校区吗？

外：没问题。你可以坐班车去，每两小时发一辆。

王：请问下一辆什么时候发车？

外：大约10分钟后。

王：在哪儿上车呢？

外：就在门外。

王：请问回来乘什么车？

外：回来也乘班车。班车在那个校区的终点就是它返程的起点。返程班车也是每两小时一辆。

王：多谢了。

外：不用客气。

Unit 4
Rescue Operations
救助

Verbal directions in English are imperative for Chinese police officers when rescuing foreigners injured in accidents, suffering acute diseases or stuck in disasters such as a fire or an earthquake.

When rescuing an injured English-speaking foreigner, police officers have to find out, by questioning in English, which part of the body is injured and how bad it is, and, if possible, help to stop bleeding, bind up the wound, and/or fix the possibly fractured or a broken part of the body before sending the injured to hospital.

When rescuing an English-speaking foreigner suffering a sudden occurrence of a serious disease such as a heart attack, police officers, if conditions permit, must take any necessary measures to prevent the disease from deteriorating while calling for an ambulance or waiting for a doctor.

When rescuing English-speaking foreigners stuck in a fire or an earthquake, police officers should, in correct and clear English, keep orders, calm them down, and tell them how to protect themselves and where and how to evacuate.

In any case, inform the victim's family members and the consulate or embassy concerned as soon as possible.

中国警察在遇到外国人意外受伤、突发急病、遭受火灾、地震等险情危胁时，使用英语口头指令非常重要。

救助讲英语的伤员时，应首先使用英语询问受伤部位及伤势，根据现场条

Unit 4　Rescue Operations 救助

件适当止血、包扎、固定可能骨折的部位，然后送往医院。

　　救助讲英语的急重病人（如心脏病发作病人）时，如条件允许，应采取措施避免病情恶化，同时叫救护车或请医生。

　　救助在火灾或地震中受困的讲英语的外国人时，警察应该使用清楚明白的英语维持秩序、安定情绪、宣传自我救护方法、指明撤离路线和方法。

　　不管属于上述哪种情况，都要尽快通知被救助外国人的家属和领事馆（大使馆）。

Part I　New Words and Useful Expressions 生词与词组

rescue	英 [ˈreskjuː] 美 [ˈreskjuː]	v. 营救
imperative	英 [ɪmˈperətɪv] 美 [ɪmˈperətɪv]	adj. 必要的
stick	英 [stɪk] 美 [stɪk]	vt. 卡住
fracture	英 [ˈfræktʃə(r)] 美 [ˈfræktʃər]	vt. 使破裂 n. [外科] 骨折
deteriorate	英 [dɪˈtɪərɪəreɪt] 美 [dɪˈtɪrɪəreɪt]	vi. 恶化，变坏
bandage	英 [ˈbændɪdʒ] 美 [ˈbændɪdʒ]	n. 绷带 vt. 用绷带包扎
sleeve	英 [sliːv] 美 [sliːv]	n. 袖子
bleed	英 [bliːd] 美 [bliːd]	vi. 流血
inform	英 [ɪnˈfɔːm] 美 [ɪnˈfɔːrm]	vt. 通知
dislocate	英 [ˈdɪsləkeɪt] 美 [ˈdɪsloʊkeɪt, dɪsˈloʊkeɪt]	vt. 使脱臼
sweat	英 [swet] 美 [swet]	vi. 出汗
complain	英 [kəmˈpleɪn] 美 [kəmˈpleɪn]	vi. 诉说
ambulance	英 [ˈæmbjələns] 美 [ˈæmbjələns]	n. [车辆] [医] 救护车
nitroglycerin	美 [ˈnaɪtrəˈglɪsərɪn]	n. 硝酸甘油
swallow	英 [ˈswɒləʊ] 美 [ˈswɑːloʊ]	vt. 吞下
stretcher	英 [ˈstretʃə(r)] 美 [ˈstretʃər]	n. 担架
direction	英 [daɪˈrekʃn; dɪ-] 美 [dəˈrekʃn; (also) daɪˈrekʃn]	n. 指导，指挥
corridor	英 [ˈkɒrɪdɔː(r)] 美 [ˈkɔːrɪdɔːr]	n. 走廊

elevator	英[ˈelɪveɪtə(r)] 美[ˈelɪveɪtər]	n. 电梯
stairway	英[ˈsteəweɪ] 美[ˈsterweɪ]	n. 阶梯，楼梯
aftershock	英[ˈɑːftəʃɒk] 美[ˈæftərʃɑːk]	n. 余震
evacuate	英[ɪˈvækjueɪt] 美[ɪˈvækjueɪt]	vi. 疏散；撤退
priority	英[praɪˈɒrəti] 美[praɪˈɔːrəti]	n. 优先考虑的事
designate	英[ˈdezɪɡneɪt] 美[ˈdezɪɡneɪt]	vt. 指定；指派
collapse	英[kəˈlæps] 美[kəˈlæps]	v.（突然）倒塌
scare	英[skeə(r)] 美[sker]	v.（使）害怕；受惊吓
intensity	英[ɪnˈtensəti] 美[ɪnˈtensəti]	n. 强度
epicenter	英[ˈepɪsentə(r)] 美[ˈepɪsentər]	n. 震中

verbal direction 口头指令

bind up the wound 包扎伤口

in any case 无论如何

stay put 待在原地别动

stay away from 远离

force one's way out 挤出去

let go of 释放，松手放开

fall off 跌落

roll up 卷起

emergency exit 安全出口

fire engine 消防车

evacuation area 疏散地

on the Richter scale 里氏震级

Part II Useful Sentence Patterns
常用句型

■ Don't worry. Let me help you. 别急，我来帮你。

■ Hold on. Everything will be all right. 坚持一下。会好的。

Unit 4 Rescue Operations 救助

- Looks like he is having a heart attack. 他看上去像心脏病发作了。
- Would you like me to inform the consulate (or embassy) of your country? 需要我通知贵国领事馆（或大使馆）吗？
- Stay calm and follow my directions! 别慌，听我指挥！
- Get down and crawl to the emergency exit! 趴下！向紧急出口爬！
- No pushing! Don't force your way out! 不要挤！不要往外挤！
- There's a danger of aftershocks. You must evacuate! I'll guide you to a safer place.
  可能会有余震。你们必须撤离。我带大家到安全的地方去。
- Stay away from the building! 离楼房远一点儿！
- Don't be scared! There will be aftershocks but no more quakes of this intensity.
  不要害怕！虽然有余震，但不会像刚才那样强烈。

Part III Situational Dialogues 情景对话

情景 1 | Helping a Foreigner Who Hurt Himself in the Street 街头救助受伤外国人

Michael Olden: Ouch!

Police: Have you hurt yourself?

O: Yes. I fell off my bicycle and hurt my arm.

P: Don't worry. Let me help you. Roll up your sleeve and let me have a look.

O: Ouch! I can't move my right arm.

P: Oh! It's bleeding! We have to bandage your arm. Hold on. Everything will be all right.

O: Maybe I've broken my arm.

P: I'll take you to the hospital. Tell me your name and the phone number of your family, please. We'd better inform your family.

O: My name is Michael Olden. Just call my wife. Her phone number is 17701343951.

P: (To his mobile phone) Hello! Is that Mrs. Olden?

Mrs. Olden: Yes. Who is calling?

P: This is the patrol police of Yuetan Police Station. Your husband fell off his bike and hurt his arm. We're now on the way to the People's Hospital. Please come over to the hospital at once.

Mrs. Olden: Oh. Thank a lot.

(After medical treatment)

O: I'm feeling much better now.

P: Glad to hear that.

(Mrs. Olden arrived)

Mrs. Olden: Oh, poor Mike! Is your arm still hurting?

O: Not a lot after the medical treatment the doctor gave me.

Mrs. Olden: What did the doctor say?

P: The doctor said Mr. Olden's right arm was just dislocated instead of fractured and he had put the bone back into the joint. Mr. Olden needs to have a good rest and avoid carrying heavy objects.

Mrs. Olden: It's very kind of you to help us, officer.

P: My pleasure. Now I have to leave him to you, Mrs. Olden.

Mrs. Olden: OK. Thank you very much for your kindness.

迈克尔·奥尔登：哎哟！

警察：您受伤了吧?

奥：是的。我从自行车上摔下来，胳膊摔伤了。

警：别急，我来帮您。把袖子卷起来让我看看。

奥：哎哼！我的右胳膊动不了了。

警：噢！出血了。得先包扎一下。坚持一下。会好的。

奥：我的胳膊可能骨折了。

警：我送您去医院。您叫什么名字？家里电话号码是多少？我们还是通知您的

Unit 4 Rescue Operations 救助

家人吧。

奥：我叫迈克尔·奥尔登。给我太太打电话就行。她的电话号码是17701343951。

警：(对着移动电话) 喂！奥尔登太太吗？

奥尔登太太：是我。您是哪一位？

警：我是月坛派出所的巡警。您丈夫从自行车上摔了下来，胳膊受了伤，我们现在正在去往人民医院的路上。请马上到人民医院来。

奥尔登太太：好的，谢谢。

(医院里，检查处置后)

奥：我觉得好多了。

警：太好了。

(奥尔登太太来到了医院)

奥尔登太太：哎呀！你还疼吗？

奥：医生帮我治疗后不怎么疼了。

奥尔登太太：医生是怎么说的？

警：医生说奥尔登先生右胳膊脱臼了，好在没有骨折，他已经将关节复位。回家后注意多休息，不要提重物。

奥尔登太太：多亏您帮忙，谢谢您，警官先生。

警：别客气。现在我就把他交给您了。

奥尔登太太：好的，多谢了。

情景2 | Rescuing a Foreign Tourist Suffering from a Heart Attack
救助突发心脏病的外国游客

Mrs. Johnson: Excuse me, officer. Please come and help us!

Police: What can I do for you?

Mrs. Johnson: There's something wrong with my husband.

Police: Oh! He looks rather pale. Sweating, too.

Mrs. Johnson: He said he has severe pain in his chest.

Mr. Johnson: I...I feel like I can't...breathe.

Police: Is it a heart attack?

Mrs. Johnson: Maybe. He complained of difficulty breathing before.

Police: Looks like he is having a heart attack.

Mrs. Johnson: What shall we do, then?

Police: Don't worry. Let him lie still. I'll call 120 for an ambulance.

(After the phone call) The ambulance will be here in about 10 minutes.

Mrs. Johnson: Oh! Good!

Police: By the way, do you have any nitroglycerin tablets with you?

Mrs. Johnson: No.

Police: (To other foreign tourists nearby) Who has any nitroglycerin tablets? We need some to save this gentleman.

A tourist: I have some. Here you are.

Police: Thank you. (To Mr. Johnson) Open your mouth. Place it under your tongue. Don't swallow it.

(10 minutes later) Look! Here comes the ambulance!

First Aid Doctor: Where is the patient?

Police: Here! Let's help him get onto the stretcher!

(In the ambulance)

Police (**To Mrs. Johnson**): Could you tell me your names and nationality?

Mrs. Johnson: He is Edward Johnson and I'm Susan Johnson. We are from South Africa.

Police: Would you like me to inform the consulate (or: the embassy) of your country?

Mrs. Johnson: Yes, please. Thank you very much.

约翰逊太太：对不起，警官先生。请过来帮帮我们。

警察：我能帮您做些什么？

约翰逊太太：我丈夫有点儿不对劲儿。

警：噢！脸色这么苍白！而且在出汗。

约翰逊太太：他说胸部疼得厉害。

约翰逊先生：我觉得……心口……闷得慌。

Unit 4 Rescue Operations
救助

警：是不是心脏病发作？

约翰逊太太：可能是。他之前说过心脏有些不舒服。

警：他看上去像心脏病发作了。

约翰逊太太：那可怎么办呀？

警：别急。让他躺着别动。我打120叫救护车。

（打过120后）救护车10分钟后就到。

约翰逊太太：太好了！

警：请问你们带硝酸甘油了吗？

约翰逊太太：没有。

警：（对附近游客）请问谁带硝酸甘油片了？我们需要一些来抢救这位先生。

一游客：我带了。给。

警：谢谢。（对约翰逊先生）请张嘴。放在舌下。别咽下去。

（10分钟后）看！救护车来了！

急救医生：病人在哪里？

警：这里！我们一起把病人抬上担架！

（在救护车上）

警：（对约翰逊太太）请告诉我两位的姓名和国籍。

约翰逊太太：他叫爱德华·约翰逊，我是他妻子，叫苏珊·约翰逊。我们来自南非。

警：好的，需要我通知贵国领事馆（或：大使馆）吗？

约翰逊太太：好的，麻烦您通知一下，非常感谢！

情景3 Rescuing English-speaking Foreigners Stuck in a Fire
火灾中急救外国人

Foreigners：Fire! Fire!

Police: This is the police! Stay calm and follow my directions!

Foreigner 1：Help! Help!

P: The emergency exit is at the end of the corridor. It's on your left!

F1：Oh! Smoke! (Begins to cough)

P: Cover your nose and mouth with a wet towel! Get down and crawl to the emergency exit!

F1: Can I take the elevator?

P: No! Use the stairway!

(More foreigners come rushing to the exit)

P: No pushing! Don't force your way out! Exit one by one!

Foreigner 2: Help! Help! I'm on the balcony!

P: Stay there and wait for the rescue! Don't go inside! Don't jump down! It's too high!

F2: Oh! Look! A fire engine is coming!

外国人:着火啦!着火啦!

警察:我是警察!别慌,听我指挥!

外国人1:救命!救命!

警:紧急出口在走廊尽头,在你的左侧!

外1:烟太大了!(开始咳嗽)

警:用湿毛巾捂住鼻子和嘴!趴下!向紧急出口爬!

外1:能乘电梯吗?

警:不行!走楼梯!

(又有许多外国人拥向出口)

警:不要挤!不要往外挤!一个一个地出去!

外国人2:救命!救命!我在阳台上呢!

警:别动!等待救援!别进屋!不要往下跳!太高了!

外2:哇!看!消防车来了!

| 情景4 | Rescuing English-speaking Foreigners Stuck in an Earthquake
地震中急救外国人

Foreigner: Earthquake! Earthquake!

Police: Stay calm and follow my directions!

Unit 4   Rescue Operations
救助

F: What shall we do now?

P: There's a danger of aftershocks. You must evacuate! I'll guide you to a safer place.

F: Wait! I must go back to get something.

P: Don't take anything with you! The top priority is your life!

F: Where are we going?

P: The park nearby. That's a designated evacuation area.

F: Oh! The building is collapsing!

P: Stay away from the building! Don't let go of your child's hand!

F: My God! We shall all be killed!

P: Don't be scared! There will be aftershocks but no more quakes of this intensity.

(In the designated evacuation area)

P: Here we are. Wait here for further directions and don't worry. Everything will be OK.

(Hours later)

F: Officer, what was the intensity of today's quake?

P: 6 degrees on the Richter scale.

F: Where was the epicenter?

P: A small village 60 kilometers to the west of this city.

外国人：地震了！地震了！

警察：别慌！听我指挥！

外：我们怎么办呀？

警：可能会有余震。你们必须撤离。我带大家到安全的地方去。

外：等一等！我回去取点儿东西。

警：什么东西也不要带。最重要的是生命！

外：我们到哪儿去？

警：附近的公园。那里是指定的疏散地点。

外：不好了！楼房要倒！

警：离楼房远一点儿！拉住您的孩子！

外：天呐！我们全会没命的！

警：不要害怕！虽然有余震，但不会像刚才那样强烈的。

(在疏散地)

警：到了。请在这里等候进一步通知。不要担心，一切问题都会解决的。

(几小时后)

外：警官，今天的地震有几级？

警：里氏6级。

外：震中在哪里？

警：城西60公里的一个小村庄。

Part IV   Creative Work
创造性练习

Situation： 民警在街头救助一位受伤的外国人。

听录音，请在听到提示音后开始口译。

哈丁（Harding）：请帮帮我！

警察：怎么了？

哈丁：我的腿受伤了。

警察：疼吗？

哈丁：疼。

警察：别急。我送您去医院。

哈丁：我动不了。

警察：我扶您。

(在车上)

警察：您叫什么名字？哪国人？

哈丁：杰克·哈丁，新加坡人。

警察：家里电话号码是多少？

哈丁：请打电话给我太太。她手机号是……

Unit 4 Rescue Operations
救助

警察：(对着手机) 喂！哈丁太太吗？

哈丁太太：是我。请问您是哪一位？

警察：我是警察。您丈夫受伤了。请马上到……医院来。

哈丁太太：好的。伤得严重吗？

警察：不严重。

(哈丁太太来到医院)

哈丁太太：医生是怎么说的？

警察：骨折。(对哈丁) 感觉好点儿了吗？

哈丁：好多了。

警察：我该走了。多保重。

哈丁夫妇：多谢了。

警察：别客气。再见。

哈丁夫妇：再见。

Unit 5
Handling Reports
接警

In China, as in all other countries throughout the world, foreigners may experience such cases as robbery, traffic accidents and burglary. They need to report to the police by dialing 110 hotline or going to the police station in person. Police officers should speak appropriate English to ask for some important information including the address, number of people involved and telephone number of the reporter. Moreover, they ought to try their best to comfort the case reporters and ask them not to touch anything in order to protect the crime scene. In this unit, there are some sample dialogues showing how to handle such reports.

在中国，如同在世界其他各地一样，外国人可能会遭遇抢劫、交通事故或入室盗窃等侵害案件，他们需要拨打110或到派出所亲自报警。因此，接警员必须采用正确的英语问清楚一些重要信息，包括案件发生地点、涉案人数和报警人的联系方式等内容。除此之外，必要时，接警员还应该尽力安慰报警人保持冷静并保护好犯罪现场等。本单元将通过一些案例向接警员展示如何处置外国人的报警。

Part I New Words and Useful Expressions
生词与词组

accident　　英[ˈæksɪdənt] 美[ˈæksɪdənt] *n.* 事故；意外

Unit 5 Handling Reports 接警

burglary 英 [ˈbɜːgləri] 美 [ˈbɜːrgləri] n. 入室偷窃
untouched 英 [ʌnˈtʌtʃt] 美 [ʌnˈtʌtʃt] adj. 保持原样的，未动过的
contact 英 [ˈkɒntækt] 美 [ˈkɑntækt] vt. 使接触，联系
SUV 越野车
VIN 车架识别号
in person 亲自
the crime scene 犯罪现场
keep in touch with 与……保持联系
toll station 收费站
the emergency lane 应急车道
parking lot 停车场

Part II Useful Sentence Patterns
常用句型

- Mr. Smith, when and where were you robbed?

  史密斯先生，请问您被抢的时间和地点？

- Mr. Smith, please keep calm. An officer will be around in 5 minutes. We will keep in touch with you all the time.

  史密斯先生，请您别慌，警察将在5分钟之内到达。我们将随时与您联系。

- Please put a warning board 150 meters behind the car and tell everybody present to stay at a safe place in the emergency lane.

  请在车后150米处放置警示牌，并确保所有在场人员转移到应急车道的安全位置。

- Please keep calm and don't touch anything.

  请保持冷静并保护好现场，不要碰任何东西。

- I'll contact you as soon as I get any clue about your car.

  一有你车的任何消息，我都会跟您联系的。

Part III   Situational Dialogues
情景对话

|情景 1| Handling a Robbery Report
              抢劫案的接警

P: Hello, this is 110. Can I help you?

F: Hello, I have been robbed.

P: Your name, please?

F: John Smith.

P: Mr. Smith, when and where were you robbed?

F: Just a few minutes ago on Xicui Road.

P: Could you please tell me more about the exact place?

F: It's about 100 meters west of Walmart.

P: Would you please describe the robber, please?

F: He looks very strong and about 5.7 feet high wearing a black jacket. He has curly hair.

P: In what way did he go?

F: He ran eastward along Xicui Road.

P: OK, Mr. Smith, please keep calm. An officer will be around in 5 minutes. We will keep in touch with you all the time. What's your phone number, please?

F: It's …

P: All right, please stay there and wait for the officer's arrival.

F: Thank you.

P: You are welcome.

警：您好，这里是110指挥中心，请讲。

外：您好，我被抢劫了。

警：请问您的姓名？

外：约翰·史密斯。

警：史密斯先生，请问您被抢的时间和地点？

Unit 5 Handling Reports
接警

外：几分钟之前，就在西翠路上。

警：请提供一下具体地址。

外：大约在沃尔玛超市以西100米。

警：您能描述一下犯罪嫌疑人吗？

外：他看上去很壮实，身高大约5.7英尺，身穿一件黑色夹克，留着卷发。

警：抢劫之后他朝什么方向跑了？

外：沿着西翠路朝东跑掉了。

警：好的，史密斯先生，请您别慌，警察将在5分钟之内到达。我们将随时与您联系，请问您的电话号码是多少？

外：我的手机号是……

警：好的，请您待在原地等待警察。

外：好的，谢谢。

警：不客气。

情景2 Handling a Traffic Accident Report
道路交通事故的接警

P: Hello, this is 110. What can I do for you?

F: Hello, I've just had an accident.

P: Sorry to hear that. Tell me your name and the exact location, please.

F: I'm Tom White driving from north to south on Jingkai Highway. The accident happened about 10 kilometers south of the toll station.

P: Is there anybody injured?

F: Yes, an old lady and a child were seriously injured. I've called 120.

P: OK. Please put a warning board 150 meters behind the car and tell everybody present to stay at a safe place in the emergency lane. An officer will arrive in 5 minutes.

F: All right, thank you.

P: You're welcome.

警：您好，110指挥中心，请讲。

外：您好，我这里刚刚发生了一场交通事故。

警：请问您的姓名和事故具体地点？

外：我叫汤姆·怀特，在京开高速上由北向南行驶，事故发生地点在收费站以南大约10公里处。

警：有人受伤吗？

外：是的，一名老人和一名儿童受伤严重，我已经拨打了120急救电话。

警：好的，请在车后150米处放置警示牌，并确保所有在场人员转移到应急车道的安全位置。警察将在5分钟之内到达。

外：好的，谢谢。

警：不客气。

| 情景 3 | Handling a Burglary Report
入室盗窃案的接警

P：Hello, this is Qingdao110. Can I help you?

F：Hello, my apartment has been broken in.

P：Where do you live?

F：Room 3201 Building 2 in No. 186 Zhujiang Road.

P：When did you find the burglary?

F：When I got home from vacation, just a few minutes ago.

P：What was stolen?

F：All my jewelry and a laptop were gone, and 10,000 yuan cash too.

P：How did they get in?

F：They forced to open the window.

P：All right. An officer will be around in about 5 minutes. Please keep calm and don't touch anything.

F：OK, thank you very much.

P：You are welcome.

警：您好，这里是青岛110指挥中心，请讲。

外：您好，我家被盗了。

警：请问您住在哪里？

外：珠江路186号2号楼3201室。

警：什么时候发现的？

外：刚才外地旅游回来，就在几分钟之前。

Unit 5 Handling Reports
接警

警：被盗的物品有哪些？
外：所有的珠宝首饰、一台笔记本电脑，还有1万元现金。
警：他们怎么进去的？
外：他们是从窗户进来的。
警：好的，警察会在5分钟之内到达。请保持冷静并保护好现场，不要碰任何东西。
外：好的，谢谢。
警：不客气。

|情景4| Handling an Auto Theft Report
机动车被盗案的接警

P: Hello, what can I do for you, Madam?
F: Hello, my car has been stolen.
P: Please sit down and tell me when you found the car stolen.
F: This morning when I wanted to drive to work.
P: Where did you park it?
F: I parked it in the parking lot on the street near my house last night when I got home from a party.
P: Please tell me more about your car.
F: My car is a red 2016 Lexus SUV.
P: What is the plate number and its VIN?
F: JYX886 and BHVJR52U85S110284.
P: OK. Please leave your name, address, mobile phone number. I'll contact you as soon as I get any clue about your car.
F: Thank you so much.
P: You're welcome.

警：您好，女士，请问有什么事情？
外：您好，我的车被偷了。
警：请坐，您是什么时候发现车被偷的？
外：今天早上打算开车上班时发现的。
警：您把车停在哪里了？

外：昨晚聚会回来，我就停在我家附近的路边停车场了。

警：请详细描述一下您的车。

外：那是一辆红色2016款的雷克萨斯城市越野车。

警：请问车牌号和车架识别号分别是什么？

外：车牌是JYX886，车架识别号是BHVJR52U85S110284。

警：好的，请留下您的姓名、地址、联系电话，一有消息，我就会跟您联系的。

外：好的，谢谢您。

警：不客气。

Part IV　Creative Work
创造性练习

Situation：一位澳大利亚人遭遇抢劫后打电话报警。

▶ 听录音，请在听到提示音后开始口译。

警：您好，这里是北京110指挥中心，请问需要什么帮助？

外：您好，我的钱被人抢了。

警：别急，请把事情经过详细描述一下。

外：今天早上十点左右，我从银行取了一万元钱。刚刚走出银行大约100米的时候，一个人冲过来，对我拳打脚踢，并把装钱的包抢走了。

警：哪个银行，具体什么位置？

外：工商银行白云路支行，就在白云桥北面大约500米。

警：抢劫之后他朝什么方向跑了？

外：沿着白云路朝北跑掉了。

警：好的，先生，警察将在5分钟之内到达。我们将随时与您联系，请告诉我您的手机号码。

外：18810453878。

警：好的，请您待在原地等待警察。

外：好的，谢谢。

警：不客气。

Unit 6
Lost and Found
受理报失与失物招领

When a foreigner reports a loss, police officers usually express their sympathy first, by saying "I'm sorry to hear that" before making out a report, which includes the natural information of the person who lost things such as his or her name, nationality, passport number, address in China and phone number, time and place of the loss and detailed description of the lost items.

If a check or a credit card is lost, remind the person who lost it to notify his bank or credit card company as soon as possible.

If foreigners report the loss of their passports, police officers should give them a receipt for the report and tell them to apply for a confirmation of reporting the loss of passports in the local Exit-Entry Administration Service Center. With the confirmation, they can apply to their consulate or embassy in China for a new passport and then get the new passport visaed by the local Exit-Entry Administration Service Center.

As soon as the lost article has been recovered, police officers have to contact the person who lost it and ask him or her to claim it, and meantime make sure what has been found is just what was lost, and ask the person to sign the Statement of Loss before returning it.

受理外国人报失时，民警应先说"I'm sorry to hear that"表示同情，然后进行登记，记下失主的个人信息，如姓名、国籍、护照号码、在中国的现住址和电话号码，以及遗失的时间、地点和遗失物品的详细描述。

遗失物品中如有支票或信用卡，应提醒失主马上向有关银行或信用卡公司挂失。

如果遗失的是护照，应给失主出具一份《护照丢失报案回执》，让其持该回执去当地出入境管理部门办理《护照报失证明》，然后去其本国驻华使馆或领事馆补办新护照，最后再到当地公安机关出入境管理部门补办签证。

报失的物品找到后，应马上通知失主携带有效身份证件前来认领。归还前应确认一下找到的物品是否与报失的物品相符。确认无误后应请失主登记签字。

Part I New Words and Useful Expressions
生词与词组

sympathy 英[ˈsɪmpəθi] 美[ˈsɪmpəθi] n. 同情

description 英[dɪˈskrɪpʃn] 美[dɪˈskrɪpʃn] n. 描述，描写

certificate 英[səˈtɪfɪkɪt] 美[sərˈtɪfɪkɪt] n. 证明

recover 英[rɪˈkʌvə(r)] 美[rɪˈkʌvər] vt. 重新找回

canvas 英[ˈkænvəs] 美[ˈkænvəs] adj. 帆布制的

sneaker 英[ˈsniːkə(r)] 美[ˈsniːkər] n. 运动鞋

souvenir 英[ˌsuːvəˈnɪə(r)] 美[ˌsuːvəˈnɪr, ˈsuːvənɪr] n. 纪念品

cloisonne 英[klɔɪˈzɒneɪ] 美[ˌklɔɪzəˈne] n.（法）景泰蓝瓷器 adj.（法）景泰蓝制的

receipt 英[rɪˈsiːt] 美[rɪˈsiːt] n. 收据

fare 英[feə(r)] 美[fer] n.（乘客支付的）公共交通费

appreciate 英[əˈpriːʃieɪt] 美[əˈpriːʃieɪt] vt. 感激

terrific 英[təˈrɪfɪk] 美[təˈrɪfɪk] adj. 极好的

in charge of 负责；主管

make out 填写

terracotta figures 兵马俑

plate number 车牌

get in touch with 同……取得联系

Unit 6　Lost and Found
受理报失与失物招领

confirmation of reporting the loss of passport 护照报失证明

reapply for 重新申请，补办

round-the-clock *adj.* 全天的

Part II　Useful Sentence Patterns
　　　　　　常用句型

- But don't worry. We'll do our best to find it for you.

  不过别急，我们会尽量帮您找。

- We'll contact you as soon as we recover your bag.

  包找到之后我们马上和您联系。

- Your lost bag has been recovered. Please come to collect it.

  您丢失的包找到了，请来认领。

- Please check your bag and see if everything is there.

  看一看您的包，里面缺什么没有。

- You should go to the embassy of your country in China to reapply for a passport with this confirmation.

  您应该拿着这份《护照报失证明》到贵国驻华使馆申请补办护照。

Part III　Situational Dialogues
　　　　　　情景对话

| 情景 1 |　Handling a Report of the Loss of a Bag
　　　　　　受理报失

P: Hello, sir. What can I do for you?

F: Hello, officer. I've lost my bag.

P: I'm sorry to hear that. But don't worry. We'll do our best to find it for you.

F: That's very kind of you.

P: Let me make out a report. What's your name?

F: Stevens Johnson.

P: How do you spell that?

F: S-T-E-V-E-N-S, Stevens; J-O-H-N-S-O-N, Johnson.

P: Nationality?

F: Canada.

P: Show me your passport, please.

F: Here you are.

P: Where are you staying?

F: Phoenix Hotel.

P: Which room?

F: 808.

P: The number of your cell phone?

F: It's…

P: OK. Now describe your bag. What kind of bag is it?

F: A canvas traveling bag.

P: What color is it?

F: Blue.

P: And the size?

F: About 40 inches long, 20 inches wide, and 30 inches high.

P: What's in it?

F: Oh, let me think. A video camera, a pair of sneakers, 2 pairs of pants, and 2 T-shirts.

P: Anything else?

F: Oh, I almost forget. There are also some souvenirs, including a cloisonne bowl and some terracotta figures.

P: When did you find out your bag missing?

F: The moment I got to the hotel.

P: Where did you lose it?

F: It's hard to say. Perhaps on the way to the hotel from the airport.

Unit 6　Lost and Found
受理报失与失物招领

P: Is it possible that you left it in the taxi?

F: Oh! That's quite possible! I remember I put it on the back seat of the taxi, but I'm not sure whether I took it with me when I got off because I carried so much luggage.

P: Have you kept the receipt of your taxi fare?

F: Yes, right in my pocket. Here it is.

P: Good. It has the plate number of the taxi and the phone number of the driver on it. We can easily get in touch with the taxi driver with the help of this receipt.

F: Really? Terrific!

P: We'll contact you as soon as we recover your bag.

F: Thank you for the trouble.

P: No trouble at all.

警：您好，先生。有什么可以帮您的？

外：您好，警官。我的包丢了。

警：真遗憾。不过别急，我们会尽量帮您找。

外：太好了。

警：我来登记一下。您叫什么名字？

外：史蒂文斯·约翰逊。

警：怎么拼？

外：S-T-E-V-E-N-S，史蒂文斯；J-O-H-N-S-O-N，约翰逊。

警：国籍？

外：加拿大。

警：请出示一下您的护照。

外：给您。

警：现在住在哪里？

外：凤凰饭店。

警：房间号？

外：808。

警：您的手机号码？

外：我的手机号码是……

警：嗯。现在说一下您的包吧。是什么样的包？

外：帆布旅行包。

警：什么颜色？

外：蓝色。

警：多大尺寸？

外：大约40英寸长，20英寸宽，30英寸高。

警：里面有些什么？

外：噢，让我想想。一台摄像机、一双旅游鞋、两条裤子、两件T恤衫。

警：还有别的吗？

外：噢，差一点儿忘了。还有些旅游纪念品，包括一只景泰蓝碗和一些兵马俑。

警：什么时候发现包没了？

外：一到饭店就发现了。

警：可能丢在哪儿了？

外：很难说。可能丢在从机场到饭店的路上了。

警：会不会忘在出租车上了？

外：噢！太有可能了！我记得把包放在出租车的后座上，因为我随身带的行李太多，记不清下车时拿没拿了。

警：出租车车费收据您保存了没有？

外：保存了，就在衣兜里。给。

警：好！收据上有出租车的牌号和司机的电话号码，我们可以和司机取得联系。

外：真的？太好了！

警：包找到之后我们马上和您联系。

外：麻烦您了，谢谢。

警：别客气。

|情景2| Returning the Lost Article that Has Been Found
归还失物

P: Hello, is Mr. Johnson there?

F: Yes. Who is calling?

P: Officer Chen of Huanghe Police Station. Your lost bag has been recovered.

Unit 6 Lost and Found
受理报失与失物招领

Please come to collect it.

F: Oh, great! What time would you like me to come?

P: Any time will do. We offer round-the-clock service.

F: All right. I'll come at nine tomorrow morning.

P: Please bring your passport or ID with you when you come.

F: OK. See you tomorrow morning, then.

P: See you.

...

F: Hello, officer.

P: Hello, sir.

F: I'm Stevens Johnson, the person you called yesterday afternoon. I have come here for my lost bag.

P: May I have your passport, please?

F: OK. Here it is.

P: To make sure, please tell me what's in the bag.

F: A video camera, a pair of shoes, some clothes and souvenirs.

P: Absolutely right. Please check your bag and see if everything is there.

F: Everything is here.

P: Sign your name in the form, please.

F: All right. How and where did you find it?

P: We called the driver of the taxi you took. The driver said he had found a bag on the back seat of his car and reported it to the taxi company.

F: Thank you very much. I really appreciate your efforts.

P: It's our pleasure.

警：喂，请问是约翰逊先生吗？

外：是我。您是哪位？

警：我是黄河派出所民警，姓陈。您丢失的包找到了，请来认领。

外：噢，真的呀！我什么时候去好呢？

警：什么时候都可以。我们全天24小时提供服务。

外：那么我明天上午9点去。

警：来时请携带护照或其他身份证明材料。

外：好的。明天上午见。

警：明天上午见。

……

外：警官您好。

警：您好，先生。

外：我叫史蒂文斯·约翰逊，昨天下午你们打电话让我来认领我丢的包。

警：请把护照给我看一下。

外：好的。给您。

警：请告诉我包里有些什么物品，我确认一下。

外：有一台摄像机、一双鞋、一些衣服和旅游纪念品。

警：完全正确。这是您的包，看一看里面缺什么没有。

外：不缺什么。

警：请在这个登记表上签字。

外：好的。你们是怎么找到的？在哪儿找到的？

警：我们给出租车司机打了电话。司机说他发现后座上有个包并报告了公司。

外：多谢了。你们费了这么多事真不容易。

警：不用谢，应该的。

情景3 Handling a Report of the Loss of Passport
受理护照丢失报案

P: Hello, madam. What can I do for you?

F: Hello, officer. I have lost my passport.

P: Sorry to hear that. Do you know where you lost it?

F: I'm not sure. I had been carrying it with me in my purse, but after I visited the Great Wall last weekend, I couldn't find it anywhere.

P: It may be difficult to find it because one week has passed since the time you lost it.

F: Oh, no. I've come to China for a tour and there still are many places I want

Unit 6 Lost and Found
受理报失与失物招领

to visit. What should I do?

P: You have to reapply for one.

F: Could you please tell me how to reapply?

P: Sure. Today I will give you a receipt for the report. You have to go to the Administration Division of Exit and Entry of the Beijing Municipal Public Security Bureau to apply for a confirmation of reporting the loss of passport with this receipt, a copy of your passport or other ID cards such as your driver's license and two 2-inch photos.

F: Thank you. What else should I do then?

P: You should go to the embassy of your country in China to reapply for a passport with this confirmation.

F: OK, thank you. Where do I reapply for a visa?

P: The Administration Division of Exit and Entry of the Beijing Municipal Public Security Bureau.

F: What papers are required for a visa?

P: Your new passport.

F: I see. Thank you very much.

P: You're welcome.

警：您好，女士。请问有什么事吗？

外：您好，警官。我的护照丢了！

警：请问知道在什么地方丢了吗？

外：不知道，我一直放在挎包里，上周末爬完长城回来后就找不到了。

警：护照丢失到现在都已经过去一个周了，所以找回来了的可能性不大。

外：噢，不会吧。我来中国旅游，还有很多地方要去呢，护照找不回来的话，那我可怎么办呢？

警：您可以补办一个护照。

外：您能告诉我怎么补办吗？

警：当然可以。我给您一份护照丢失报案回执，您拿着这份回执、护照复印件或其他能够证明您身份的证件（比如驾照），还有两张两寸照片去北京市公安局出入境管理局办理《护照报失证明》。

外：明白了，谢谢您！然后，我该怎么做呢？

警：拿着这份《护照报失证明》到贵国驻华使馆申请补办护照。

外：好的，谢谢您！我应该去哪里补办签证呢？

警：北京市公安局出入境管理局。

外：需要带什么材料呢？

警：新补办的护照就行。

外：我明白了。谢谢。

警：别客气。

Part IV　　Creative Work
创造性练习

Situation：某外国人钱包丢失后向我民警报失。

▶ 听录音，请在听到提示音后开始口译。

警：您好，先生。请问有什么可以帮您的？

外：您好，警官。我的钱包丢了。

警：我来给您登记一下。

外：好的，谢谢。

警：请问您的姓名？

外：罗伯特·韦德。

警：怎么拼呢？

外：R-O-B-E-R-T，W-A-D-E。

警：请问您的国籍？

外：美国。

P：您现在住在哪里？

外：友谊宾馆321房间。

警：手机号？

外：13712374177。

Unit 6　Lost and Found
受理报失与失物招领

警：大约什么时间丢的？
外：今天上午10点到11点之间。
警：在哪里丢的？
外：友谊商店。
警：什么样的钱包？
外：皮的。
警：什么颜色？
外：黑色。
警：里面有什么？
外：120美元现金、2000美元旅行支票。
警：旅行支票？哪一家银行的？
外：美国银行。
警：请告知那家银行。
外：我会的。
警：还有什么？
外：一张信用卡。
警：请向信用卡公司挂失。
外：我会的。
警：就这些吗？
外：是的，就这么多。
警：钱包找到后我们会通知您的。
外：麻烦您了。
警：别客气。

Unit 7
Security Inspection
安全检查

With the increase of international terrorist attacks and drug trafficking, it becomes more and more imperative to carry out security inspections at border crossings. If security inspectors find something wrong with passengers or their belongings or passengers refuse to be inspected, the inspectors will call the police for help. In order to smoothly handle such situations involving English speakers, the police officers concerned are required to have a good command of English. The aim of this unit is to help police officers to learn some useful phrases and sentences necessary to deal with problems involving English speakers in the process of security inspection.

全球恐怖袭击和国际贩毒日益猖獗，在各出入境口岸对过往旅客进行安检日显重要。如果安检人员发现过境乘客或他们随身携带的行李有问题时，或者乘客拒绝接受安检时，他们都会请警察前来处理。如果以上情况涉及外国人的话，警察们需要熟练掌握英语，才能成功处理。本单元将会帮助警察掌握一些必要的短语和句子，以便成功应对安检过程中出现的问题。

Part I New Words and Useful Expressions
生词与词组

increase 英[ɪnˈkriːs] 美[ɪnˈkriːs] v. 增加

terrorist 英[ˈterərɪst] 美[ˈterərɪst] n. 恐怖主义者，恐怖分子

Unit 7 Security Inspection 安全检查

单词	英式音标	美式音标	词性 释义
trafficking	[ˈtræfɪkɪŋ]	[ˈtræfɪkɪŋ]	n. 非法交易（尤指毒品买卖）
security	[sɪˈkjʊərəti]	[sɪˈkjʊrəti]	n. 安全，安全性
inspection	[ɪnˈspekʃn]	[ɪnˈspekʃn]	n. 检查
belongings	[bɪˈlɒŋɪŋz]	[bɪˈlɔːŋɪŋz] / [bɪˈlɔːŋɪŋz]	n. 所有物，行李
handle	[ˈhændl]	[ˈhændl]	v. 处理
involve	[ɪnˈvɒlv]	[ɪnˈvɑːlv]	vt. 牵涉
command	[kəˈmɑːnd]	[kəˈmænd]	n.（尤指对语言的）掌握
process	[ˈprəʊses]	[ˈprɑːses]	n. 过程
board	[bɔːd]	[bɔːrd]	vt. 上（飞机、车、船等）
forbid	[fəˈbɪd]	[fərˈbɪd]	vt. 禁止
restrict	[rɪˈstrɪkt]	[rɪˈstrɪkt]	vt. 限制
confiscate	[ˈkɒnfɪskeɪt]	[ˈkɑːnfɪskeɪt]	vt. 没收
marijuana	[ˌmærəˈwɑːnə]	[ˌmærəˈwɑːnə]	n. 大麻；大麻毒品
meth	[meθ]	[meθ]	abbr. 甲基苯丙胺，冰毒
luggage	[ˈlʌɡɪdʒ]	[ˈlʌɡɪdʒ]	n. 行李
option	[ˈɒpʃn]	[ˈɑːpʃn]	n.[计] 选项
Illicitly	[ɪˈlɪsɪtli]	[ɪˈlɪsɪtli]	adv. 违法地
ammunition	[ˌæmjuˈnɪʃn]	[ˌæmjuˈnɪʃn]	n. 弹药
crossbow	[ˈkrɒsbəʊ]	[ˈkrɔːsboʊ]	n. 弩
dagger	[ˈdæɡə(r)]	[ˈdæɡər]	n. 匕首
concurrently	[kənˈkʌrəntli]	[kənˈkɜːrəntli]	adv. 同时地
ridiculous	[rɪˈdɪkjələs]	[rɪˈdɪkjələs]	adj. 可笑的；荒谬的
necessity	[nəˈsesəti]	[nəˈsesəti]	n. 必需品
suspicious	[səˈspɪʃəs]	[səˈspɪʃəs]	adj. 可疑的
innocent	[ˈɪnəsnt]	[ˈɪnəsnt]	adj. 无辜的；无罪的

terrorist attack 恐怖袭击

drug trafficking 贩卖毒品

security inspector 安检员

have a good command of 熟练掌握

deal with 处理

in the process of security inspection 在安检过程中
be suspected of illegally holding 涉嫌非法持有
carry-on luggage 随身携带的行李
be crazy about 热衷于
in question 成问题的
mean to break the law 故意违法
put it to a test 对……进行检验
according to the law 根据法律
be suspicious of drug trafficking 涉嫌贩毒
on a business trip 出差
belong to 属于

Part II　Useful Sentence Patterns　常用句型

- According to the law of China, every passenger has to go through a safety inspection before boarding planes.
根据中国法律，所有旅客在登机之前都需要接受安检。

- You have two options now. The first one is to be inspected. The other is not to board the plane.
您现在有两个选择，一是接受安检，二是放弃登机。

- This knife is too long and restricted in China, so it can't be carried along with you and it must be confiscated.
这把刀太长了，属于管制刀具，不能随身携带，所以，我将依法对其进行没收。

- According to the law of China, I have to check the suspicious suitcase.
根据我国法律，我必须对可疑行李进行检查。

- Our test has proved it to be heroin which weighed 2 kg. You are illegally holding the drug.
经过检验，我们已经证实这是海洛因，重达2公斤，你涉嫌非法持有毒品。

Unit 7　Security Inspection
安全检查

Part III　Situational Dialogues
情景对话

|情景 1|　Persuading a Lady into being Inspected at the Airport
劝说机场女乘客接受安检

P: Hello, Miss. Could you show me your passport, please?

F: Here you are.

P: OK, Miss White. Why do you refuse to be inspected?

F: Well, I don't like to be touched by others.

P: According to the law of China, every passenger has to go through a safety inspection before boarding planes.

F: I don't care. I simply hate to be touched by strangers.

P: Well, we'll arrange for a woman inspector to do the inspection.

F: No. I don't want to be touched by others, not even by a woman.

P: If so, I'm sorry to say that I can't help you with this. You have two options now. The first one is to be inspected. The other is not to board the plane. Please think it over.

F: My luggage has been checked already. Is it absolutely necessary to search me?

P: Yes, absolutely. Just to ensure the safety of every passenger.

F: All right. Please do it quickly for I have to hurry to catch the flight.

P: Thank you for your cooperation.

警：您好，女士。请出示您的护照。

外：给。

警：怀特女士，请问您为什么拒绝接受安检？

外：我不喜欢别人碰我。

警：根据中国法律，所有旅客在登机之前都需要接受安检。

外：我不管。我就是讨厌陌生人碰我。

警：我们会帮您安排一位女性安检员进行安检。

外：不行，我不想别人碰我，即使女性也不行。

警：如果这样的话，很抱歉，我也帮不了您了。您现在有两个选择，一是接受安检，二是放弃登机。您考虑一下吧。

外：我的行李都已经安检过了，还有必要对我进行安检吗？

警：是的，非常有必要，目的就是为了确保每位乘客的安全。

外：那好吧。请抓紧时间，我还要赶飞机呢。

警：谢谢您的配合。

| 情景 2 | Handling a Case in Which a Long Knife is Found During the Inspection
安检中查获管制刀具的处置

Situation: At Baiyun Airport, an officer was asked to handle a situation in which a security inspector found a long knife in a passenger's carry-on luggage and decided to confiscate it, but the passenger refused and quarreled with him.

P: Good morning, sir. What's your name and nationality, please?

F: Good morning. My name is Ben Park and I'm from the U. S.

P: Mr. Park, could you show me your passport, please?

F: Here it is.

P: OK, thank you. Is this knife yours?

F: Yes, I bought it as a gift for my father who is crazy about collecting all kinds of knives.

P: This knife is too long and restricted in China, so it can't be carried along with you and it must be confiscated.

F: No, you can't do that. It's a gift for my father.

P: According to Article 32 of Public Security Administration Punishments Law of the People's Republic of China, Anyone who illicitly carries any gun, ammunition, crossbow, dagger or any other tool controlled by the state shall be detained for not more than 5 days, and maybe concurrently fined 500 yuan. If the case is not so serious, the person in question shall be

Unit 7　Security Inspection
安全检查

given a warning or be fined not more than 200 yuan. Anyone who illicitly carries any gun, ammunition, crossbow, dagger or any other tool controlled by the state into a public place or vehicle shall be detained for more than 5 days but not less than 10 days, and maybe concurrently fined 500 yuan.

F：Sorry, officer. I don't mean to break the law, and I didn't know the law before for this is my first time to China.

P：All right. But I have to confiscate the knife according to the law.

F：OK. Here you are.

P：Thank you for your cooperation.

警：上午好，先生。请问您叫什么名字，来自哪个国家？

外：我叫本·帕克，来自美国。

警：请出示一下您的护照。

外：给。

警：好的，谢谢。请问这把刀是您的吗？

外：是的，这是我给父亲买的礼物，他特别喜欢收藏世界上各种各样的刀具。

警：这把刀太长了，属于管制刀具，不能随身携带，所以，我将依法对其进行没收。

外：不行，你不能收走。这是我买给父亲的礼物。

警：对不起，我必须依法办事。根据《中华人民共和国治安管理处罚法》第三十二条，非法携带枪支、弹药或者弩、匕首等国家规定的管制器具的，处五日以下拘留，可以并处五百元以下罚款；情节较轻的，处警告或者二百元以下罚款。非法携带枪支、弹药或者弩、匕首等国家规定的管制器具进入公共场所或者公共交通工具的，处五日以上十日以下拘留，可以并处五百元以下罚款。

外：对不起，警官。我不是想故意违法，只是之前对贵国法律并不了解，这是我第一次来中国。

警：好吧。对于这把管制刀具我必须依法予以没收。

外：那好吧，给你。

警：谢谢您的配合。

| 情景 3 | Handling a Case in Which Drug is Found in a Passenger's Suitcase at Ruili Border Checkpoint
在瑞丽边检站查获毒品的处置

Situation: At Ruili border checkpoint, a passenger was found suspicious of drug trafficking when he had his suitcase checked by the machine, so the inspector called the police for help.

P: Good afternoon, Sir. Show me your passport, please.

F: OK. Here you are.

P: Is this your first time to China?

F: Yes.

P: What for?

F: I'm on a business trip.

P: All right. Come with me to the office over there.

F: Why?

P: I'm going to do a thorough check of your suitcase.

F: I don't think it's necessary since it's been checked by the machine. Furthermore, I'm in a hurry to catch a flight.

P: The machine shows there's something wrong with your suitcase, so I will check it by hand.

F: It's ridiculous. I only put some necessities for my trip and nothing else.

P: According to the law of China, I have to check the suspicious suitcase. Hope you can cooperate.

F: OK.

(In the office, the police officer found some suspicious white powder that weighed 2 kg and put it to a test. The result showed it was heroin.)

P: What's this? Where did you get it?

F: I don't know. This suitcase belongs to one of my friends who asked me to bring it to China.

Unit 7 Security Inspection
安全检查

P: Our test has proved it to be heroin which weighed 2 kg. You are illegally holding the drug. According to Criminal Law of the People's Republic of China, you have to go to Ruili municipal public security bureau with us for further investigation.

F: I'm innocent. There must be some misunderstanding.

P: Everything will be clear after our investigation.

警：下午好，先生。请出示您的护照。

外：好的，给你。

警：第一次来中国吧？

外：是的。

警：来干什么？

外：出差。

警：请跟我到那边的办公室来一下。

外：为什么？

警：我需要仔细检查一下您的行李箱。

外：刚才都已经在安检机检查过了，没有必要了吧？而且，我还要着急赶飞机呢。

警：机器显示箱子有问题，所以我需要手工检查一下。

外：无稽之谈。我的箱子里只装了一些旅行必需品，没有其他的。

警：根据我国法律，我必须对可疑行李进行检查。请您配合。

外：好吧。

（在办公室里，警察在行李箱的夹层里查获一些可疑白色粉末，后经检验确认为海洛因，重量达2公斤。）

警：这些是什么？哪来的？

外：不知道。这个箱子是一个朋友托我带到中国来的。

警：经过检验，我们已经证实这是海洛因，重达2公斤，你涉嫌非法持有毒品，根据中华人民共和国刑法，我们现依法对您进行传唤，跟我们到瑞丽市公安局接受进一步的调查。

外：我是无辜的，你们误会了。

警：经过调查之后，一切都会清楚的。

Part IV　Creative Work
创造性练习

Situation：随身物品安检。

听录音，请在听到提示音后开始口译。

警：上午好，先生。请问您叫什么名字，来自哪个国家？

外：上午好，我叫克里斯·史密斯，来自美国。

警：史密斯先生，请出示一下您的护照。

外：给。

警：好的，谢谢。请问这把枪是您的吗？

外：是的，这是一把玩具枪，送给儿子的礼物，他特别喜欢各种各样的枪。

警：在我国，这种枪属于管制器具，不能随身携带，所以，我将依法对其进行没收。

外：不行，您不能收走。这是我买给儿子的礼物。而且，在我们国家，携带枪支是合法的。

警：对不起，中国法律不同于美国法律。根据《中华人民共和国治安管理处罚法》第三十二条，非法携带枪支、弹药或者弩、匕首等国家规定的管制器具的，处五日以下拘留，可以并处五百元以下罚款；情节较轻的，处警告或者二百元以下罚款。非法携带枪支、弹药或者弩、匕首等国家规定的管制器具进入公共场所或者公共交通工具的，处五日以上十日以下拘留，可以并处五百元以下罚款。

外：对不起，警官。我不是想故意违法，只是之前对贵国法律并不了解，这是我第一次来中国。

警：好吧。对于这把管制枪我必须依法予以没收。此外，请跟我到派出所接受进一步调查。

外：那好吧。

警：谢谢您的配合。

Unit 8
Police Patrol and Traffic Stops
巡逻与盘查

Police patrol and traffic stop play an important role in preventing crimes and catching suspects. When doing so, police officers should, on the one hand, remain alert because the suspect may be an armed felon, and, on the other hand, avoid using rude and provocative language as a provoked foreigner may not cooperate. To ensure cooperation and avoid misunderstanding, it is absolutely necessary for police officers to use polite, clear and correct English.

巡逻与盘查在犯罪预防及追捕犯罪嫌疑人等方面起着非常重要的作用。民警在对步行或驾车的外国人实施盘查时，一方面应保持警惕，注意自身安全，因为盘查对象有可能是带武器的重罪犯；同时要避免使用粗暴和刺激性语言，因为一旦被激怒，被盘查的外国人有可能拒绝配合。为了确保被盘查者的配合，避免产生误解，警察要使用礼貌、清晰、正确的英语。

Part I New Words and Useful Expressions
生词与词组

patrol	英[pəˈtrəʊl] 美[pəˈtroʊl]	n. 巡逻
suspect	英[səˈspekt] 美[səˈspekt]	n. 嫌疑犯
alert	英[əˈlɜːt] 美[əˈlɜːrt]	adj. 警惕的，警觉的
felon	英[ˈfelən] 美[ˈfelən]	n. 重罪犯
provoke	英[prəˈvəʊk] 美[prəˈvoʊk]	vt. 激怒

provocative	英[prəˈvɒkətɪv] 美[prəˈvɑːkətɪv]	adj. 挑衅的
ensure	英[ɪnˈʃʊə(r)] 美[ɪnˈʃʊr]	vt. 保证，确保
investigation	英[ɪnˌvestɪˈgeɪʃn] 美[ɪnˌvestɪˈgeɪʃn]	n. 调查；调查研究
temporary	英[ˈtemprəri] 美[ˈtempəreri]	adj. 暂时的，临时的
routine	英[ruːˈtiːn] 美[ruːˈtiːn]	adj. 常规的，例行的
license	英[ˈlaɪsns] 美[ˈlaɪsns]	n. 执照，许可证
suitcase	英[ˈsuːtkeɪs; ˈsjuːtkeɪs] 美[ˈsuːtkeɪs]	n. 手提箱，行李箱
cooperate	英[kəʊˈɒpəreɪt] 美[koʊˈɑːpəreɪt]	vi. 合作，配合
certificate	英[səˈtɪfɪkət] 美[sərˈtɪfɪkət]	n. 证书，证明
coercive	英[kəʊˈɜːsɪv] 美[koʊˈɜːrsɪv]	adj. 强制的
checkpoint	英[ˈtʃekpɔɪnt] 美[ˈtʃekpɔɪnt]	n. 检查站，关卡
gesture	英[ˈdʒestʃə(r)] 美[ˈdʒestʃər]	n. 手势
property	英[ˈprɒpəti] 美[ˈprɑːpərti]	n. 财产
illegal	英[ɪˈliːgl] 美[ɪˈliːgl]	adj. 非法的；违法的
stab	英[stæb] 美[stæb]	vt. 刺；刺伤
intersection	英[ˌɪntəˈsekʃn] 美[ˌɪntərˈsekʃn]	n. 十字路口
crossing	英[ˈkrɒsɪŋ] 美[ˈkrɔːsɪŋ]	n. 十字路口
direction	英[dəˈrekʃn; daɪˈrekʃn] 美[dəˈrekʃn, daɪˈrekʃn]	n. 方向
frightened	英[ˈfraɪtnd] 美[ˈfraɪtnd]	adj. 害怕的；受惊的

to the point 扼要；切题

driver's license 驾照

the trunk/boot of the car 后备箱

take coercive measures 采取强制措施

pull over 靠边停车

roll down 摇下

set up temporary checkpoint 设置临时关卡

the crime scene 犯罪现场

what's up 什么事

run into 撞上

the plate number of the car 车牌号

Unit 8 Police Patrol and Traffic Stops
巡逻与盘查

Part II Useful Sentence Patterns
常用句型

- We are police officers from Yangfangdian police station and these are our police ID cards. Please go with us to the police station for further investigation.

  我们是羊坊店派出所的警察,这是我们的警官证。请跟我们到派出所接受进一步调查。

- Go with us, or we'll take coercive measures!

  跟我们走,不然我们就采取强制措施了!

- In China, if necessary, the police have the right to check anyone and anything suspicious by law.

  在中国,必要情况下,警察有权依法检查任何可疑人员和物品。

- This is a temporary check. Please show me your driver's license.

  临时检查,请出示一下您的驾照。

- We are searching for two men and a car. Please take a look at the pictures. Have you ever seen them?

  我们正在搜寻两个人和一辆车。请您看一下这些照片,看看是否见过他们。

Part III Situational Dialogues
情景对话

|情景1| Questioning a Suspicious Foreigner

盘问可疑外国人

P: Stop, sir!

F: What's up?

P: Why are you in such a hurry?

F: I'm trying to catch a movie.

P: Show me your passport, please.

F: I left it at home.

P: Do you have any other ID with you?

F: No.

P: What's your name?

F: I'm Evan Johansson.

P: What's your nationality?

F: I'm from the Philippines.

P: Is this bag yours?

F: Oh, yes.

P: But it's for a lady.

F: I know that.

P: What's in it?

F: Oh, sorry. It's my girlfriend's. I don't know what's in it.

P: We are police officers from Yangfangdian police station and these are our police ID cards. Please go with us to the police station for further investigation.

F: No! I'm in a hurry. I won't go anywhere.

P: Go with us, or we'll take coercive measures!

警：站住，先生！

外：什么事？

警：怎么这么慌慌张张的？

外：我急着去看电影。

警：请出示一下您的护照。

外：我忘带了。

警：有其他身份证件吗？

外：没有。

警：您叫什么名字？

外：埃文·约翰逊。

警：哪国人？

Unit 8 Police Patrol and Traffic Stops
巡逻与盘查

外：菲律宾。

警：这包是您的吗？

外：是的。

警：可这是一个女包。

外：我知道。

警：里面有什么？

外：哦，对不起。这包是我女朋友的，我不知道里面有什么。

警：我们是羊坊店派出所的警察，这是我们的警官证。请跟我们到派出所接受进一步调查。

外：不！我有急事。我哪儿也不去。

警：跟我们走，不然我们就采取强制措施了！

| 情景 2 | A Traffic Stop at a Routine Checkpoint
检查站内对过往车辆的常规检查

Situation：At a routine checkpoint, a police officer on duty gesticulates a driver to pull over. The driver pulls over and rolls down the window of his car.

P：Good morning, sir.

F：Good morning, officer. What's the matter?

P：This is a routine check.

F：Oh, I see.

P：Your driver's license, please.

F：Here you are.

P：What's your name, nationality?

F：I'm Harry Johnson from England.

P：Show me your passport.

F：Here it is.

P：What do you do in China?

F：I'm an English teacher.

P：Which school are you in?

F：Beijing Foreign Studies University.

P: Who is the lady beside you?

F: My wife.

P: Her passport, please.

F: OK. Here it is.

P: OK. Thank you. We need to check the boot of your car.

F: No. It's our personal property!

P: In China, if necessary, the police have the right to check anyone and anything suspicious by law.

F: There is nothing illegal or dangerous in it. You don't need to check it.

P: This is our official duty. Please cooperate.

F: All right.

P: Would you please open the suitcase?

F: Sure.

P: OK. Thank you for your cooperation.

F: May we go now?

P: Yes. Have a nice day!

警：早上好，先生。

外：早上好，警官。什么事？

警：这是例行检查。

外：噢，好的。

警：请出示驾驶证。

外：给，在这儿。

警：请问您的姓名、国籍？

外：我叫哈利·约翰逊，来自英国。

警：请出示一下您的护照。

外：给。

警：您在中国干什么？

外：在学校里当英语老师。

警：哪所学校？

外：北京外国语大学。

警：您身边这位女士是谁？

Unit 8 Police Patrol and Traffic Stops
巡逻与盘查

外：我太太。
警：请出示一下她的护照。
外：在这里，给您。
警：好的，谢谢。我们需要检查一下您车的后备箱。
外：不行，后备箱里是我们的私人物品。
警：在中国，必要情况下，警察有权依法检查任何可疑人员和物品。
外：里面没有违法物品或危险品，没必要检查了吧。
警：我们在执行公务。请配合一下。
外：好吧。
警：能否把手提箱打开让我检查一下里面的物品？
外：可以。
警：好了。谢谢您的配合。
外：我们可以走了吗？
警：可以走了。再见！

| 情景 3 | Searching for Wanted Suspects by Setting Up a Temporary Checkpoint
设置临时关卡搜寻犯罪嫌疑人

Situation：Two foreign suspects robbed a jewelry store and stabbed the owner. They ran away immediately in a white Honda. Police set up temporary checkpoints on roads around the crime scene to search for them.

P：Hello, sir.
F：Hello, officer. What's up?
P：This is a temporary check. Please show me your driver's license.
F：Here you are.
P：Thank you. We need to check the trunk of your car.
F：OK. Go ahead.
P：All right, thank you.
F：You are welcome.
P：We are searching for two men and a car. Please take a look at the

pictures. (showing him the pictures of the two men and the car) Have you ever seen them?

F: Yes, I've seen the guy who has long hair. He was driving a black Mazda, so fast that he almost ran into my car at the intersection.

P: When?

F: About ten minutes ago.

P: Where?

F: At the crossing between Yangzhou Road and Taizhou Road.

P: In which direction did he go?

F: To the west along Yangzhou Road.

P: Do you remember the plate number of the car?

F: Not completely. I got scared at that moment and could only remember the last two digits are 2 and 6.

P: Thank you so much, sir. You've been a big help.

F: My pleasure.

警：您好，先生。

外：您好，警官。什么事？

警：临时检查，请出示一下您的驾照。

外：给。

警：谢谢。我们需要检查一下您车的后备箱。

外：好的。

警：检查完了，谢谢您的配合。

外：不客气。

警：我们正在搜寻两个人和一辆车。请您看一下这些照片，看看是否见过他们。

外：我见过这个留着长头发的人，他开的是一辆黑色的马自达。当时他的车速特别快，经过十字路口时，差点儿撞上我的车。

警：什么时候？

外：大约10分钟之前。

警：在哪里？

外：就在扬州路和泰州路的交叉路口。

警：他朝哪个方向开走了？

Unit 8 Police Patrol and Traffic Stops
巡逻与盘查

外：沿着扬州路朝西走了。

警：您记得那辆车的车牌号吗？

外：没有记全。当时太害怕了，只记得车牌后两位数是2和6。

警：非常感谢，您给我们提供了很大的帮助。

外：愿意效劳。

Part IV Creative Work
创造性练习

听录音，请在听到提示音后开始口译。

警：您好，先生。

外：您好，警官。什么事？

警：例行检查，请出示您的驾驶证。

外：给您。

警：您的驾驶证已经过期了。

外：不会吧？

警：已经过期三个月了。

外：噢，实在对不起，我没有意识到已经过期了。

警：请出示一下这辆车的行驶证。

外：给您。

警：为什么行驶证上登记的车牌号与车上悬挂的车牌号不符？

外：不知道，这辆车是我借朋友的。

警：您的朋友叫什么名字，怎么联系他？

外：他叫汤尼·弗林，手机号是13301344851。

警：好的，请跟我们到交警队接受进一步的调查。

外：我真不知道这是怎么回事。

警：把发动机关掉！下车！

外：好吧。

Unit 9
Traffic Directions and Control
道路交通秩序管理

It is true that in modern cities worldwide, traffic is mostly controlled by the electronic systems automatically, but still quite a few situations, such as car accidents, literally require police officer's presence to issue directions, to ensure safe and smooth traffic flow. To English-speaking foreign drivers in China, these directions and commands must be given in English so that they can understand and follow the instructions without difficulties. This unit provides some commonly used English sentence patterns and model conversations about traffic directions and control.

尽管全球各大城市的交通大多都由电子系统自动控制，但在某些场合下，比如发生交通事故或道路修建时，仍然需要警察到场，指挥疏导交通。对那些说英语的司机下达口头交通指令时，交警应该使用英语，这样才能确保他们听懂并迅速执行指令。本单元将练习实施交通疏导和交通管制时常用的英语句型和典型对话。

Part I New Words and Useful Expressions
生词与词组

automatically 英[ˌɔːtəˈmætɪkli] 美[ˌɔːtəˈmætɪkli] adv. 自动地
literally 英[ˈlɪtərəli] 美[ˈlɪtərəli] adv. 确实地
ensure 英[ɪnˈʃʊə(r); ɪnˈʃɔː(r)] 美[ɪnˈʃʊr] vt. 保证，确保

Unit 9　Traffic Directions and Control
道路交通秩序管理

provide	英[prəˈvaɪd]	美[prəˈvaɪd]	vt. 提供
allow	英[əˈlaʊ]	美[əˈlaʊ]	vt. 允许
temporarily	英[ˈtemprərəli]	美[ˌtempəˈrerəli]	adv. 临时地
marathon	英[ˈmærəθən]	美[ˈmærəθɑːn]	n. 马拉松赛跑
announcement	英[əˈnaʊnsmənt]	美[əˈnaʊnsmənt]	n. 公告；通告
avoid	英[əˈvɔɪd]	美[əˈvɔɪd]	vt. 避免；避开
actually	英[ˈæktʃuəli]	美[ˈæktʃuəli]	adv. 实际上
release	英[rɪˈliːs]	美[rɪˈliːs]	v. 发布
navigation	英[ˌnævɪˈɡeɪʃn]	美[ˌnævɪˈɡeɪʃn]	n. 导航系统
fault	英[fɔːlt]	美[fɔːlt]	n. 错误
detour	英[ˈdiːtʊə(r); ˈdiːtɔː(r)]	美[ˈdiːtʊr]	n. 迂回路；临时绕行道路
Jaywalker	英[ˈdʒeɪwɔːkə(r)]	美[ˈdʒeɪwɔːkə(r)]	n. 不守交通规则；乱穿马路的人
pedestrian	英[pəˈdestriən]	美[pəˈdestriən]	adj. 徒步的
underpass	英[ˈʌndəpɑːs]	美[ˈʌndərpæs]	n. 地下通道
stall	美[stɔːl]		v. 突然熄火；（发动机）突然熄火
vehicle	英[ˈviːəkl]	美[ˈviːəkl, ˈviːhɪkl]	n. 车辆
garage	英[ˈɡærɑːʒ; ˈɡærɑːdʒ; ˈɡærɪdʒ]	美[ɡəˈrɑːʒ, ɡəˈrɑːdʒ]	n. 车库；汽车修理厂
assistance	英[əˈsɪstəns]	美[əˈsɪstəns]	n. 援助，帮助

traffic flow 交通流量

follow the instruction 执行指令

be towed away 被拖走

be closed to traffic 实施交通管制

do me a favor 帮我个忙

a couple of minutes 几分钟

traffic jam 交通堵塞

pay parking lot 收费停车场

on the scene 现场的

pedestrian overpass 步行天桥

take the underpass 走地下通道

break down 发生故障

Part II　Useful Sentence Patterns
常用句型

- Parking is not allowed here from 8:00 a.m. to 8:00 p.m.

  此处早8点到晚8点禁止停车。

- Illegal parking would cause traffic jams. I would have it towed away if you parked it here.

  违章停车会造成交通堵塞。如果您停在这儿，我会叫拖车把它拖走的。

- The road is temporarily closed to traffic.

  这条路暂时实行交通管制了。

- We released a notice on our official website and Traffic Radio yesterday afternoon.

  昨天下午就在官网和交通台上发布了交通管制通知。

- You can take the pedestrian overpass or underpass.

  你可以走天桥或地下通道。

Part III　Situational Dialogues
情景对话

|情景1|　Stop Illegal Parking

　　　　　阻止违章泊车

P: Hello, madam. You cannot park here.

F: Why not?

P: Parking is not allowed here from 8:00 a.m. to 8:00 p.m.

Unit 9 Traffic Directions and Control
道路交通秩序管理

F: It's only five past 8:00 a.m., and I'll be back pretty soon. Could you do me a favor and let me park the car here for a couple of minutes?

P: I'm sorry I can't. This is a busy street. Illegal parking would cause traffic jams. I would have it towed away if you parked it here.

F: OK. Could you tell me where the nearest parking lot is?

P: There is a pay parking lot in front of the supermarket over there.

F: Thank you.

P: My pleasure.

警：您好，女士。您不能在这儿停车。

外：为什么？

警：此处早8点到晚8点禁止停车。

外：现在是早上8点刚刚过5分钟，而且我马上就回来。求求您让我在这儿停几分钟吧。

警：对不起，真的不行。这儿是繁忙街道，违章停车会造成交通堵塞。如果您停在这儿，我会叫拖车把它拖走的。

外：那好吧。能告诉我离这儿最近的停车场在哪儿吗？

警：那边的超市前面有个收费停车场。

外：谢谢。

警：不客气。

| 情景 2 | Traffic Control
          交通管制

Situation: Some roads are closed to traffic because of the city marathon. A foreign driver didn't get the news in advance and was stopped. He asked the police on the scene for help.

F: Hello, officer. What's the matter?

P: The road is temporarily closed to traffic.

F: Why?

P: There is a city marathon going on now and this road is one part of the route.

F: I see. I wish there was an announcement beforehand, so I could avoid choosing this road.

P: Actually, we have done that. We released a notice on our official website and Traffic Radio yesterday afternoon. Besides, we used some cellphone apps such as Baidu Navigation to notify the public.

F: Oh, it's my fault. I should have checked my cellphone before starting. Could you please tell me how to get to the Second Ring Road?

P: Sure. But you have to make a detour.

F: How?

P: Turn right here. Go along that street and turn left at the first crossing. Then drive straight ahead for about 500 meters and you will get there.

F: Thank you.

P: You're welcome.

外：您好，警官。请问这是怎么回事？

警：这条路暂时实行交通管制了。

外：为什么？

警：今天举行城市马拉松比赛，这条路是比赛路线的一部分。

外：我明白了。真希望你们提前发布交通管制通知，那样我就不会走这条路了。

警：我们已经提前发了通知。昨天下午就在官网和交通台上发布了管制信息。而且，我们还借助百度导航等手机客户端发布了相关信息通知。

外：噢，那怪我了，我应该在出发前看看手机提醒信息就好了。麻烦您告诉我怎样才能上二环，好吗？

警：没问题。但您得绕一下。

外：怎么绕呢？

警：这个地方右转弯，沿着那条街往前开，第一个十字路口往左拐。再往前开大约500米就能上二环路了。

外：谢谢。

警：别客气。

Unit 9　Traffic Directions and Control
道路交通秩序管理

|情景 3|　Stop Jaywalkers
阻止乱穿马路的人

P: Hello, sir. Please don't cross the road from here.

F: Why?

P: It's too dangerous.

F: How can I get to the other side of the road?

P: You can take the pedestrian overpass or underpass.

F: Where is the overpass? Is it far away from here?

P: Walk straight ahead about 200 meters.

F: OK. Thank you.

P: You are welcome. The underpass is a bit closer from here.

F: How far?

P: Walk backward for about 150 meters.

F: All right, thank you. I will take the underpass then.

P: My pleasure.

警：您好，先生。请不要从这里横穿马路。

外：为什么？

警：从这里过马路太危险了。

外：我需要到马路对面去，怎样才能过去呢？

警：可以走天桥或地下通道。

外：天桥在哪儿？离这里远吗？

警：就在前面，大约200米。

外：好的，谢谢您。

警：不客气。地下通道离这儿稍微近一些。

外：大约要走多远？

警：往回走大约150米就到了。

外：好的，那我还是走地下通道吧，谢谢。

警：不客气。

| 情景 4 | **Help to Move a Stalled Vehicle**
协助转移故障车

P: Hello, sir. Can we help you?

F: Yes. My car's broken down.

P: Is it movable?

F: I think so.

P: Let's push the car to the side of the road.

F: All right.

P: Do you need a tow truck?

F: Yes. I'd like to have it towed to the nearest garage.

P: There is a garage about 2 kilometers from here. You can have your car fixed there.

F: Thank you for your assistance.

P: It's our pleasure.

警：您好，先生。需要帮忙吗？

外：需要。我的车坏了。

警：您的车子可以动吗？

外：我看没问题。

警：我们把它推到路边去。

外：好的。

警：需要拖车吗？

外：需要。我想把它拖到离这儿最近的修车厂去。

警：离这儿两公里左右有修车厂。

外：谢谢帮忙。

警：别客气。

Unit 9　Traffic Directions and Control
道路交通秩序管理

Part IV　Creative Work
创造性练习

▶ 听录音，请在听到提示音后开始口译。

1. 交通管制

外：您好，警官。怎么回事？

警：您好，先生。这条路临时实行交通管制。

外：为什么？

警：一个外国使团的车队将从这儿通过。

外：管制多长时间？

警：大约半个小时。

外：我着急去西单大悦城看电影呢，快到时间了。

警：如果着急的话，可以绕一下，走其他的路。

外：怎么走呢？

警：从这个地方右转，顺这条街往前走，第一个十字路口左拐，再往前走大约500米就到了。

外：谢谢。

警：别客气。

2. 阻止违章停车

警：您好，先生。请不要在这儿停车。

外：为什么？这儿没有禁止停车的标志呀。

警：现在这里交通流量太大，停车会造成交通堵塞。

外：我就停一会儿，马上开走。

警：一分钟也不能停，如果违章停车的话，您的车将会被拖走而且还要交罚款。

外：那好吧。请问附近有停车场吗？

警：前面不远处就有一个。

外：怎么去那儿？

警：向前开500米左右然后右转，您就能看到停车场的标志了，就在您的右手边。

Unit 10
Community Policing Management Involving Foreigners 涉外社区警务管理

As is well known, neighborhood watch plays a very important role in preventing crimes. With the number of foreign residents in China increasing, community policing in China relies on the cooperation of not only Chinese but also foreign residents. Therefore, community police officers should keep contact with foreign residents and foreign companies or joint-venture enterprises in their communities, communicate with them and constantly remind them to protect themselves and prevent crime. What's more, officers should encourage them to help police in the investigation when a crime occurs. Good command of English, of course, plays an important role in communicating with English-speaking foreigners in three basic crime-prevention approaches, namely, human prevention, physical protection and technical prevention.

众所周知，邻里守望在犯罪预防方面起着非常重要的作用。由于在华外籍居民人数不断增加，中国的社区警务不仅要依靠中国居民，也要依靠外籍居民。因此，社区警察应该保持与所在社区内外国人和合资企业的联系，与他们交流沟通，动员他们自我保护和预防犯罪。此外，还要鼓励他们当犯罪发生时积极帮助警方进行调查。当然，在落实三防（人防、物防和技防）与外国人交流时，较高的英语水平至关重要。

Unit 10 Community Policing Management Involving Foreigners
涉外社区警务管理

Part I New Words and Useful Expressions
生词与词组

therefore 英[ˈðeəfɔː(r)] 美[ˈðerfɔːr] adv. 因此；所以

suspicious 英[səˈspɪʃəs] 美[səˈspɪʃəs] adj. 可疑的

disturb 英[dɪˈstɜːb] 美[dɪˈstɜːrb] vt. 打扰

burglary 英[ˈbɜːɡləri] 美[ˈbɜːrɡləri] n. 入室偷窃

delivery 英[dɪˈlɪvəri] 美[dɪˈlɪvəri] n. 递送

intruder 英[ɪnˈtruːdə(r)] 美[ɪnˈtruːdər] n. 侵入者

securely 英[sɪˈkjʊəli] 美[sɪˈkjʊrli] adv. 安全地；牢固地

peddler 英[ˈpedlə(r)] 美[ˈpedlər] n. 小贩

peephole 英[ˈpiːphəʊl] 美[ˈpiːphoʊl] n. 猫眼，窥视孔

release 英[rɪˈliːs] 美[rɪˈliːs] v. 松开

promptly 英[ˈprɒmptli] 美[ˈprɑːmptli] adv. 迅速地

headquarter 英[ˌhedˈkwɔːtə(r)] 美[ˌhedˈkwɔːrtər] n. 指挥中心

recommend 英[ˌrekəˈmend] 美[ˌrekəˈmend] vt. 建议

install 英[ɪnˈstɔːl] 美[ɪnˈstɔːl] vt. 安装

competitive 英[kəmˈpetətɪv] 美[kəmˈpetətɪv] adj. 有竞争力的

prosper 英[ˈprɒspə(r)] 美[ˈprɑːspər] vi. 繁荣，昌盛

infrared 英[ˌɪnfrəˈred] 美[ˌɪnfrəˈred] adj. 红外线的

monitoring 英[ˈmɒnɪtərɪŋ] 美[ˈmɑːnɪtərɪŋ] n. 监控

sense 英[sens] 美[sens] vt. 感觉到；检测

neighborhood watch 邻里联防，邻里守望

in the service of 为……服务

fill out 填写

on vacation 度假

none of your business 不关你的事

keep...in your mind 把……记在心中

Part II　Useful Sentence Patterns
常用句型

- We learned that you are newcomers here, so we're here to see if there is anything we can do for you.

  知道您刚搬到这里，特来拜访，想了解一下能为您做些什么。

- We are visiting every home to learn about the residents.

  为了解每一户的情况，我们对每一家都要走访。

- Tell us what's happening and maybe we can help you.

  我们是警察，告诉我们发生了什么，或许能帮到您。

- There have been some burglaries in this area recently. Be sure to lock the doors when you leave home.

  最近，这一带地区发生了几起盗窃案。出门时一定把门关好。

- Most burglars gain access through unlocked front and back doors or windows. Be sure to check the house carefully before going to bed or going out.

  多数盗贼都是从忘了上锁或没有关上的前后门、窗户进入室内的。睡前和外出前一定要检查一下。

- If you notice an intruder, keep calm, note his features, and notify us immediately.

  如果发现有盗贼入室，要保持冷静，记住他的长相和特征，尽快找机会报警。

- In case your house was broken into and some properties were stolen, leave the area as it is and dial 110 to report to the police promptly.

  如果家中进了小偷，丢了东西，一定要保护好现场，尽快拨打110报警。

- We have English speaking officers on duty at 110 headquarters.

  110指挥中心有英语值班员。

- We're police officers assigned to this neighborhood.

  我们是这个社区的社区民警。

Unit 10　Community Policing Management Involving Foreigners
涉外社区警务管理

- Many burglars can open them easily because they're equipped with advanced technology and tools.

现在很多入室盗窃犯拥有先进技术和工具，轻易就可以打开防盗门窗。

Part III　Situational Dialogues
情景对话

|情景 1|　Calling on Foreign Residents
拜访外籍居民

Police: Good morning, sir. I'm officer Li from Rose Garden Police Station. And this is officer Wang.

Foreigner: Good morning, officer. I'm Stephen McDonald.

P: We're in the service of this neighborhood. We learned that you are newcomers here, so we're here to see if there is anything we can do for you.

F: Oh, that's very nice of you. Nice to meet you.

P: Nice to meet you, too. We are visiting every home to learn about the residents. Would you please fill out this form?

F: What for?

P: It will help us to provide you with better service. Could you please fill it out now?

F: I see. But I'm very busy just now.

P: That's all right. You may keep it for a few days.

F: OK, thank you.

P: You are welcome. When will you finish it?

F: In three or four days. OK?

P: Fine, thank you. We'll come to get it then. Well, we must go. Sorry for disturbing you.

F: Not at all.

P: Good-bye, Mr. McDonald.

F: Good-bye, officer.

警察：早上好，先生。我是玫瑰园派出所的小李。这位是小王。

外国人：您好。我是斯蒂文·麦克唐纳。

警：我们是这一片的社区民警。知道您刚搬到这里，特来拜访，想了解一下能为您做些什么。

外：太好了。很高兴见到你们。

警：我们也很高兴见到您。为了了解每一户的情况，我们对每一家都要走访。请您填一下这个表好吗？

外：干什么用的？

警：为了帮助我们更好地为您服务，把我们的工作做得更好。

外：我明白了，但是我现在没时间填。

警：没关系，您先拿着，有时间再填也行。

外：好的，谢谢。

警：不客气，您大约什么时间可以填完？

外：三四天好吗？

警：好的，谢谢，到时候我们再来取。我们告辞了，打扰了。

外：不客气。

警：再见，麦克唐纳先生。

外：再见，警官先生。

| 情景2 | Helping a Foreign Girl Having Run Away from Home at Night

帮助晚上离家出走的外籍女孩

P: Hi! What are you doing here, little girl?

F: It's none of your business. Leave me alone.

P: What's the matter with you? You look unhappy. We are police officers. Tell us what's happening and maybe we can help you.

F: I've said it's none of your business. Please go away.

Unit 10   Community Policing Management Involving Foreigners
涉外社区警务管理

P: No. We can't leave you here alone at this moment of the night. It's very dangerous. May I know your name?

F: Susan.

P: OK, Susan. Tell us why you're standing here alone in the middle of the night.

F: Because I don't want to go home.

P: Where is your home?

F: A few blocks away.

P: What's your parents' cellphone number? They must be worrying about you right now.

F: I don't think so. They don't care about me at all.

P: Impossible. None of the parents in the world don't love their kids.

F: I do have the feeling that they don't love me.

P: There must be some misunderstandings. Come on, tell me your parents' phone number.

F: The cellphone number of my mum is 17765432231. But please don't call her. I hate her.

P: I'll call her just to let her know that you are safe with us.

(After calling her mother)

P: Your parents are worried to death and looking for you everywhere. You see, they do love you and care about you.

F: Maybe you are right.

P: They are hurrying here. We'll stay with you till they arrive.

F: Thank you.

P: My pleasure. Please keep it in mind that your parents love you very much. Talk to them more and you'll understand what they have done for you.

F: OK, thank you. I will do that.

P: You are welcome. We are so happy to hear that.

警：你好，小姑娘！在这儿做什么呢？

外：不关你的事。别管我！

警：遇到什么不顺心的事情了？你看上去好像不开心。我们是警察，告诉我们发生了什么，或许能帮到你。

外：我说了不关你们的事。请走开。

警：不行，天这么晚了，我们不能让你一个人待在这里。这很危险。你叫什么名字？

外：苏珊。

警：好了，苏珊。告诉我们这么晚了为什么一个人待在这里。

外：因为我不愿回家。

警：家在哪儿？

外：过几栋楼就是。

警：你父母的手机号是多少？你不回家，他们现在肯定特别担心你。

外：不会的，他们一点儿都不关心我。

警：不可能不关心你的。天底下哪有父母不爱自己的孩子的？

外：我就是觉得他们一点儿也不爱我。

警：你们之间肯定有一些误会。快点儿，跟我说一下你父母的手机号。

外：我妈妈的手机号是17765432231。不要给她打电话，我讨厌她。

警：我给她打个电话，告诉她你现在跟我们在一起，很安全。

（打完电话后）

警：你父母担心死了，现在到处找你呢。你看，他们的确非常关心你、爱你。

外：也许是吧。

警：他们正着急往这儿赶呢。他们到之前，我们会一直陪着你的。

外：谢谢。

警：不客气。请一定记住你父母非常爱你。平时多跟他们聊聊，你会明白他们的良苦用心的。

外：好的，谢谢，我会的。

警：不客气。听到你这么说，我们真的很高兴。

Unit 10　Community Policing Management Involving Foreigners
涉外社区警务管理

|情景 3| Giving Advice to a Foreign Resident on Self-protection and Crime Prevention
为外籍居民提供自我防范建议

P: Good morning, Mrs. Brown.

F: Good morning, officers.

P: Haven't seen you for a long time. How have you been doing?

F: Fine, thank you.

P: We want to talk to you for a couple of minutes if you aren't too busy.

F: All right.

P: There have been some burglaries in this area recently. Be sure to lock the doors when you leave home.

F: Sure.

P: When you are away on vacation, make sure that thieves do not notice your absence. I suggest you have newspaper delivery stopped, for example.

F: Oh, good idea.

P: Most burglars gain access through unlocked front and back doors or windows. Be sure to check the house carefully before going to bed or going out. Never forget to lock the house securely.

F: OK, I've got it.

P: Do not let peddlers or salesmen into the house. Speak to them through the small window or the peephole in the door and do not release the safety-chain.

F: All right.

P: If you notice an intruder, keep calm, note his features, and notify us immediately.

F: I see.

P: In case your house was broken into and some properties were stolen, leave the area as it is and dial 110 to report to the police promptly.

F: I can't speak Chinese. May I call at 110 in English?

P: Certainly. We have English speaking officers on duty at 110 headquarters.

F: OK. Thank you for letting me know.

P: My pleasure.

警：早上好，布朗太太。

外：早上好，警官。

警：好久不见了。最近好吗？

外：挺好的，谢谢。

警：方便的话我们想和您谈谈。

外：好的。

警：最近，这一带地区发生了几起盗窃案。出门时一定把门关好。

外：好的。

警：如果外出度假长时间不在家的话，千万不要让小偷知道家里没人。比如，可以先暂时停止送报。

外：好主意。

警：多数盗贼都是从忘了上锁或没有关上的前后门、窗户进入室内的。睡前和外出前一定要检查一下，不要忘记锁门关窗。

外：好的，明白了。

警：不要让小贩和推销员进屋。最好通过小窗口、猫眼洞同他们交谈，不要打开安全链。

外：我会注意的。

警：如果发现有盗贼入室，要保持冷静，记住长相和特征，尽快找机会报警。

外：明白。

警：如果家中进了小偷，丢了东西，一定要保护好现场，尽快拨打110报警。

外：我不会讲汉语，用英语打110电话可以吗？

警：可以。110指挥中心有英语值班员。

外：太好了。谢谢。

警：应该的。

Unit 10 Community Policing Management Involving Foreigners
涉外社区警务管理

|情景 4| Giving a Foreign Company Advice on Crime Prevention
为外企预防犯罪提供建议

P: Hello, Sir.

F: Hello, officers.

P: We're police officers assigned to this neighborhood. Nice to see you.

F: Nice to see you, too.

P: We'd like to talk to you for a few minutes if you don't mind.

F: All right. What is it?

P: We're glad your company has moved here to our neighborhood. For the safety of your company, we recommend that you install an alarm system.

F: Is it necessary? I know the crime rate here is very low.

P: But it doesn't mean that there is no crime at all here. Your company is very competitive, and it has a brilliant future. I'm sure it will develop and prosper here for a long time. So in the long run, it pays to install an alarm system such as infrared alarm devices and monitoring cameras.

F: But we have already installed burglary-resisting doors and windows.

P: That's not enough. Many burglars can open them easily because they're equipped with advanced technology and tools. If an infrared alarm device is installed, it can send out a loud alarming sound when sensing an intruder. This can frighten burglars away and help to protect your company.

F: That's true. Thank you for your advice. We'll do it accordingly as soon as possible.

P: Thank you for your cooperation. This is my business card, with the telephone number of our police station on it. Call us if you need any help.

F: Thanks again. Bye-bye.

P: Bye-bye.

警：您好，先生。

外：您好，警官。

警：我们是这个社区的社区民警。见到您很高兴。

外：见到您我也很高兴。

警：如果不介意的话，我们想和您聊一会儿。

外：可以。聊什么？

警：贵公司搬到我们社区，我们都很高兴。为了贵公司的安全，我们建议安装报警系统。

外：有必要吗？据我们了解，这里的犯罪率很低。

警：犯罪率低并不代表没有犯罪。贵公司很有竞争力，前途无量，我敢肯定贵公司将在这里获得长期稳步的发展。因此从长远来看，安装红外线报警装置和监视录像是值得的。

外：我们已经安装了防盗门和防盗窗。

警：仅仅安装防盗门窗还不够。现在很多入室盗窃犯拥有先进的技术和工具，轻易就可以打开防盗门窗。安装红外线报警装置以后，如果感应到入室盗窃犯后，就会自动发出警报，吓跑窃贼，从而起到保护公司的作用。

外：您说得对。谢谢您的建议。我们马上按您说的去做。

警：谢谢合作。这是我的名片，上面有报警电话，保持联系。

外：再次感谢。再见。

警：再见。

Part IV Creative Work
创造性练习

Situation：几个外国籍少年在住宅小区里骑改装助动车飙车，居民反映说这样做太吵而且不安全。作为社区民警兼国际学校的校外指导员前去制止，讲清危害，让他们今后不要这样做。

▶ 听录音，请在听到提示音后开始口译。🎧

警：你好，小伙子！你是本社区国际学校的学生吗？

外：是的。

Unit 10　Community Policing Management Involving Foreigners
涉外社区警务管理

警：从哪个国家来的？

外：加拿大。

警：我是你们学校的校外辅导员。你的助动车改装过吧？

外：是的。

警：助动车的限速是每小时 20 公里。你们方才飙车超过了限速，噪音大而且危险。

外：但是在我们国家这是允许的，很好玩。

警：你要知道在中国这是不允许的，这样做违法。

外：哦，我以前不知道，我再也不会这样做了。

警：很好！谢谢你的合作，小伙子！

Unit 11
Administration of the Foreigner's Entry and Exit 外国人入出境管理

When Chinese nationals go abroad to study or work or only reside in a foreign country, sometimes they need a new visa or visa extension. Likewise, foreigners in China may have similar experiences. In addition, they have to do something that is not required in Western countries because of the differences in regulations. For instance, in China foreigners must get their dwelling or lodging places registered with local police stations. In order to manage foreigners' entry, stay, residence and exit efficiently, Chinese police officers need to use English when communicating with English speakers. This unit contains some dialogues as well as expressions frequently used in handling foreigners' accommodation registration, application for a new visa and visa extension.

中国公民在国外居住、上学或工作时,有时需要新的签证或签证延期。同样,在中国的外国人也有类似的需求,由于国家规定不同,他们还必须做一些在西方国家不需要做的事情。例如,在中国,外国人必须到当地派出所办理住宿登记手续。为了高效做好外国人入境、停留或居留、出境等方面的管理工作,我国民警需要用英语与外国人交流。本单元介绍了民警在为外国人办理住宿登记、签证补办、签证延期等业务时常用的英语表达方式。

Unit 11 Administration of the Foreigner's Entry and Exit
外国人入出境管理

Part I New Words and Useful Expressions
生词与词组

accommodation	英[əˌkɒməˈdeɪʃn] 美[əˌkɑːməˈdeɪʃn]	n. 住宿
registration	英[ˌredʒɪˈstreɪʃn] 美[ˌredʒɪˈstreɪʃn]	n. 登记
specific	英[spəˈsɪfɪk] 美[spəˈsɪfɪk]	adj. 具体的
qualified	英[ˈkwɒlɪfaɪd] 美[ˈkwɑːlɪfaɪd]	adj. 合格的
extend	英[ɪkˈstend] 美[ɪkˈstend]	vt. 延长
extension	英[ɪkˈstenʃn] 美[ɪkˈstenʃn]	n. 延长
undergo	英[ˌʌndəˈɡəʊ] 美[ˌʌndərˈɡoʊ]	vt. 经历
accumulated	英[əˈkjuːmju‚leɪtɪd] 美[əˈkjʊmjə‚letɪd]	adj. 累计的
duration	英[djuˈreɪʃn] 美[duˈreɪʃn]	n. 持续的时间
specify	英[ˈspesɪfaɪ] 美[ˈspesɪfaɪ]	vt. 详细说明
notice	英[ˈnəʊtɪs] 美[ˈnoʊtɪs]	n. 通知

confirmation of reporting the loss of passport 护照报失证明

be informed of 收到……通知

visa extension 签证延期

Foreign Permanent Residence ID Card 外国人永久居留证件

a certificate of kinship 亲属关系证明

Part II Useful Sentence Patterns
常用句型

- He has to conduct accommodation registration within 24 hours of his arrival.
  他应在入住后24小时内办理住宿登记。

- Please fill in the Visa Application Form.
  请填一张《外国人签证证件申请表》。

- This is a letter of notice for you and you will be informed of the result of your application in seven workdays.

这是您的业务受理通知单，工作人员会在7个工作日内通知您审核结果。

- We take either card or cash.

  我们接受现金或银行卡付款。

- If the duration could be extended, the accumulated length of extension must not exceed the original duration of stay specified in your visa.

  如果您的申请得到批准，延长的停留期限，累计不得超过签证原注明的停留期限。

Part III Situational Dialogues
情景对话

情景 1 Handling Foreigner's Accommodation Registration
受理外国人住宿登记

P: Hello! Sir. Can I help you?

F: Hello officer. My brother came to Beijing from London to visit me. He arrived yesterday and stayed at my house. I've heard that he is supposed to report to the local police station for accommodation registration. Is that right?

P: Yes. According to the law, he has to do it within 24 hours of his arrival. Has he come here with you?

F: No. I'll do that for him.

P: Please show me your passport.

F: Here you are.

P: Thanks. Mr. Brown, what's your brother's name, nationality and birth date?

F: He's Jacob Brown, a British. He was born on September 5, 1990.

P: Have you brought his passport?

F: Yes. Here it is.

P: What's his job and workplace?

F: He is a teacher at London University.

P: What's his purpose for coming to China?

Unit 11　Administration of the Foreigner's Entry and Exit
外国人入出境管理

F：For travelling.

P：Did he begin to live at your house yesterday? What's the specific address?

F：Yes. My address is Building 3 Room 1306 in Muxidi Nanli.

P：When will he leave?

F：In three days.

P：What is your phone number?

F：My phone number is…and his is…

P：All right, Mr. Brown. The registration is done.

F：Thank you. Good-bye.

P：You are welcome. Good-bye.

警：您好，先生。请问有什么可以帮您的？

外：我弟弟从伦敦来北京看我，昨天下午刚到，现住在我家里，我听说需要来公安机关办理住宿登记，对吧？

警：是的。按规定他应在入住后24小时内办理住宿登记。他跟您一起来了吗？

外：没有，我来替他办。

警：看一下您的护照。

外：给。

警：谢谢，布朗先生。请问您弟弟的姓名、国籍、出生日期？

外：雅各布·布朗，英国人，出生于1990年9月5日。

警：他的护照带来了吗？

外：带来了，给你。

警：他的职业和工作单位是什么？

外：他在伦敦大学教学。

警：他来中国的目的是什么？

外：旅游。

警：他是昨天下午入住您家的，是吧？具体地址在哪儿？

外：是的。我家地址是木樨地南里3号楼1306室。

警：他什么时间离开？

外：三天后。

警：你们两人的手机号分别是什么？

外：我的手机号是……他的是……

警：好的，布朗先生，已经登记好了。

外：谢谢您，警官，再见。

警：不客气，再见。

|情景 2| Handling Application for a New Visa
受理签证补发申请

P: Good morning, sir. What can I do for you?

F: Good morning, officer. I want to apply for a new visa because I lost my passport several days ago.

P: Have you got the confirmation of reporting the loss of passport and a new passport?

F: Yes, I've got both of them. Here you are.

P: OK, Mr. Smith, please fill in the Visa Application Form. Besides, please submit a qualified photo.

F: All right, I'll fill it in right now. This is my photo.

P: Mr. Smith, this is a letter of notice for you and you will be informed of the result of your application in seven workdays. You can come here to pick up your passport then.

F: Thank you, I see. How much should I pay?

P: The fee is 160 RMB.

F: Can I pay with a credit card?

P: Sure, we take either card or cash.

F: OK, thank you.

P: You're welcome.

警：早上好，先生。请问您要办理什么业务？

外：早上好，警官。前段时间我的护照丢了，我想申请补发一个签证。

警：请问您有护照报失证明和新护照吗？

外：都有，在这儿。

警：好的。请填一张《外国人签证证件申请表》，并提交一张符合规定要求的照片。

Unit 11　Administration of the Foreigner's Entry and Exit
外国人入出境管理

外：好的，我马上填。这是我的照片，给您。
警：好的。史密斯先生，这是您的业务受理通知单，工作人员会在7个工作日内通知您审核结果，到时候您凭此通知单前来领取您的护照。
外：谢谢，我需要付多少钱？
警：160元人民币。
外：我能刷信用卡吗？
警：可以，卡和现金都可以。
外：好的，非常感谢，再见。
警：不客气，再见。

|情景 3|　Handling Application for Visa Extension
受理签证延期申请

P: Good morning, madam. What can I do for you?

F: Good morning, officer. I would like to extend my visa.

P: Have you brought your passport with you? What type of visa do you have?

F: Yes, here you are. My visa is Q2.

P: What is your reason for extending?

F: I came to visit my brother who is holding a permanent residence permit in China and had planned to go back to the U.S. next month. But unfortunately, my brother got a heart attack and underwent an operation. He is still in the hospital. I have to stay here longer to take care of him but my visa will expire soon.

P: Sorry about your brother. Well, Miss Smith, please fill in the Visa Application Form first and then submit one qualified photo, a certificate of kinship between you and your brother, and your brother's Foreign Permanent Residence ID Card.

F: OK, I will fill in the form right now. These are the materials needed. Here you are.

P: OK. If the duration could be extended, the accumulated length of extension must not exceed the original duration of stay specified in your visa, that is to say, 120 days.

F: Thank you, I see. I think that will be enough. How much should I pay?

P: The fee is 160 RMB.

F: Can I pay with a credit card?

P: Sure, we take the card.

F: OK, thank you.

P: Miss Smith, this is a letter of notice for you and you will be informed of the result of your application in seven workdays. You can come here to pick up your passport then.

F: Thank you so much.

P: You're welcome.

警：早上好，女士。请问您要办理什么业务？

外：早上好，警官。我想申请签证延期。

警：请问您的签证类型是什么？带护照了吗？

外：Q2字签证。带了，给您。

警：好的。请问您的申请延期的理由是什么呢？

外：我哥哥已经取得了在中国的永久居留证，我这次来中国看他，原本打算下个月就回美国的。不幸的是，他突发严重心脏病，做了手术，现在还躺在医院里，所以我不得不多待一段时间来照顾他，但是，我签证上的停留期限马上就要到期了。

警：很遗憾听到你哥哥的事。史密斯女士，您需要填一张《外国人签证证件申请表》。此外，您要提供一张符合规定要求的照片、您和哥哥之间亲属关系证明以及您哥哥的《外国人永久居留证》。

外：好的，我马上填。这些都是需要的相关材料，我已经准备好了，给您。

警：好的，谢谢。如果您的申请得到批准，延长的停留期限，累计不得超过签证原注明的停留期限，也就是说，不能超过120天。

外：谢谢，我明白。我想120天应该足够了。我需要付多少钱？

警：签证延期费用是160元人民币。

外：我能刷信用卡吗？

警：可以。

外：好的，非常感谢。

警：史密斯女士，这是您的业务受理通知单，工作人员会在7个工作日内通知

Unit 11 Administration of the Foreigner's Entry and Exit
外国人入出境管理

您审核结果,到时候您凭此通知单前来领取您的护照。

外:明白了,谢谢。

警:不客气。

Part IV Creative Work
创造性练习

听录音,请在听到提示音后开始口译。

警:您好,先生。请问有什么可以帮您的?

外:您好,警官。我从旧金山来看我弟弟,昨天刚到,现住在他家里,我听说需要来公安机关办理住宿登记,对吧?

警:是的。按规定您应在入住后24小时内办理住宿登记。请问您的姓名、国籍、出生日期?

外:我叫雅各布·布朗,美国人,出生于1992年9月5日。

警:看一下您的护照。

外:给。

警:您的职业和工作单位是什么?

外:我在斯坦福大学教学。

警:您来中国目的是什么?

外:出差。

警:您是昨天下午开始住在您弟弟家的,是吧?具体地址在哪儿?

外:是的。我弟弟家的地址是白云路3号楼1306室。

警:您什么时间离开?

外:三天后。

警:你们两人的手机号分别是什么?

外:我的手机号是……他的是……

警:好的,布朗先生,已经登记好了。

外:谢谢您,再见。

警:不客气,再见。

Unit 12

Handling Cases of Illegal Immigration
外国人"三非"案件处置

　　Illegal immigration is a transnational headache. Traditionally, the destinations of immigrants are mainly the United States, Canada, and Australia. But over recent years more and more illegal immigrants have been sneaking into China chiefly because of good money-making opportunities brought about by her fast development and economic prosperity. These people are mostly from South and Southeast Asian countries. A large number of them tend to commit crimes and thus cause disturbances in Chinese society. Although these illegal migrants have their own mother tongues, many of them speak English too. There are also illegal immigrants from some Western countries. They came to China for traveling, but continued to stay after their visas expired. They can survive comparatively easily by teaching or tutoring English without proper work permits since the language is extremely hot and English teachers, especially native speakers, are welcome almost everywhere in our country. To sum up, illegal immigration refers to illegal entry, illegal residency and illegal employment. The cases in these categories are handled by the Exit-Entry Administration Law of the People's Republic of China and Regulation of the People's Republic of China on the Administration of the Entry and Exit of Foreign Nationals. When investigating or questioning foreigners involved in such a case, police officers need to speak clear and appropriate English to determine the foreigners' identities, state the penalty decisions and the legal basis, and inform them of their rights if necessary.

Unit 12　Handling Cases of Illegal Immigration
外国人"三非"案件处置

　　非法移民是一个令人头疼的跨国问题。传统移民目的地主要包括美国、加拿大和澳大利亚。但近年来，因为中国的快速发展和经济繁荣带来了很多赚钱机会，越来越多的非法移民偷偷进入中国，这些人大多来自南亚和东南亚国家，极有可能在中国从事各种违法犯罪活动，从而给中国社会安全带来威胁。虽然这些非法移民有自己的母语，但他们中的许多人也说英语。此外，还有一些非法移民来自西方国家，他们来中国旅行，发现在中国英语学习非常热门，以英语为母语的英语教师深受欢迎，即便在没有工作许可的情况下，他们也可以通过教英语来轻松谋生，所以有些人签证到期后选择继续留在中国。综上所述，外国人"三非"案件包括非法入境、非法居留或非法就业。此类案件的处置依据主要是《中华人民共和国出境入境管理法》《中华人民共和国外国人入境出境管理条例》等。处置此类案件时，我国民警需要正确使用英语，以便能够及时查清涉案外国人身份，宣布处罚决定及其所依据的法律条款，必要时告知其所享有的诉权。

Part I　New Words and Useful Expressions
生词与词组

destination	英[ˌdestɪˈneɪʃn] 美[ˌdestɪˈneɪʃn]	n. 目的地，终点
prosperity	英[prɒˈsperəti] 美[prɑːˈsperəti]	n. 繁荣
disturbance	英[dɪˈstɜːbəns] 美[dɪˈstɜːrbəns]	n. 骚乱
comparatively	英[kəmˈpærətɪvli] 美[kəmˈpærətɪvli]	adv. 比较地
tutor	英[ˈtjuːtə(r)] 美[ˈtuːtər]	v. 辅导
extremely	英[ɪkˈstriːmli] 美[ɪkˈstriːmli]	adv. 非常地
repatriate	英[ˌriːˈpætrieɪt] 美[ˌriːˈpeɪtrieɪt]	v. 遣返
injure	英[ˈɪndʒə(r)] 美[ˈɪndʒər]	vt. 伤害
contract	英[ˈkɒntrækt] 美[ˈkɑːntrækt]	n. 合同
scope	英[skəʊp] 美[skoʊp]	n. 范围
penalty	英[ˈpenəlti] 美[ˈpenəlti]	n. 处罚

sneak into 偷偷摸摸地进入

tend to commit crime 极有可能犯罪

a large number of 大量的

continued to do sth. 继续做某事

work permit 工作许可证

to sum up 总而言之

illegal entry 非法入境

illegal employment 非法就业

illegal residence 非法居留

clear up the matter 把事情弄清楚

be suspected of 涉嫌

Alien Employment Permit 外国人就业证

sign a contract 签订合同

request for administrative reconsideration 申请行政复议

lodge an administrative lawsuit 提起行政诉讼

Part II Useful Sentence Patterns
常用句型

- You are suspected of illegal entry.

  您涉嫌非法入境。

- you will be repatriated and you may not enter China within five years from the day of repatriation.

  决定将您遣送出境,自被遣送出境之日起5年内不准入境。

- You should have applied to the local exit and entry administration bureau for an extension.

  您本应该在到期之前去出入境管理部门办理延期手续的。

- Have you signed a contract with the school?

  您和学校签合同了吗?

Unit 12

Handling Cases of Illegal Immigration
外国人"三非"案件处置

- You have been suspected of working illegally, so please come to the police station with us to be questioned.

  您已经涉嫌非法就业,现在我们口头传唤您到公安局接受继续盘问。

- If you don't accept the penalty, you have the right to apply for administrative reconsideration within 60 days or lodge an administrative lawsuit within 3 months according to law.

  如果对此处罚决定有异议的话,您有权在60日内申请行政复议或3个月内提起行政诉讼。

- This is the written penalty decision, we'll read it to you in English, and then please sign it.

  这是处罚决定书,我们会用英语为您宣读一遍,听完之后,请签字。

Part III   Situational Dialogues
情景对话

情景 1 Handling Cases of Foreigners' Illegal Entry
外国人非法入境案件处置

P: Hello, sir. We are police officers from Yuetan police station of Xicheng District, please show your passport.

F: Oh, I have left it at the hotel.

P: Do you have any other ID?

F: No.

P: What's your name and nationality?

F: I'm Sven Grooten from the Philippines.

P: When did you come to China?

F: Last month.

P: The exact date?

F: Sorry, I've forgotten.

P: Where did you enter China?

F: At Baiyun airport in Guangzhou.

P: What is your purpose for coming to China?

F: For a tour.

P: Where do you stay now in China?

F: I'm staying in the hotel just across the street.

P: Please take us to your room and show us your passport since it's not far away from here.

F: Well, to tell you the truth, I've lost it.

P: Then please come with us to the police station.

F: Why?

P: You have neither passport nor any other ID. You are suspected of illegal entry.

F: Oh, no.

P: To clear up the matter, you must come to the police station with us to be questioned.

F: OK.

(After further investigation, the police found out that the foreigner entered China illegally by using a fake passport and visa.)

P: After a thorough investigation, we have proved that you entered China illegally. According to Article 71 of the Exit-Entry Administration Law of the People's Republic of China, you'll be fined RMB 4000. If you don't accept the penalty, you have the right to apply for administrative reconsideration within 60 days or lodge an administrative lawsuit within 3 months according to law. This is the written penalty decision, I'll read it to you in English, and then please sign it.

F: OK. I accept the penalty.

P: According to Article 62 of Exit-Entry Administration Law of the People's Republic of China, you will be repatriated and you may not enter China

Unit 12 Handling Cases of Illegal Immigration
外国人"三非"案件处置

within five years from the day of repatriation. If you don't accept the decision, you have the right to apply for administrative reconsideration within 60 days.

F：OK. I see.

警：您好，先生。我们是西城区月坛派出所的民警，请出示您的护照。

外：我没带，放在宾馆里了。

警：您有其他身份证件吗？

外：没有。

警：您叫什么名字？哪国人？

外：我叫斯文·格罗腾，菲律宾人。

警：您是什么时候来中国的？

外：上个月。

警：具体哪一天？

外：我不记得了。

警：从哪里入境的？

外：广州白云机场。

警：来中国干什么？

外：我来旅游。

警：您现在住在哪里？

外：就在街对面的宾馆里。

警：既然这么近，那就带我们去房间看一下您的护照吧。

外：说实话，我的护照丢了。

警：您没有护照，又没有其他身份证件，涉嫌非法入境，我们现在口头传唤您到公安局接受进一步调查。

外：好吧。

（经进一步询问和调查，证实该外国人使用伪造的护照和签证入境，确属非法入境。）

警：经过全面调查，我们已经证实您确属非法入境。根据《中华人民共和国出境入境管理法》第71条规定，我们决定对您处以罚款人民币4000元。如果对此处罚决定有异议的话，您有权在60日内申请行政复议或3个月内提起行政诉讼。这是处罚决定书，我们会用英语为您宣读一遍，听完之后，请签字。

外：噢，好吧，我接受处罚。

警：根据《中华人民共和国出境入境管理法》第62条规定，决定将您遣送出境，自被遣送出境之日起5年内不准入境。如不服本决定，可在60日内申请行政复议。

外：好的，我知道了。

| 情景2 | Handling Cases of Illegal Residence
非法居留案件处置

P: Hello, madam. We are police officers from Jinsong police station of Chaoyang District. Show me your passport, please.

F: OK. Here it is.

P: When and where did you enter China?

F: I entered China at Beijing Capital International Airport on August 4.

P: The duration after entry specified in your visa is 30 days, so you have to leave China before september 3, but it's september 25 today.

F: I'm sorry. I came here to visit my son who's an overseas student and I had planned to leave on August 30. Unfortunately, my son was seriously injured in an accident on 28th that month, so I had to stay to take care of him.

P: You should have applied to the local exit and entry administration bureau for an extension of stay.

F: I know, but I was so busy that I just forgot to do so.

P: You are suspected of illegal residence because you didn't exit China on time or extend the visa 7 days before it expires. Please come with me to the police station to be questioned.

F: OK.

(After further investigation, the foreigner is proved of illegal residence but no other offence.)

Unit 12　Handling Cases of Illegal Immigration
外国人"三非"案件处置

P: You have illegally stayed in China for 22 days. According to Article 78 of Exit and Entry Administration Law of the People's Republic of China, you shall be fined 10000 RMB. If you don't accept the penalty, you have the right to apply for administrative reconsideration within 60 days or lodge an administrative lawsuit within 3 months according to law. This is the written penalty decision, we'll read it to you in English, and then please sign it.

F: OK. I accept the penalty.

警：您好，女士，我们是朝阳区劲松派出所的民警。请出示一下您的护照。

外：好的，给您。

警：请问您是什么时间从哪个口岸入境的？

外：8月4日从北京机场入境的。

警：您签证上注明的入境后停留期限为30天，也就是说您应该最晚于9月3日出境，但今天都已经是9月25日了。

外：对不起。我是来看望在中国留学的儿子的，本来打算8月30日回国，但我儿子在8月28日不幸发生了车祸，受伤非常严重，我不得不留下来照顾他。

警：您本应该在到期之前去出入境管理部门办理延期手续的。

外：我知道，但是这段时间我太忙了，就给忘了。

警：您没有按期内出境或在停留期限满七日前办理延期，已经涉嫌非法居留，请跟我到公安局接受继续盘问。

外：好吧。

（经过进一步的调查，证实改外国人确属非法居留，但没有其他违法行为。）

警：经过调查，我们已经证实您在中国非法居留达22天。根据《中华人民共和国出境入境管理法》78条规定，我们将对您处以罚款人民币5000元。如果对此处罚决定有异议的话，您有权在60日内申请行政复议或3个月内提起行政诉讼。这是处罚决定书，我们会用英语为您宣读一遍，听完之后，请签字。

外：好吧，我接受处罚。

| 情景 3 | Handling Cases of Illegal Working
　　　　　处置非法就业

P: Hello, sir. We are police officers from Chaoyang branch of Beijing municipal public security bureau. Show us your passport, please.

F: OK, here you are.

P: Do you work here?

F: Yes, I teach English here.

P: How did you get the job?

F: A friend of mine introduced me here.

P: How long have you been working here?

F: Almost two months.

P: Have you signed a contract with the school?

F: No.

P: Do you have a work permit?

F: Yes.

P: Show us your Alien Employment Permit.

F: OK.

P: The working place stated in your permit is Beijing Foreign Studies University instead of this English training school.

F: Yes, I just do a part-time job here.

P: According to Article 43 of the Exit-Entry Administration Law of the People's Republic of China, foreign nationals are working illegally if they work in China beyond the scope specified in work permits.

F: Oh no. It's just a part-time job.

P: A part-time job is a job too. You are suspected of working illegally, so please come to the police station with us to be questioned.

F: OK.

警：您好，先生，我们是北京市公安局朝阳分局的民警。请出示一下您的护照。

外：好的，给您。

Unit 12　Handling Cases of Illegal Immigration
外国人"三非"案件处置

警：您在这儿工作吗?

外：是的，我在这儿教英语。

警：怎么得到这份工作的?

外：一个朋友介绍我来的。

警：在这工作多长时间了?

外：大约两个月了。

警：签合同了吗?

外：没有。

警：有工作许可证吗?

外：有。

警：给我们看一下。

外：好的。

警：您工作许可证上的工作单位是北京外国语大学，不是这家外语培训机构。

外：是的，我在这儿只是兼职。

警：根据《中华人民共和国出境入境管理法》，如果工作地址与许可证上注明地址不同，就属于非法就业。

外：没有那么严重吧? 我只是兼职而已。

警：兼职也是工作，您已经涉嫌非法就业，现在我们口头传唤您到公安局接受继续盘问。

外：好吧。

Part IV　Creative Work
创造性练习

▶ 听录音，请在听到提示音后开始口译。 🎧

警：您好，先生，我们是北京市公安局海淀分局的民警。您在这儿工作吗?

外：是的，我在这儿教英语。

警：您是怎么得到这份工作的?

外：一个朋友帮我介绍的。

警：在这工作多长时间了？

外：大约两个月了。

警：签过合同吗？

外：没有。

警：看一下您的护照。

外：给您。

警：您持有的是X1签证，是留学生吗？

外：是的。

警：在哪个学校？

外：北京语言大学。

警：看一下您的居留许可证。

外：请稍等，我找一下。

警：您的居留许可证并未加注勤工助学或实习，因此是不能在校外工作的。

外：对不起，我以前不知道有这样的规定。

警：根据《中华人民共和国外国人入境出境管理条例》第22条规定，您已经涉嫌非法就业，现在我们口头传唤您到公安局接受继续盘问。

外：好吧。

Unit 13
Handling Public Security Cases Involving Foreigners 涉外治安案件查处

Security cases involving foreigners refer to cases of disrupting public order, encroaching upon the right of individuals or property and impairing social administration. They are tackled in accordance with the Public Security Administration Punishments Law of the People's Republic of China. In this unit, police officers will learn some useful expressions and sentences needed to interrogate English speakers involved in public security cases, to inform them of the penalty with its legal basis, and their legal right to apply for administrative reconsideration or to appeal.

常见的涉外治安案件有扰乱公共秩序、侵犯人身权利或财产权利、妨害社会管理等。此类案件一般依照《中华人民共和国治安管理处罚法》进行处置。本单元将学习如何用英语询问违反治安管理的外国行为人，宣布处罚决定及其法律依据，并告知其依法申请行政复议或诉讼的权利。

Part I New Words and Useful Expressions 生词与词组

disrupt	英[dɪsˈrʌpt] 美[dɪsˈrʌpt]	vt. 破坏
encroach	英[ɪnˈkrəʊtʃ] 美[ɪnˈkroʊtʃ]	vi. 侵犯
impair	英[ɪmˈpeə(r)] 美[ɪmˈper]	vt. 损害

tackle	英[ˈtækl] 美[ˈtækl]	vt. 应付，处理
proceeding	英[prəˈsiːdɪŋ] 美[prəˈsiːdɪŋ]	n. 诉讼
respective	英[rɪˈspektɪv] 美[rɪˈspektɪv]	adj. 分别的，各自的
strike	英[straɪk] 美[straɪk]	vt. 打
fault	英[fɔːlt] 美[fɔːlt]	n. 过错
maliciously	英[məˈlɪʃəsli] 美[məˈlɪʃəsli]	adv. 有敌意地，恶意地
bleeding	英[ˈbliːdɪŋ] 美[ˈbliːdɪŋ]	adj. 流血的
witness	英[ˈwɪtnəs] 美[ˈwɪtnəs]	n. 证人
interview	英[ˈɪntəvjuː] 美[ˈɪntərvjuː]	vt. 询问
sign	英[saɪn] 美[saɪn]	vt. 在……上签名
punch	英[pʌntʃ] 美[pʌntʃ]	vt. 用拳猛击
bruise	英[bruːz] 美[bruːz]	vt. 使受瘀伤
dislodge	英[dɪsˈlɒdʒ] 美[dɪsˈlɑːdʒ]	vt. 使……移动
mediate	英[ˈmiːdieɪt] 美[ˈmiːdieɪt]	vi. 调解
agreement	英[əˈɡriːmənt] 美[əˈɡriːmənt]	n. 协议
fulfill	英[fʊlˈfɪl] 美[fʊlˈfɪl]	vt. 履行
privacy	英[ˈprɪvəsi] 美[ˈpraɪvəsi]	n. 隐私
private	英[ˈpraɪvət] 美[ˈpraɪvət]	adj. 私人的
prostitute	英[ˈprɒstɪtjuːt] 美[ˈprɑːstɪtuːt]	n. 妓女
resist	英[rɪˈzɪst] 美[rɪˈzɪst]	vt. 抵抗
attractive	英[əˈtræktɪv] 美[əˈtræktɪv]	adj. 吸引人的；有魅力的
continue	英[kənˈtɪnjuː] 美[kənˈtɪnjuː]	vi. 继续

refer to 指的是

encroaching upon the right of the person 侵犯他人人身权利

impairing social administration 妨害社会管理

in case 以防，万一

off and on 时不时地

hit the roof 勃然大怒

overseas student 留学生

China University of Geosciences 中国地质大学

Unit 13   Handling Public Security Cases Involving Foreigners
涉外治安案件查处

in detail 详细地

break up with my girlfriend 同女朋友分手

in a low mood 情绪低落

cheer myself up 使自己高兴起来

be dumped by 被甩了

lose one's temper 发脾气

as compensation 作为赔偿

complain about 投诉

record of this interrogation 询问笔录

Part II   Useful Sentence Patterns
常用句型

- We are going to ask you a few questions in accordance with the law.
  现依法对你进行询问。

- Please tell the truth and you have a legal responsibility for what you say.
  你要如实回答并对自己所讲的话承担法律责任。

- It's their fault. They started it!
  他们的错,是他们挑起来的。

- I saw one of them got a bleeding nose.
  我看到他们当中有一个人鼻子出血了。

- You are suspected of having violated Public Security Administration Punishments Law of the People's Republic of China.
  你们涉嫌违反《中华人民共和国治安管理处罚法》。

- Tell us in detail what happened.
  详细讲讲事情经过。

- After investigation, we learned that your punches bruised his face and dislodged one of his teeth.

经调查我们得知，你把室友打得面部青肿，一颗牙齿脱落。

- We can mediate for you if both of you want us to do so.

  如果你俩都愿意，我们可为你们调解。

- I am the officer in the service of this community.

  我是这个社区的社区民警。

- We have received a call from your neighbor complaining about loud noise in your house

  我们收到您的邻居打来举报电话，投诉您家中噪音太大。

Part III Situational Dialogues
情景对话

情景 1 Handling a Case of Fighting Involving Overseas Students
处理留学生打架斗殴案件

P: Stop fighting! We are police officers from Haidian branch of Beijing municipal public security bureau!

F: It's their fault. They started it!

P: Come with us to the police station to be questioned!

(At the Police Station)

P: We are police officers from Haidian branch of Beijing municipal public security bureau. We are going to ask you a few questions in accordance with the law. Please tell me the truth. You have a legal responsibility for what you say.

F: I see.

P: What's your name and nationality?

F: Jack Thompson from Australia.

P: Show me your passport, please.

F: Here you are.

Unit 13

Handling Public Security Cases Involving Foreigners
涉外治安案件查处

P: When did you come to China and what for?

F: We came here last month for travelling.

P: Where are you staying?

F: Beijing Home Inn Plus.

P: Are you all from Australia?

F: Yes.

P: Tell me the names of the other two.

F: John Lewis and Angela Davis.

P: Why were you fighting with them?

F: Because they talked about and laughed at my girlfriend Angela.

P: How many of them were there?

F: Two.

P: Did they speak English?

F: No. I didn't know what language they spoke. Spanish, perhaps.

P: Do you understand Spanish?

F: No, I don't.

P: Then how could you tell they were talking about your girlfriend?

F: We were having dinner at a restaurant and they sat next to us. At first, I didn't notice them. My girlfriend told me that both of them stared at her and smiled maliciously. Later, I found they did stare at her off and on and whisper to each other. I really hit the roof and went over to fight with them.

P: Did you all attack them?

F: Yes.

P: Did you use any weapons?

F: No. We used our fists.

P: Did they fight back?

F: Yes.

P: Are you injured?

F: No.

P: Do you know what injures you've caused the other two?

F: Well, I saw one of them got a bleeding nose.

P: And another got a black eye.

F: Oh, really?

P: Did you have any witnesses?

F: Yes, there were some other customers eating at another table. Besides, the waiters were all there.

P: OK. Do you have anything else to say?

F: No.

P: You are suspected of having violated Public Security Administration Punishments Law of the People's Republic of China.

F: Sorry we didn't realize that.

P: Don't leave China before the decision is made. This is the record of this interview. I'll read it to you in English and then please sign it if everything is correct.

F: OK.

P: Please return here at 3 tomorrow afternoon for the decision.

F: All right.

(At 3 o'clock the next afternoon)

P: Haidian branch of Beijing municipal public security bureau has investigated the case of your beating others and has made public security punishment decisions. According to Article 43 of Public Security Administration Punishments Law of the People's Republic of China, you shall be detained for 5 days and fined 500 yuan. You have the rights to apply for administrative reconsideration within 60 days or lodge an administrative lawsuit within 3 months according to law. This is a written decision. I'll read the English translation to you and then you sign your name if there is nothing wrong.

F: All right. I see.

警：快住手！我们是北京市公安局海淀分局的民警！

外：是他们挑起来的。

警：现在我口头传唤你们到公安机关接受调查。

Unit 13　Handling Public Security Cases Involving Foreigners
涉外治安案件查处

（在公安局）

警：我们是北京市公安局海淀分局的民警，现依法对你进行询问，你要如实回答并对自己所讲的话承担法律责任。

外：我知道。

警：你叫什么名字？哪国人？

外：杰克·汤普森，澳大利亚人。

警：看一下你的护照。

外：给，在这里。

警：什么时候来中国的？来干什么？

外：我们来旅游，上个月到的。

警：现在住哪儿？

外：北京如家精选宾馆。

警：你们几个都是澳大利亚人吗？

外：是的。

警：另外两个叫什么名字？

外：约翰·刘易斯，安吉拉·戴维斯。

警：因为什么打起来的？

外：他们背后谈论并嘲笑我女朋友。

警：他们有几个人？

外：2个人。

警：他们讲的是英语吗？

外：不是。我不知道他们讲的是什么语言。好像是西班牙语。

警：你能听懂西班牙语？

外：听不懂。

警：那你们怎么知道他们是在谈论你女朋友呢？

外：当时我们三个正在饭馆吃饭，他们两人坐在邻桌。一开始我并没有注意到他俩，但我女朋友说那两个人一直盯着她看，并不怀好意地朝她笑。我女朋友比较胖，所以很敏感，她认为那两个人在笑话她。后来，我发现他们俩确实时不时地盯着我女朋友看并小声说着什么。当时我就火冒三丈，跑过去跟他们扭打在一起了。

警：你们全都动手了吗？

外：是的。

警：你们怎么打的他们？用拳头还是用什么东西？

外：只用拳头。

警：他们还手了吗？

外：还了。

警：你受伤了吗？

外：没有。

警：把对方打成什么样了？

外：我看到他们当中有一个人鼻子出血了。

警：另一个人被打得眼眶淤青。

外：噢，真的吗？

警：有没有人看见你们打架？

外：有，当时还有一桌人在吃饭，饭店服务员也在场。

警：好的，还有没有要补充说明的？

外：没有了。

警：你们的行为涉嫌违反《中华人民共和国治安管理处罚法》。

外：对不起，我们没有意识到这点。

警：做出处罚决定之前，不得离境。这是询问笔录，我会用英语读给你听，如果没有问题，请签字。

外：好的。

警：请于明天下午3点到这里听候处罚决定。

外：好的。

（第二天下午3点）

警：北京市公安局海淀分局对你们殴打他人一案进行了调查，并依法对你们作出了治安处罚决定。根据《中华人民共和国治安管理处罚法》第（43）条，对你们处以拘留5天和罚款500元。对这一决定你们有权在60日内依法提起行政复议或者在3个月内申请行政诉讼。这是处罚决定书，我将用英语为你宣读一遍，听后请签字。

外：好吧。我明白了。

Unit 13　Handling Public Security Cases Involving Foreigners
涉外治安案件查处

| 情景 2 |　Handling a Case Involving Foreigners by Mediating
　　　　　调解处置涉外纠纷案件

P: We are police officers from Chaoyang branch of Beijing municipal public security bureau. We are going to ask you a few questions in accordance with the law. Please tell the truth and you have a legal responsibility for what you say.

F: I see.

P: What's your name and nationality?

F: I'm Aven Thompson from Canada.

P: Show me your passport, please.

F: Here you are.

P: Are you an overseas student? When did you come to China?

F: Yes. I came here this past August.

P: Where are you studying now?

F: China University of Geosciences.

P: Where are you living?

F: Room 206 of the dormitory building for overseas students in that university.

P: Do you know why you have been brought here?

F: Yes. And I'm very sorry. I shouldn't have hit my roommate.

P: Tell us in detail what happened.

F: I just broke up with my girlfriend a few days ago and I was in a low mood. In order to cheer me up, I went to a bar to have some drinks this afternoon.

P: Which bar?

F: A bar named "Midnight" on Sanlitun Street.

P: How much did you drink?

F: I drank 2 bottles of wine.

P: Were you drunk?

F: Yeah. I went to my dormitory and wanted to sleep. At that time, my roommate was watching TV and it was noisy. I asked him to turn down the

TV. He not only refused to do so, but also laughed at me for I was being dumped by my girlfriend. I lost my temper and punched him.

P: How many times did you punch him?

F: One on the mouth and the other two on the face.

P: Did he fight back?

F: Yes.

P: Are you injured?

F: No.

P: After investigation, we learned that your punches bruised his face and dislodged one of his teeth.

F: I drank too much and couldn't control myself.

P: You have broken the law for fighting others.

F: I'm so sorry for what I've done. I'd like to apologize to him and pay him some money as compensation.

P: We can mediate for you if both of you want us to do so. If an agreement is reached and fulfilled successfully, you will be free of punishment. If no agreement is reached or the agreement is not fulfilled, you will be punished according to law.

F: OK, I see.

P: This is the record of this interrogation. I'll read it to you in English and then please sign your name if there is nothing wrong.

警：我们是北京市公安局朝阳分局的民警，现依法对你进行询问，你要如实回答并对自己所讲的话承担法律责任。

外：我明白。

警：你叫什么名字？哪国人？

外：我叫埃文·汤普森，来自加拿大。

警：看一下你的护照。

外：给，在这里。

警：你是留学生？什么时候来中国的？

外：是的，今年八月份。

Unit 13   Handling Public Security Cases Involving Foreigners
涉外治安案件查处

警：在哪个学校？

外：中国地质大学。

警：现在住哪儿？

外：中国地质大学留学生宿舍楼206室。

警：知道为什么被带到这儿来吗？

外：知道。很抱歉，我不应该打人。

警：详细讲讲事情经过。

外：因为前几天刚跟女朋友分手，心情特别不好，今天下午去了酒吧，想喝点儿酒散散心。

警：哪家酒吧？

外：位于三里屯路上的"夜半时分"酒吧。

警：喝了多少？

外：2瓶红酒。

警：喝醉了吗？

外：醉了。回到宿舍后我想睡觉，但我室友还在看电视，而且声音开得特别大，我让他调小点儿。他不但不调，还嘲笑我被女朋友甩了。我特别生气，就动手打了他。

警：打哪儿了？

外：一拳打在嘴上，另两拳打在脸上。

警：他还手了吗？

外：还了。

警：把你打伤了吗？

外：没有。

警：经调查我们得知，你把室友打得面部青肿，一颗牙齿脱落。

外：我当时喝多了，没有控制住自己。

警：你殴打他人，触犯了中国法律。

外：我知道错了，我愿意向他道歉并赔偿他的损失。

警：如果你俩都愿意，我们可为你们调解，达成调解协议并履行的话，我们可以不处罚你。达不成协议或者达成协议不履行的，我们会依法对你作出处罚决定。

外：好的。我明白了。

警：这是询问笔录。我用英语读给你听，没有什么问题的话，签上你的名字。

外：好的。

| 情景 3 | Handling a Case Involving a Foreigner's Whoring
            处理涉外嫖娼案件

P: We are police officers from Xicheng branch of Beijing public security bureau. We are going to ask you a few questions. You will have to take legal responsibility for what you say, so please tell the truth. Is that clear?

F: Quite clear.

P: What's your name and nationality?

F: I'm Edward White from the U. S.

P: Show me your passport.

F: Here you are.

P: When and where did you enter China?

F: Last week at Beijing airport.

P: What for?

F: On business.

P: Please tell us what you did in the hotel last night.

F: Oh, it's my privacy.

P: It may be against the law, so it's not a private matter at all.

F: All right. Last night, when I was about to go to bed, I got a telephone call.

P: What was the exact time?

F: Ten o'clock.

P: Who called you?

F: A young lady.

P: Do you know her?

F: No.

P: What did she say?

Unit 13   Handling Public Security Cases Involving Foreigners
涉外治安案件查处

F: She asked if I needed someone to chat with.

P: What language did she speak?

F: English. Very poor English.

P: Did you know what she really meant?

F: Yes. I could tell she was a prostitute.

P: What did you say to her?

F: Well, I couldn't resist… Her voice was so sweet and attractive. So I let her in.

P: When did she get to your room?

F: At about ten thirty.

P: What happened next?

F: You can tell what we did. We…we had sex.

P: Did you pay her money?

F: Yeah.

P: How much did you pay?

F: 500 dollars.

P: Have you done this before?

F: No. This is my first time.

P: Is there anything else you want to say?

F: No.

P: This is the record of this interrogation. I will read it to you in English and then you sign your name if there is nothing wrong.

F: OK.

警：我们是北京市公安局西城分局的民警，现依法对你进行询问，你要如实回答并对自己所讲的话承担法律责任，听清楚了吗？

外：清楚了。

警：你叫什么名字？哪国人？

外：我叫爱德华·怀特，来自美国。

警：看一下你的护照。

外：给，在这里。

警：什么时候从哪个口岸入境中国的？

外：上周刚到，我从北京入境的。

警：来做什么？

外：出差。

警：说说昨晚你在旅馆干了些什么。

外：哦，那是私事。

警：这件事涉嫌违法，因此绝不是什么私事。

外：好吧，我说。昨晚我刚要睡觉的时候接到一个电话。

警：当时是几点？

外：大约10点。

警：谁来的电话？

外：一个年轻女子。

警：你认识她吗？

外：不认识。

警：她说了些什么？

外：她问我是否需要有人陪着聊天。

警：她讲的是哪国语言？

外：英语。很糟糕的英语。

警：你当时知道她的真正用意吗？

外：知道。我猜她是妓女。

警：你是怎样回的电话？

外：怎么说呢？我难以抗拒……她的声音是那么甜美，那样有魅力。因此我让她到我房间来。

警：她到达你房间是什么时间？

外：大约十点半。

警：接着发生了什么？

外：我们发生了性关系。

警：付钱给她了吗？

外：付了。

警：付了多少钱？

Unit 13 Handling Public Security Cases Involving Foreigners
涉外治安案件查处

外：500 元。

警：以前做过这事吗？

外：没有，这是第一次。

警：还有其他要补充的吗？

外：没有了。

警：这是询问笔录。我用英语读给你听，没有什么问题的话，签上你的名字。

外：好的。

| 情景 4 | Handling a Case of Noise Complaint
处理噪音投诉

P: (Knocking at the door.) Hello, is there anyone at home?

F: Hello, officer.

P: I am the officer in the service of this community. Could you show me your passport?

F: Sure. Wait a moment and I am getting it.

P: Good. Mrs Black, We have received a call from your neighbor complaining about loud noise in your house.

F: I'm sorry. My friends and I are having a party. Perhaps the music is too loud.

P: It's OK to have a party. But please keep the music down. It is midnight now.

F: Oh, I'm terribly sorry. We didn't notice it's already that late.

P: Please turn the music down now.

F: All right. We'll keep it low.

P: Thank you for your cooperation. According to the law, noisemakers will be fined not less than RMB 200 and not more than RMB 500 yuan if they continue to do so after being warned.

F: I promise it won't happen again.

警：（边敲门边问）请问有人在家吗？

外：您好，警官。

警：您好，我是这个社区的社区民警，请出示一下您的护照。

外：好的，没问题，请稍等，我去拿一下。

警：布莱克先生，我们收到您的邻居打来的举报电话，投诉您家中噪音太大。

外：抱歉，我和朋友正在家里聚会，可能是音乐声音太大了。

警：可以在家里聚会，但一定要把音乐声音调小点儿，都已经半夜了。

外：实在是对不起，我们没有意识到已经这么晚了。

警：请现在就把音乐声音调低。

外：好的，我马上就去。

警：谢谢您的配合。根据我国相关法律，噪音制造者受到警告处罚之后，仍然不改的将被处以 200 元以上 500 元以下罚款。

外：放心吧，不会再发生类似的事情了。

| 情景 5 | Handling a Case of Drug Abuse
吸毒案件的查处

P：We're police officers of Chaoyang branch of Beijing public security bureau. We're going to interrogate you in the light of law. You should answer honestly instead of trying to conceal facts or lying to us. Otherwise, you have to take legal responsibility. You have the right to refuse to answer questions irrelevant to the case. Am I understood?

F：Yes, I've got it.

P：Why are you brought to the police station?

F：Because I took drugs.

P：Tell us the incident in detail, please.

F：Last Sunday, my friends and I had a party in KOKOMO Bar. We got together in a private room, singing, dancing and drinking. One of my friends took a mysterious small ball, telling me it's fancy to take it and persuaded me to have a try. I didn't believe him at first. Seeing more and more friends began to try it, I lost my control and took one. Later I knew it

Unit 13　Handling Public Security Cases Involving Foreigners
涉外治安案件查处

was Ecstasies. Suddenly that night, some police officers broke in and found we were taking drugs and then brought us to the police station for further investigation. I took a urine drug test, and the result was positive.

P: Is this your first time taking the drug?

F: Yes.

P: Do you have anything else to say?

F: No.

P: Did you tell the truth?

F: Yes, everything is true.

P: We've read the record of interrogation in English to you. Is it the same as what you've said?

F: Yes.

P: Please sign it.

F: OK.

警：我们是北京市公安局朝阳分局的警察，现在依法对你进行询问，你要如实回答，不能隐瞒作假，否则要承担法律责任。与本案无关的问题，你有权拒绝回答，听清楚了吗？

外：听清楚了。

警：为什么被带到公安局来？

外：因为我吸毒。

警：把事情经过详细说一下。

外：上周日，我和朋友在KOKOMO酒吧聚会。我们一直在包厢里唱歌、跳舞、喝酒，期间，一位朋友吞了一颗神秘的小球，他说感觉特别棒，并劝我也试一试。一开始我并不相信他。但后来发现越来越多的朋友都吃了，我便没有忍住，也尝了一颗，后来我才知道那是摇头丸。不久之后，一些警察闯了进来，发现我们在吸毒，便把我们带到警察局做进一步的调查。警察对我进行毒品尿检之后结果呈阳性。

警：这是你第一次吸毒吗？

外：是的。

警：你还有其他要补充的吗？

外：没有了。

警：以上回答是否属实？

外：是事实。

警：以上询问笔录刚才我们已经用英语读给你听了，记录的内容是否和你说的一致？

外：一致。

警：签个字。

外：好的。

Part IV　Creative Work
创造性练习

Situation：处置外国人殴打他人案件。

听录音，请在听到提示音后开始口译。

警：我们是北京市公安局朝阳分局的民警，现依法对你进行询问，你要如实回答并对自己所讲的话承担法律责任。

外：我明白。

警：你叫什么名字？哪国人？

外：我叫爱德华·史密斯，来自加拿大。

警：看一下你的护照。

外：给。

警：什么时候来中国的？来干什么？

外：今年八月份来的，我是来工作的。

警：现在在哪个单位工作？

外：在中国科技大学教英语。

警：现在住哪儿？

外：中国科技大学外教宿舍楼206室。

警：知道为什么被带到这儿来吗？

Unit 13　Handling Public Security Cases Involving Foreigners
涉外治安案件查处

外：知道。很抱歉，我不应该打收银员。

警：详细讲讲事情经过。

外：因为前几天刚跟女朋友分手，心情特别不好，所以今天下午来到这家酒吧喝酒散散心。

警：喝了多少？

外：2瓶红酒。

警：喝醉了吗？

外：醉了。我当时迷迷糊糊的，不小心把杯子碰到地上摔碎了。结账时，收银员让我赔50元钱，我嫌赔得太多了，就没给她。我要走，她不让我走，我们就吵起来了。后来，我特别生气，就动手打了她。

警：打哪儿了？

外：一拳打在嘴上，另两拳打在脸上。

警：她还手了吗？

外：没有。

警：经调查我们得知，你把收银员打得面部青肿，一颗牙齿脱落。

外：我当时喝多了，没有控制住自己。

警：还有其他要补充的吗？

外：没有了。

警：这是询问笔录。我用英语读给你听，没有什么问题的话，签上你的名字。

外：好的。

Unit 14

Dealing with Traffic Violations and Accidents Involving Foreigners
涉外道路交通违法行为和交通事故处理

It is common sense that smooth and safe driving is a combination of skill, alertness, and luck, which depends upon some uncontrollable factors like weather, road conditions, and other drivers. Sometimes no matter how careful you are violations or accidents may happen unavoidably. When foreigners unfortunately run into such a situation, they have to rely on Chinese police officers to solve the cases. On these occasions, our traffic officers are required to have a good command of spoken English. Otherwise, the language barrier will make it difficult for them to manage traffic, determine the causes and responsibilities through investigations, and come up with fare judgements. This unit presents some examples of how to handle traffic offenses and accidents involving English speaking foreigners in the hope of assisting the officers in need.

众所周知，平稳、安全驾驶是技巧、机警和运气的结合，同时还取决于一些人为无法控制的因素，如天气、路况和其他司机等。有时不管你多么小心，难免会出现一些交通违法行为或发生交通事故。当外国人在中国违章或不幸发生交通事故时，需要我国交通警察来处理。这种情况下，我们的交警必须具备良好的英语口语能力。否则，语言障碍将使他们很难高效管理交通、快速展开调查、确定事故原因和责任、作出公平判断。本单元将举例说明如何用英语处理涉及外国人的交通违法和交通事故，以期对办案民警有所帮助。

Unit 14 Dealing with Traffic Violations and Accidents Involving Foreigners
涉外道路交通违法行为和交通事故处理

Part I New Words and Useful Expressions
生词与词组

lane 英 [leɪn] 美 [leɪn] n. 车道
detector 英 [dɪˈtektə(r)] 美 [dɪˈtektər] n. 探测器；检测器
priority 英 [praɪˈɒrəti] 美 [praɪˈɔːrəti] n. 优先考虑的事
breathalyzer 英 [ˈbreθəˌlaɪzər] 美 [ˈbreθəˌlaɪzər] n. 呼气式酒精检测仪
ambulance 英 [ˈæmbjələns] 美 [ˈæmbjələns] n. [车辆][医] 救护车
unexpectedly 英 [ˌʌnɪkˈspektɪdli] 美 [ˌʌnɪkˈspektɪdli] adv. 出乎意料地，意外地
total 英 [ˈtəʊtl] 美 [ˈtoʊtl] vt. (美俚) 使完全损坏
photograph 英 [ˈfəʊtəɡrɑːf] 美 [ˈfoʊtəɡræf] v. 拍照
diplomatic immunity 外交豁免权
motor vehicle driving permit 机动车行驶证
exceed the speed limit 超速
under no circumstances 无论如何都不
DUI: Driving Under the Influence 酒后驾驶
crash into 撞上
tow truck 拖车

Part II Useful Sentence Patterns
常用句型

- Pull over, please. 请靠边停车。

- You illegally changed lanes just now. 你刚才违法变道了。

- Do you have diplomatic immunity? 你享有外交豁免权吗?

- If you accept the penalty decision, please go to the Industrial and Commercial Bank of China and pay the fine within 15 days.
如果对处罚决定没有异议的话，请你在 15 日内到中国工商银行缴纳罚款。

- The speed detector recorded your speed of 110 kilometers per hour, but the speed limit there is 80 kilometers per hour.

  测速监控探头记录了你当时的速度,高达每小时 110 公里,而那条路限速每小时 80 公里。

- Under no circumstances should you speed.

  无论如何都不能超速。

- You must be responsible for your safety and that of others.

  你必须对自己和他人的安全负责。

- This is a breathalyzer. Please blow into it until I tell you to stop.

  这是呼气式酒精检测仪,使劲往里吹气,叫你停再停。

- The breathalyzer shows that the alcohol in your breath is 60 mg/100ml and you are suspected of DUI.

  检测仪显示,你呼吸中的酒精含量为 60 毫克/百毫升,涉嫌饮酒后驾驶。

- Please come along with us to the traffic police station for further investigation.

  请跟我们到交警队,配合我们进一步调查。

Part III　Situational Dialogues
情景对话

|情景 1|　Handling Illegal Lane Changing
　　　　　查处违章变道

P: Hello, we are police officers from Chaoyang division of Beijing traffic police bureau. Pull over, please.

F: Hi, officer. What's the matter?

P: You illegally changed lanes just now.

F: Oh, sorry. I just wanted to turn right.

P: If you want to turn right, you have to change lanes in advance instead of doing it when the lane line is solid.

Unit 14 Dealing with Traffic Violations and Accidents Involving Foreigners
涉外道路交通违法行为和交通事故处理

F: I don't know the road very well. It was too late to change lanes in advance when I realized I had to take the rightest lane.

P: You should have paid attention to the signs on the road all the time.

F: Yes, but I just forgot to do so.

P: Show us your driver's license, motor vehicle driving permit and your passport please.

F: Here you are.

P: Do you have diplomatic immunity?

F: No.

P: According to Article 90 of Road Traffic Safety Law of the People's Republic of China, you will be fined 200 RMB. If you don't accept the decision, you have the right to appeal to Beijing traffic police bureau for administrative reconsideration within 60 days or lodge an administrative lawsuit to Chaoyang people's court within 3 months according to law. This is the written decision. I'll read the English translation to you and then please sign your name if there is nothing wrong.

F: OK.

P: If you accept the penalty decision, please go to the Industrial and Commercial Bank of China and pay the fine within 15 days.

P: I see.

F: Is that all?

P: That's all. You may go now.

警：你好，我是北京市交警朝阳支队的民警，请靠边停车。

外：您好，警官，怎么了？

警：你刚才违法变道了。

外：噢，对不起。我想右转弯。

警：右转车辆必须提前进入右转车道，不能压实线变道。

外：我不太熟悉这儿的路，等我意识到需要走右转车道时，已经来不及提前变道了。

警：你应该时刻关注交通标志、地上的标记线。

外：是的，但我忘记看了。

警：请出示一下你的驾驶证、行驶证和护照。

外：好的，给您。

警：你享有外交豁免权吗？

外：没有。

警：依据《中华人民共和国道路交通安全条例》第九十条之规定，你将被处以罚款人民币200元。对这一处罚决定有异议的话，你有权在60日内向北京市交警总队依法提起行政复议或者在6个月内向朝阳区人民法院申请行政诉讼。这是行政处罚决定书，我用英语为你宣读一遍，听完之后如果没有什么问题，请签字。

外：好吧。

警：如果对处罚决定没有异议的话，请你在15日内到中国工商银行缴纳罚款。

外：明白。

外：没其他事了吧？

警：没了，你可以走了。

| 情景 2 | Handling Speeding
            处理超速行驶

P: Hello, sir. What can I do for you?

F: Hi, officer. I received a text message notifying me that I exceeded the speed limit.

P: Let me check it for you. Give me your driver's license and the motor vehicle driving permit, please.

F: OK, here you are.

P: According to the information in the system, on October 10, you were speeding on the 3rd Ring main Road when you drove from south to the part of Gongzhufen.

F: I didn't feel I was driving fast.

P: The speed detector recorded your speed of 110 kilometers per hour, but

Unit 14 Dealing with Traffic Violations and Accidents Involving Foreigners
涉外道路交通违法行为和交通事故处理

the speed limit there is 80 kilometers per hour. Take a look at the pictures, please.

F: Oh, I get it. I was in a hurry to meet my mother at the airport on that day. So I was speeding without knowing it.

P: Safety is always the first priority, so under no circumstances should you speed. You must be responsible for your safety and that of others.

F: Sorry, officer. I promise this will never happen again.

P: According to Article 90 of Road Traffic Safety Law of the People's Republic of China, you will be fined 200 RMB for exceeding the speed limit by less than 50%. If you don't accept the decision, you have the right to appeal for administrative reconsideration within 60 days or lodge an administrative lawsuit within 3 months according to law. This is a written decision. I'll read it to you in English before you sign your name if there is nothing wrong.

F: OK, I accept the decision.

P: If you accept the penalty decision, please go to the Industrial and Commercial Bank of China and pay the fine within 15 days.

F: OK. I've got it.

警：你好，先生。有什么可以帮你的？

外：你好，警官。我收到一条违章提醒短信，提醒我驾车时超速了。

警：请给我你的驾驶证和行驶证，我帮你查一下。

外：好的，谢谢。

警：根据系统信息，你于10月11日在北京三环主路公主坟路段，由南向北行驶时超速。

外：我当时感觉开得不快。

警：测速监控探头记录了你当时的速度，高达每小时110公里，而那条路限速每小时80公里，你看一下这几张照片。

外：哦，我想起来了。我当时着急去机场接我妈妈，可能不知不觉就超速了。

警：安全驾驶第一，无论如何都不能超速。你必须对自己和他人的安全负责。

外：对不起，我以后不会超速了。

警：根据《中华人民共和国道路交通安全法》第九十条规定，超过规定时速百分之五十以下的，处以二百元罚款。对这一决定有异议的话，你有权在60日内向北京市公安局交警总队依法提起行政复议或在6个月内向西城区人民法院申请行政诉讼。这是行政处罚决定书，我用英语为你宣读一遍，听完之后如果没有什么问题，请签字。

外：哦，我没有异议。

警：如果对处罚决定没有异议的话，请你在15日内到中国工商银行缴纳罚款。

外：明白。

| 情景 3 | Handling Foreigners' DUI
             处置外国人酒后驾驶

F: Hi, officer. What's the matter?

P: Hello, sir, we are police officers from Xicheng division of Beijing traffic police bureau and this is a routine check. Please show us your driver's license, motor vehicle driving permit and passport.

F: OK. Here you are.

P: Have you drunk?

F: No.

P: This is a breathalyzer. Please blow into it until I tell you to stop.

F: OK.

P: The breathalyzer shows the alcohol in your breath is 60 mg/100ml and you are suspected of DUI. Step out of the car, please.

F: Fine. I'll do it.

P: This is the printed result of the test. A Signature, please.

F: I haven't drunk any alcohol today. I had some the day before yesterday. There must be something wrong with the breathalyzer.

P: If you have any doubt about the result, we can take you to the hospital for a test on the alcohol content in your blood.

F: OK. I will go to the hospital to have another test.

外：你好，警官。什么事？

Unit 14　Dealing with Traffic Violations and Accidents Involving Foreigners
涉外道路交通违法行为和交通事故处理

警：你好，先生，我们是北京市西城交警支队的民警，例行检查，请出示一下你的驾照、行驶证、护照。

外：好的。

警：喝酒了吗？

外：没喝。

警：这是呼气式酒精检测仪，使劲往里吹气，叫你停再停。

外：好的。

警：检测仪显示，你呼吸中的酒精含量为60毫克/百毫升，涉嫌饮酒后驾驶，请下车。

外：真的吗？

警：这是打印出来的检测结果，请签字。

外：虽然前天喝了点酒，但我今天确实没有喝，你们的检测仪有问题吧？

警：如果对检测结果有异议的话，我们可以带你去医院抽血进行体内酒精检测。

外：好的，我要去医院重新检测一次。

| 情景 4 | Investigating a Traffic Accident
调查交通事故

P: We are police officers from Haidian division of Beijing traffic police bureau. Who called the police just now?

F: It was me, officer.

P: Who was injured? How was the injury?

F: The driver of the other car was seriously injured on the head.

P: The ambulance is coming. Get the injured man into the ambulance and take him to the hospital.

P: Show us your driver's license, motor vehicle driving permit, car insurance and passport, please.

F: OK. Here you are.

P: What happened?

F: The car crashed into my car from behind.

P: How?

F: I was driving to the north when the car in front of me made a sudden stop unexpectedly, I stepped on my brakes at once in order to avoid the collision, then the car behind me crashed into mine from behind.

P: We've photographed and recorded the damage of both vehicles. Now let's get them out of the way. Is your car movable?

F: I think so.

P: Move your car to the right side of the road.

F: How about the other car? It's totaled. I don't think it's movable.

P: I've called the tow truck. It'll come soon.

F: OK.

P: Please come along with us to the traffic police station for further investigation.

F: OK.

警：我们是北京市海淀交警支队的民警,刚才谁报的警?

外：我报的,警官。

警：几个人受伤?伤者是谁?伤情怎么样?

外：对方车辆司机一个人受伤了,他的头部受伤很严重。

警：救护车来了,快把伤者抬到救护车上,送他去医院。

警：请出示一下你的驾照、行驶证、汽车保险保单和护照。

外：好的。

警：事故怎么发生的?

外：那辆车从后面撞上了我的车。

警：怎样撞上的?

外：当时我从南面开过来,不知道什么原因,我前面的车突然急刹车。为了避免撞上,我也立即踩了刹车,停了下来。后面这辆车就撞到我车上了。

警：我们已拍过照,做了标记,记下了两辆车的损坏情况。现在把车子挪到路边去。你的车还能开吗?

外：能。

警：把你的车开到路边。

外：那辆车怎么办?损坏太严重了。我看是不能开了。

警：我已叫了拖车,很快就到。

Unit 14　Dealing with Traffic Violations and Accidents Involving Foreigners
涉外道路交通违法行为和交通事故处理

外：哦。

警：请跟我们到交警队，配合我们进一步调查。

Part IV　Creative Work
创造性练习

Situation：交通事故调查。

▶ 听录音，请在听到提示音后开始口译。

警：我们是北京市朝阳交警支队的民警，刚才谁报的警？

外：我报的，警官。

警：伤者是谁？伤情怎么样？

外：摩托车司机受伤了，他的头部伤得很严重，救护车已经送他去医院了。

警：请出示一下你的驾照、行驶证、汽车保险保单和护照。

外：好的。

警：事故怎么发生的？

外：我当时由西向东行驶，当我到达这个路口中央时一辆摩托车从右边撞了过来。

警：你当时刹车了吗？

外：刹了，但当我看见他时，已经太晚了，没有刹住。

警：你进入路口前是红灯还是绿灯？

外：绿灯。

警：你当时的车速是多少？

外：每小时50公里左右。

警：我们已拍过照，做了标记，现在把车子挪到路边去。你的车还能开吗？

外：能。

警：把你的车开到路的右边。

外：好的。

警：请跟我们到交警队，配合我们做进一步调查。

外：好的。

Unit 15
Handling Other Administrative Cases Involving Foreigners
其他涉外行政案件查处

　　While it is natural for tourists to photograph scenes from their trips abroad, China and some other countries are particularly sensitive about photographs, and photographing police and military installations is strictly forbidden. Conducting interviews without permits is also illegal in China. Foreign nationals may do something against Chinese laws unknowingly if they aren't familiar with the regulations. Whether they break the rules purposefully or not, police officers have to interfere. This unit provides some dialogues for Chinese officers' reference when they take action to stop foreigners' activities that violate Chinese laws and harm the interests of the public and security of the country. Hopefully, these examples can help them solve such problems with appropriate and concise English.

　　游客在国外旅行时遇到自己喜欢的景色经常会拍照留念，但中国和其他一些国家对于拍照有着严格的规定，严禁在军事区域拍照。而且，在中国未经许可进行采访也是违法的。外国人如果不熟悉中国法律，可能会做出违反中国法律的事情。不管他们是否故意，我国警察都必须立即制止其违法行为，并作出相应处罚。本单元提供了一些对话，为我国民警执法提供参考，希望他们可以运用恰当、简洁的英语制止外国人危害我国公共利益和国家安全的违法行为。

Unit 15　Handling Other Administrative Cases Involving Foreigners
其他涉外行政案件查处

Part I　New Words and Expressions
生词和词组

interview　　　英[ˈɪntəvjuː]　美[ˈɪntərvjuː]　n. 采访
delete　　　　英[dɪˈliːt]　美[dɪˈliːt]　vt. 删除
recording　　　英[rɪˈkɔːdɪŋ]　美[rɪˈkɔːrdɪŋ]　n. 录音
military　　　　英[ˈmɪlətri]　美[ˈmɪləteri]　adj. 军事的
photographer　英[fəˈtɒgrəfə(r)]　美[fəˈtɑːgrəfər]　n. 摄影师
scenery　　　　英[ˈsiːnəri]　美[ˈsiːnəri]　n. 风景；景色

conduct interview　新闻采访
military forbidden zone　军事禁区
No photographing　禁止拍照

Part II　Useful Sentence Patterns
常用句型

■ You are gathering news here, aren't you?
　你是在这里采访，对吧？

■ You are not allowed to conduct interviews with an F visa.
　你持有F签证，是不允许进行新闻采访的。

■ Please delete all the photos and recordings you've got in this interview.
　请把这次采访的照片和录音删除。

■ Didn't you see the sign that says "Military Forbidden Zone and No Photographing" over there?
　难道你没看见那边的牌子上写着"军事禁区，禁止拍照"？

■ You've taken photos in a military forbidden zone and violated Chinese law.
　你在军事禁区拍照，已经违反了中国法律。

■ Whatever purpose it is, your action is against Chinese law.

不管出于什么目的,你的行为都违反了中国法律。

Part III   Situational Dialogues
情景对话

|情景 1| Handling a Case of Gathering News Illegally
处置非法采访案件

P: Excuse me, sir. We are police officers from Shinan branch of Qingdao public security bureau. What are you doing here?

F: I'm chatting with them.

P: What's your name and nationality?

F: I'm Evan Muncie coming from Australia.

P: When and where did you enter China?

F: I entered China at Beijing Capital International Airport on February 25.

P: What's your purpose for coming to China?

F: I'm a visiting scholar at Qingdao University.

P: Show me your passport, please.

F: Here it is.

P: You are gathering news here, aren't you?

F: Oh, yeah, you can say that.

P: You are not allowed to conduct interviews with an F visa.

F: I'm really sorry. I didn't know that.

P: Please delete all the photos and recordings you've got in this interview.

F: OK.

警:对不起,先生,我们是青岛市公安局市南分局的民警。请问你在这儿干什么?

外:和他们聊聊。

Unit 15　Handling Other Administrative Cases Involving Foreigners
其他涉外行政案件查处

警：请问你的姓名和国籍？

外：我叫埃文·曼西，来自澳大利亚。

警：你是什么时间、从哪个口岸入境的？

外：今年2月25日从北京首都国际机场入境。

警：你来中国干什么？

外：我是青岛大学的访问学者。

警：看一下你的护照。

外：给。

警：你是在这里采访，对吧？

外：哦，是的，可以这样说。

警：你持有F签证，是不允许进行新闻采访的。

外：实在对不起，我不知道这个规定。

警：请把这次采访的照片和录音删除。

外：好吧。

情景2　Handling a Case of Foreigner's Taking Photos in Military Forbidden Areas
处置禁区拍照案件

P：Excuse me, sir. We are police officers from Yangfangdian Police Station of Beijing public security bureau. Please stop taking pictures.

F：Why?

P：This is a military forbidden zone.

F：A military forbidden zone?

P：Yes. Didn't you see the sign that says "Military Forbidden Zone and No Photographing" over there?

F：Sorry, I didn't see it.

P：What is your name and nationality?

F：I'm Homer Simpson from Canada.

P：What's your purpose for coming to China?

F: For travelling.

P: What do you do?

F: I'm a photographer.

P: Show me your passport, please.

F: OK. Here you are.

P: Mr. Simpson, you've taken photos in a military forbidden zone and violated the Chinese law. Come to the police station with me for further investigation.

F: I did take some photos here, but it's just because I really like the buildings and scenery here. There is no other purposes.

P: Whatever purpose it is, your action is against Chinese law.

F: OK.

警：对不起，先生，我是北京市公安局海淀分局羊坊店派出所的民警，请停止拍照。

外：为什么？

警：这是军事禁区。

外：军事禁区？

警：是的。你没看到那边的牌子上写着"军事禁区，禁止拍照"吗？

外：对不起，我没看到。

警：请问你的姓名和国籍？

外：我叫霍默·辛普森，来自加拿大。

警：你来中国干什么？

外：旅游。

警：你的职业是什么？

外：我是一名摄影师。

警：看一下你的护照。

外：好的，给你。

警：辛普森先生，你在军事禁区拍照违反了中国法律，现在口头传唤你跟我们到派出所接受进一步调查。

外：我的确拍了些照片，因为我太喜欢这儿的建筑和景色了，并非出于其他目的。

Unit 15　Handling Other Administrative Cases Involving Foreigners
其他涉外行政案件查处

警：不管出于什么目的，这样做都违反了中国有关法律。

外：好吧。

Part IV　Creative Work
创造性练习

▶ 听录音，请在听到提示音后开始口译。

警：对不起，先生。你在这儿干什么？

外：和他们聊聊。

警：请问你的姓名和国籍？

外：我叫埃文·怀特，来自加拿大。

警：你来中国干什么？

外：我是常驻记者。

警：请出示一下你的护照。

外：给。

警：你是在这里采访吗？

外：哦，是的，可以这样说。

警：看一下你的记者证。

外：对不起，我忘记带了。

警：根据中国法律，未携带证件进行采访属于非法采访。

外：实在对不起，我早上出门走得太急了。

警：请把这次采访的照片和录音删除。

外：好吧。

Unit 16
Handling Drug-related Crime Cases Involving Foreigners
涉外毒品案件查处

Global drug-related criminal cases are increasing ceaselessly and sweeping both developed and developing countries. With an estimated annual value of between $300 billion and $400 billion, international illegal drug trafficking dwarfs the value of many staple legal commodities in the global economy. These drug dealers constantly provide funds for various entrenched criminal organizations, bribe and corrupt some of law enforcement personnel, cause regional unrest, and thus pose a great threat to national security. In order to maintain social stability, law enforcement agencies at all levels double their efforts in cracking down on illegal drug trafficking. Generally speaking, China has achieved great success in the battle against drug-related crimes. But the war against drugs is an arduous, complicated, and long-term task. It still faces huge challenges. Although trafficking of heroin, the traditional drug in China's market, has largely been brought under control, some new drugs keep coming up above water. And more and more cocaine smugglers from South America have also chosen China as their transfer station. There are more and more drug-related cases involving foreigners. Obviously English serves as an increasingly important tool. This unit aims to help anti-drug police officers to get familiar with some expressions regarding how to deal with Illicit Drug Trafficking involving foreigners.

全球涉毒案件日益攀升，已经席卷发达国家和发展中国家。据估计，全球

Unit 16　Handling Drug-related Crime Cases Involving Foreigners
涉外毒品案件查处

每年涉毒资金高达 3000 亿到 4000 亿美元，跨国贩毒案的涉案资金数额远远超过全球经济中很多主要合法商品的价值。毒贩们不断为犯罪组织提供资金支持，贿赂部分执法人员，严重影响到地区安全，从而给国家安全稳定带来极大威胁。为了维护社会稳定，各级执法机关加大了对贩毒犯罪活动的打击力度。总体而言，我国在打击毒品犯罪方面取得了巨大的成功，但仍然面临巨大挑战，这是一项艰巨、复杂和长期的任务。虽然传统毒品海洛因在中国已基本得到控制，但一些新型毒品却不断涌现，而且，中国已经成为南美毒贩贩卖可卡因的中转站，涉外毒品案件不断增加，因此英语成为办案过程中的重要语言工具。本单元的目的在于帮助缉毒警察熟悉处置涉外毒品案件时常用的英语表达方式。

Part I　New Words and Useful Expressions
生词与词组

summon　英[ˈsʌmən]　美[ˈsʌmən]　vt. 传唤
irrelevant　英[ɪˈreləvənt]　美[ɪˈreləvənt]　adj. 不相干的
voluntarily　英[ˈvɒləntrəli]　美[ˌvɑːlənˈterəli]　adv. 自动地
confess　英[kənˈfes]　美[kənˈfes]　vt. 供认
contact　英[ˈkɒntækt]　美[ˈkɑːntækt]　n. 联系人；vt. 联系
lysergide　[laɪˈsɜːdʒaɪd]　n. 麦角酸酰二乙胺（迷幻药的一种）
contraband　英[ˈkɒntrəbænd]　美[ˈkɑːntrəbænd]　adj. 禁运的；非法买卖的
moniker　英[ˈmɒnɪkə(r)]　美[ˈmɑːnɪkər]　n. 绰号；名字
transfer　英[trænsˈfɜː(r)]　美[trænsˈfɜːr]　vt. 把（钱）转到另一账户
inject　英[ɪnˈdʒekt]　美[ɪnˈdʒekt]　vt. 注入；注射

suspected of committing a crime 涉嫌犯罪
the Notification of Rights and Obligations of Criminal Suspects
《犯罪嫌疑人权利义务告知书》
Notification of Foreigners' Rights in Cases Involving Foreigners
《涉外案件外国人权利告知书》
Statement on Consular Notification《关于领事通报的声明书》

Statement on Visit by Consular Officers 《关于领事探视的声明书》
Criminal Procedure Law of the People's Republic of China
《中华人民共和国刑事诉讼法》
keep contact with 与……保持联系
be supposed to do 应该做……
on purpose 故意地
cooperate with 与……配合/合作

Part II　Useful Sentence Patterns
常用句型

- We'd like to inform you of the fact that you've been summoned for questioning in accordance with law because you've been suspected of committing a crime.
  先向你告知你因涉嫌违法犯罪，被依法传唤。

- According to the relevant provisions of the law, criminal suspects can be treated with leniency by law if they voluntarily and truthfully confess their crimes, admit to the accused criminal facts, and are willing to be punished.
  根据法律相关规定，犯罪嫌疑人自愿如实供述自己的罪行，承认被指控的犯罪事实，愿意接受处罚的，可依法从宽处理。

- You are suspected of drug smuggling and need to be further investigated.
  你涉嫌毒品走私，我们还需要做进一步的调查。

- Are you tortured in the process of interrogation?
  讯问过程中，是否对你刑讯逼供了？

- In China, it's forbidden to take and sell heroin, so you have broken the law.
  根据中国相关法律，吸食、贩卖海洛因都是违法的，你已经涉嫌违法犯罪。

Unit 16　Handling Drug-related Crime Cases Involving Foreigners
涉外毒品案件查处

Part III　Situational Dialogues
情景对话

|情景 1| Handling Suspected Drug Smuggling
涉嫌毒品走私案的查处

P: Can you understand my English?

F: Yes, I can.

P: This is Haidian branch of Beijing municipal public security bureau. First of all, We'd like to inform you that you have been summoned for questioning in accordance with the law for suspected crimes.

F: I've got it.

P: I'll read the English translation of the following documents to you. Please listen carefully.

P: (After reading The Notification of Rights and Obligations of Criminal Suspects, Notification of Foreigners' Rights in Cases Involving Foreigners, Statement on Consular Notification, and Statement on Visit by Consular Officers.) Now, do you understand everything?

F: Yes, I do.

P: Then your signature, please. According to Criminal Procedure Law of the People's Republic of China, you are expected to answer the questions honestly. You have the right not to answer questions irrelevant to the case. Are you clear?

F: Yes, I'm clear.

P: According to the relevant provisions of the law, criminal suspects can be treated with leniency by law if they voluntarily and truthfully confess their crimes, admit to the accused criminal facts, and are willing to be punished.

F: I see.

P: What's your name and nationality?

F: I'm Aaron Smith from the U. S.

P: Please show us your passport.

F: Here you are.

P: Who is your contact in China?

F: Nobody.

P: Where did you enter China?

F: At Beijing Capital International Airport.

P: Do you know why you are brought here to the police station?

F: Sorry, I don't know.

P: Is this your suitcase?

F: Yes, why?

P: What are these?

F: They are stamps.

P: Don't try to fool us. We know what they are. Just tell the truth.

F: They are just common stamps and I have nothing to say.

P: According to the test report, they contain lysergide, known as LSD. It is a new contraband drug.

F: I really don't know they are drugs. A man I met online paid me to bring them to China.

P: What's the man's name?

F: I only knew his online moniker was Arthur King but didn't know his real name.

P: How did you contact him?

F: We use Skype to keep in contact with each other.

P: What is his Skype account?

F: It's...

P: What does he look like?

F: I don't know, for I've never met him. He asked his friend to give the stamps to me.

P: How much did he pay you?

Unit 16 Handling Drug-related Crime Cases Involving Foreigners
涉外毒品案件查处

F: He promised to give me ＄3000. He's already paid me ＄1000 and told me someone else would give me the rest of ＄2000 after I deliver them successfully.

P: Did the man tell you to whom you were supposed to give all the stuff?

F: No. He said someone would call me after I arrived here.

P: You are suspected of drug smuggling and need to be further investigated.

F: I really didn't do this on purpose and I promise I will cooperate with you.

P: Are you tortured in the process of interrogation?

F: No.

P: Are your thoughts clear when being interrogated?

F: Yes.

P: Do you have anything else to say?

F: No.

P: Did you tell the truth?

F: Yes, everything is true.

P: We've read the record of interrogation in English to you. Is it the same as what you've said?

F: Yes.

P: Please sign it.

F: OK.

警：刚才我说的英语你是否都能听明白？

外：能听明白。

警：这里是北京市公安局海淀分局，先向你告知你因涉嫌违法犯罪，被北京警方依法传唤。

外：知道了。

警：现将以下文件向你送达，我们会用英语为你宣读，请你认真听。

警：（宣读《犯罪嫌疑人权利义务告知书》《涉外案件外国人权利告知书》《关于领事通报的声明书》和《关于领事探视的声明书》等文件之后）你听明白了吗？

外：是的，全都听明白了。

警：在这些文件后面签字。根据《中华人民共和国刑事诉讼法》的有关规定，你要如实回答我们的提问，对与本案无关的内容，你有拒绝回答的权利，你听清楚了吗？

外：听清楚了。

警：根据法律的有关规定，犯罪嫌疑人自愿如实供述自己的罪行，承认被指控的犯罪事实，愿意接受处罚的，可以依法从宽处理。

外：明白。

警：你的姓名、国籍？

外：我叫亚伦·史密斯，来自美国。

警：请出示一下你的护照。

外：给你。

警：在中国的联系人是谁？

外：没有人。

警：从哪个口岸入境的？

外：北京首都国际机场。

警：知道为什么把你带到公安局来吗？

外：对不起，不知道。

警：这是你的行李箱吗？

外：是的，怎么了？

警：这些是什么东西？

外：邮票啊！

警：别想骗我们，我们已经知道那是什么了，希望你能如实交代。

外：那些真是邮票，我没有什么可说的。

警：根据检验报告，那些东西根本就不是邮票，而是一种含有麦角酸酰二乙胺的新型毒品，被称为LSD.

外：我不知道那是毒品。网上认识的一个人付钱给我，让我帮他带到中国来的。

警：那人叫什么名字？

外：我不知道真实姓名，只是知道他的网名叫"亚瑟王"。

警：你怎么跟他联系？

外：我们通过Skype保持联系。

Unit 16　Handling Drug-related Crime Cases Involving Foreigners
涉外毒品案件查处

警：他的 Skype 账号是什么？

外：是……

警：他有哪些外貌特征？

外：不知道，我从没见过他。这些东西都是他让一个朋友转交给我的。

警：他给了你多少钱？

外：他答应给我3000美元，已经给了1000美元，成功交货后还会有人再给我剩下的2000美元。

警：他告诉你把这些东西交给谁了吗？

外：没有，他说我到中国后，会有人跟我联系的。

警：根据中国法律，你涉嫌毒品走私，我们还需要做进一步的调查。

外：我真不是故意的，我一定好好配合你们的调查。

警：讯问过程中，你是否遭到了刑讯逼供？

外：没有。

警：被讯问时，你是否神智清楚？

外：清楚。

警：还有其他要补充的吗？

外：没有了。

警：以上回答是否属实？

外：属实。

警：以上讯问笔录我们已经用英语读给你听了，记录的内容是否和你说的一致？

外：一致。

警：签个字。

外：好的。

| 情景2 | Interrogating a Drug Dealer
讯问毒贩子

P: Can you understand my English?

F: Yes, I can.

P: This is Haidian branch of Beijing municipal public security bureau. First of all, we'd like to inform you of the fact that you've been summoned for questioning in accordance with law because you've been suspected of committing a crime.

F: I've got it.

P: I'll read the English translation of the following documents to you. Please listen carefully.

P: (After reading The Notification of Rights and Obligations of Criminal Suspects, Notification of Foreigners' Rights in Cases Involving Foreigners, Statement on Consular Notification, and Statement on Visit by Consular Officers.) Now, do you understand everything?

F: Yes, I do.

P: Then your signature, please. According to Criminal Procedure Law of the People's Republic of China, you are expected to answer the questions truthfully. You have the right not to answer questions irrelevant to the case. Am I understood?

F: Yes.

P: According to the relevant provisions of the law, criminal suspects can be treated with leniency by law if they voluntarily and truthfully confess their crimes, admit to the accused criminal facts, and are willing to be punished.

F: I see.

P: What is your name and nationality?

F: I am Edward Smith from the Philippines.

P: Who is your contact in China?

F: My wife.

P: How to contact her?

F: Her cell phone number is…

P: Where did you enter China?

F: At Guangzhou Baiyun International Airport.

P: What is your purpose for coming to China?

Unit 16

Handling Drug-related Crime Cases Involving Foreigners
涉外毒品案件查处

F: I teach English at an English Training School.

P: How did you get the heroin?

F: I bought it from a man I met in a QQ group.

P: What's the name of the QQ group?

F: It's Happy Pursuit of the Dream.

P: What's the man's name?

F: He's called Flying Dragon in the QQ group.

P: What's his QQ account?

F: It's 37548168.

P: What does he look like?

F: I've never met him. I usually transfer the money to him online via QQ after finding the heroin from the place where he hides it in advance.

P: What is the price for the heroin and how much have you bought?

F: It's 500 RMB per gram and I've bought 30 grams.

P: How did you deal with the heroin?

F: I took it.

P: Really? You must tell the truth.

F: I took most of it and some of it was sold.

P: How much heroin did you sell and what's the price?

F: I sold 10 grams at the price of 900 RMB per gram.

P: To whom?

F: I didn't know them. Whenever I went to the bar, they would come to me to buy heroin.

P: Which bar?

F: Many bars but the bar I often went to is *Midnight* located in Sanlitun Street.

P: When were your first time and the last time of taking drugs respectively? What kind of drug?

F: The first time was two years ago and the last time was two days ago. I took heroin at both times.

P: How and with whom did you take it?

F: The first time, I took it just like smoking a cigarette with some friends. And the last time I injected it into my body alone at home.

P: In China, it's forbidden to take and sell heroin, so you have broken the law.

F: I really regret having done these things.

P: Are you tortured in the process of interrogation?

F: No.

P: Are your thoughts clear when being interrogated?

F: Yes.

P: Do you have anything else to say?

F: No.

P: Is what you've said true?

F: Yes, all is true.

P: We've read the record of interrogation in English to you. Is it the same as what you've said?

F: Yes.

P: Please sign it.

F: OK.

警：刚才我说的英语你是否都能听明白？

外：能听明白。

警：这里是北京市公安局海淀分局，先向你告知你因涉嫌违法犯罪，被北京警方依法传唤。

外：知道了。

警：现将以下文件向你送达，我们会用英语为你宣读，请你认真听。

警：（宣读《犯罪嫌疑人权利义务告知书》《涉外案件外国人权利告知书》《关于领事通报的声明书》和《关于领事探视的声明书》等文件之后）你听明白了吗？

外：是的，全都听明白了。

警：在这些文件后面签字。根据《中华人民共和国刑事诉讼法》的有关规定，你要如实回答我们的提问，对与本案无关的内容，你有拒绝回答的权利，你听清楚了吗？

Unit 16　Handling Drug-related Crime Cases Involving Foreigners
涉外毒品案件查处

外：听清楚了。

警：根据法律的有关规定，犯罪嫌疑人自愿如实供述自己的罪行，承认被指控的犯罪事实，愿意接受处罚的，可以依法从宽处理。

外：明白。

警：你的姓名和国籍？

外：我叫爱德华·史密斯，来自菲律宾。

警：在中国的联系人是谁？

外：我妻子。

警：联系方式是什么？

外：她的手机号是……

警：你从哪个口岸入境的？

外：广州白云国际机场。

警：来中国干什么？

外：我在一所英语培训学校教英语。

警：这些白粉从哪里弄到的？

外：从QQ群里的一个人那里买的。

警：QQ群名叫什么？

外：快乐追梦。

警：那人叫什么名字？

外：他在群里的网名叫"飞龙"，不知道真实姓名。

警：他的QQ号是多少？

外：37548168。

警：那人长什么样？

外：不知道，从没见过他面。一直都是他先告诉我东西藏的地方，我找到之后再通过QQ转账付钱给他。

警：你多少钱买的？一共买了多少？

外：每克500元人民币，一共买了30克左右。

警：买回来的这些白粉你是怎么处置的？

外：我自己吸了。

警：真的吗？你要老实交代。

外：大部分自己吸了，也卖了一点儿。

警：卖了多少？多少钱卖的？

外：每克900元人民币卖的，大约卖了10克。

警：你都卖给哪些人了？

外：不认识他们。每次去酒吧，都会有很多人主动跟我买。

警：哪个酒吧？

外：很多酒吧，我常去的是位于三里屯的"午夜时分"酒吧。

警：第一次和最后一次吸毒分别是什么时间？吸的什么？

外：我第一次吸毒大约是两年前，最后一次是两天前。吸的都是白粉。

警：跟谁一起吸的？采用什么方式？

外：第一次是跟朋友一起采用吸烟方式吸的，最后一次是我自己在家用针管注射的。

警：根据中国相关法律，吸食、贩卖海洛因都是违法的，你已经涉嫌违法犯罪。

外：我非常后悔。

警：我们讯问时，是否对你刑讯逼供了？

外：没有。

警：被讯问时，你是否神智清楚？

外：清楚。

警：还有其他要补充的吗？

外：没有了。

警：以上回答是否属实？

外：属实。

警：以上讯问笔录刚才我们已经用英语读给你听了，记录的内容是否和你说的一致？

外：一致。

警：签个字。

外：好的。

Unit 16　Handling Drug-related Crime Cases Involving Foreigners
涉外毒品案件查处

Part IV　Creative Work
创造性练习

Situation：外国人通过北京首都国际机场走私毒品入境。

听录音，请在听到提示音后开始口译。

警：刚才我说的英语你是否都能听明白？

外：能听明白。

警：这里是北京市公安局海淀分局，先向你告知你因涉嫌违法犯罪，被北京警方依法传唤。

外：知道了。

警：现将以下文件向你送达，我们会用英语为你宣读，请你认真听。

警：(宣读《犯罪嫌疑人权利义务告知书》《涉外案件外国人权利告知书》《关于领事通报的声明书》和《关于领事探视的声明书》等文件之后）你听明白了吗？

外：是的，全都听明白了。

警：在这些文件后面签字。根据《中华人民共和国刑事诉讼法》的有关规定，你要如实回答我们的提问，对与本案无关的内容，你有拒绝回答的权利，你听清楚了吗？

外：听清楚了。

警：根据法律的有关规定，犯罪嫌疑人自愿如实供述自己的罪行，承认被指控的犯罪事实，愿意接受处罚的，可以依法从宽处理。

外：明白。

警：告诉我们你的姓名、国籍、出生日期。

外：我叫……，巴基斯坦人，1988年8月8日出生。

警：你在你们国家的住址在哪里？

外：伊斯兰堡格林路。

警：职业是什么？

外：在巴基斯坦……化学品公司当工人。

警：以前被判过罪吗？

外：没有。

警：因违法行为被警方调查过吗？

外：没有。在巴基斯坦和中国都没有过。

警：你从体内排出50粒海洛因，重300克；我们还从你的拖鞋中发现200克海洛因。这些你是从什么人手里得到的？

外：老板手里。

警：你的老板叫什么名字？

外：他叫……

警：是从他手里买来的吗？

外：不是。他让我把这些毒品带进中国。

警：你偷运这些毒品，老板给你钱了吗？

外：他给了我5000美元。

警：运输毒品在中国是严重犯罪，你知道吗？

外：知道，我对自己的行为感到非常懊悔，希望能得到从轻处理。

警：你只有配合我们，交代罪行，把此案的所有情况告诉我们，才有可能得到从轻处理。

外：好的。据我所知，我们老板还要派另一个人来，再带一些海洛因过来。

警：派谁？

外：派……

警：什么时间？

外：后天，同一航班。

警：你们把毒品带进中国后交给谁？

外：一个名叫……的尼日利亚人。

警：在哪里交货？

外：广州。

警：具体交货时间和地点？

外：……会打电话告诉我。

警：能带我们到广州找到他吗？

外：能。

警：今天的讯问到此结束。讯问过程中，你是否遭到了刑讯逼供？

Unit 16 Handling Drug-related Crime Cases Involving Foreigners
涉外毒品案件查处

外：没有。

警：被讯问时，你是否神智清楚？

外：清楚。

警：还有其他要补充的吗？

外：没有了。

警：以上回答是否属实？

外：属实。

警：以上讯问笔录刚才我们已经用英语读给你听了，记录的内容是否和你说的一致？

外：一致。

警：签个字。

外：好的。

Unit 17
Handling Cyber Crimes Involving Foreigners
涉外网络犯罪案件查处

Nowadays computers and cellphones are widely used for online shopping, dating, teaching, applying for a job, and many other things. Internet brings tremendous convenience to law-abiding citizens and at the same time provides handy opportunities for criminals to engage in malicious activities. Common types of cybercrime include unauthorized computer access, business trade secrets theft, identity theft, pornography, and online fraud. Frauds that are directed through mobile devices and by online users have multiplied in complexity and have been a fast-growing phenomenon in China. Since there are a large number of foreign nationals in China, it is inevitable for some of them to be involved in cybercrimes sometimes, either as offenders or victims. This unit will help police officers learn how to use appropriate English to handle such cyber crimes as marital fraud, bank card fraud, and online gambling involving foreigners.

如今，电脑、手机被广泛应用于网购、网恋、网络教学、网上求职等。互联网给人们带来了极大的便利，同时也给犯罪分子提供了犯罪机会。常见的网络犯罪包括：电脑黑客入侵、商业秘密窃取、公民个人身份信息盗取、网络色情传播和网络诈骗等。在我国，针对手机和网络用户的诈骗案件数量逐年上升，诈骗手段不断翻新。很多在中国的外国人也被卷入到网络犯罪案件当中，有人成为网络犯罪的受害者，有人参与网络犯罪。本单元将会帮助我国民警学习如何用恰当的英语查处诸如国际婚姻诈骗、银行卡犯罪和网络赌博等涉外网络犯罪案件。

Unit 17 Handling Cyber Crimes Involving Foreigners
涉外网络犯罪案件查处

Part I   New Words and Expressions
生词与词组

marital	英 [ˈmærɪtl] 美 [ˈmærɪtl]	adj. 婚姻的
fraud	英 [frɔːd] 美 [frɔːd]	n. 欺骗；诡计
personnel	英 [ˌpɜːsəˈnel] 美 [ˌpɜːrsəˈnel]	n. 人事部门
invest	英 [ɪnˈvest] 美 [ɪnˈvest]	vt. 投资
profitable	英 [ˈprɒfɪtəbl] 美 [ˈprɑːfɪtəbl]	adj. 赚钱的
stock	英 [stɒk] 美 [stɑːk]	n. 股票
update	英 [ˌʌpˈdeɪt] 美 [ˌʌpˈdeɪt]	vt. 更新
link	英 [lɪŋk] 美 [lɪŋk]	n. [计] 链接
click	英 [klɪk] 美 [klɪk]	vt. 点击
log	英 [lɒɡ] 美 [lɔːɡ]	vi. 登录
programmer	英 [ˈprəʊɡræmə(r)] 美 [ˈproʊɡræmər]	n. 程序设计员
gamble	英 [ˈɡæmbl] 美 [ˈɡæmbl]	v. 赌博
register	英 [ˈredʒɪstə(r)] 美 [ˈredʒɪstər]	vi. 注册
debt	英 [det] 美 [det]	n. 债务
ridiculous	英 [rɪˈdɪkjələs] 美 [rɪˈdɪkjələs]	adj. 可笑的；荒谬的
x–rated	英 [ˈeks reɪtɪd] 美 [ˈeks reɪtɪd]	adj. 色情的
pornographic	英 [ˌpɔːnəˈɡræfɪk] 美 [ˌpɔːrnəˈɡræfɪk]	adj. 色情的，淫秽的
encrypted	英 [ɪnˈkrɪpt] 美 [ɪnˈkrɪpt]	v. 把……加密
charge	英 [tʃɑːdʒ] 美 [tʃɑːrdʒ]	vt. 对……索费

a match-maker website 婚恋网站

hunt for 寻找

log into my account 登录账户

password 英 [ˈpɑːswɜːd] 美 [ˈpæswɜːrd] n. 密码

the phishing site 钓鱼网站

the official site 官方网站

on average 平均而言

commit suicide 自杀

make a fortune 发财，赚大钱

Part II　Useful Sentence Patterns
常用句型

- How can you explain this? We do hope you can stop telling lies.

  你怎么解释这一切？希望你不要再试图编造谎言，老老实实地把问题交代清楚。

- We've read the record of interrogation in English to you. Is it the same as what you've said?

  以上讯问笔录刚才我们已经用英语读给你听了，记录的内容是否和你说的一致？

- After you clicked it, you were actually logging in to the phishing site, and they stole your card number, password and then your money so easily.

  你点击进入银行网页之后，实际上当时登录的就是一个钓鱼网站。他们得到你的银行卡号和密码之后，就能轻而易举地把卡内的钱转走。

- Do remember not to click any suspicious link. Besides, when you want to log in to your account, make sure to use the official site of the bank.

  请切记以后不要随便点击任何不明链接，而且，如果登录银行账户的话，一定要通过银行官网进入。

- It's not that easy and we've already got some evidence. We hope you can cooperate with us and tell us the truth.

  事情并不像你说的那样简单吧？目前我们已经掌握了很多关于你们网站的证据，希望你能如实交代，配合我们的调查工作。

- It's illegal to spread pornographic materials in China and you've gone against the Chinese Criminal law.

  在中国，传播淫秽物品牟利是违法的，你已经违反了中国的刑法。

Unit 17　Handling Cyber Crimes Involving Foreigners
涉外网络犯罪案件查处

Part III　Situational Dialogues
情景对话

|情景 1| Interrogating a Suspect Involved in International Marital Fraud

讯问国际骗婚犯罪嫌疑人

P: Can you understand my English?

F: Yes, I can.

P: This is Chaoyang branch of Beijing municipal public security bureau. First of all, we'd like to inform you of the fact that you've been summoned for questioning in accordance with law because you've been suspected of committing a crime.

F: I've got it.

P: I'll read the English translation of the following documents to you. Please listen carefully.

P: (After reading The Notification of Rights and Obligations of Criminal Suspects, Notification of Foreigners' Rights in Cases Involving Foreigners, Statement on Consular Notification, and Statement on Visit by Consular Officers.) Now, do you understand everything?

F: Yes, I do.

P: Then your signature, please. According to Criminal Procedure Law of the People's Republic of China, you are expected to answer the questions honestly. You have the right not to answer questions irrelevant to the case. Are you clear?

F: Yes, I'm clear.

P: According to the relevant provisions of the law, criminal suspects can be treated with leniency by law if they voluntarily and truthfully confess their crimes, admit to the accused criminal facts, and are willing to be punished.

F: I see.

P: Tell us your name and nationality.

F: I am Edward White from New Zealand.

P: Show us your passport.

F: Here you are.

P: Who is your contact in China?

F: Nobody.

P: Where did you enter China?

F: At Beijing Capital International Airport.

P: What do you do in China?

F: I'm on a business trip.

P: Do you know the lady? (showing him the picture of the victim)

F: No, I have never seen her.

P: The young lady is Yang Hong. We've dug up some stories between you. We hope you can tell us the truth.

F: Well, it's true that we've never met each other in real life. We got to know each other on a match-maker website. With time passing by, she has fallen in love with me.

P: Do you really love her? Do you really want to marry her?

F: Sure.

P: As far as we know, you've been married. How can you marry her? You told Yang Hong that you were a personnel manager with a yearly payment of $100,000 at one of the top 500 enterprises in the world, but you've asked her to give you about $70,000. She asked to meet you so many times but you refused except this time. How can you explain this? We do hope you can stop telling lies.

F: OK, I admit I've cheated her. I heard that many Chinese women like to marry foreigners, so I decided to take advantage of this to make some money. I began to hunt for a suitable woman online and I chatted with Yang Hong one day. She told me that she was working in a foreign enterprise

Unit 17 Handling Cyber Crimes Involving Foreigners
涉外网络犯罪案件查处

with a high salary. She said she was interested in foreign cultures and hope to marry a foreigner. I told her I liked Chinese woman and pretended to be a man with a high salary. I managed to make her fall in love with me and promised to marry her this year. I told her I would take her to the United States and introduced her to work in my company and promise her a bright future after our marriage.

P: Why did she give you so much money?

F: I found she had a crush on me and thought it's time to ask money from her. At first, I told her I was going to invest in a profitable project and asked her to invest some too in order to make more money for us. She gave me $20,000. Several months later, I told her I wanted to buy a suite for our marriage in Los Angeles California but I was $50,000 short. So she gave me the money.

P: Another lady named Chen Jing reported a similar case in which you got involved. We are pretty sure that you know her.

F: Yes, she is the second lady I cheated in a similar way. I really regret what I've done.

P: Are you tortured in the process of interrogation?

F: No.

P: Are your thoughts clear when being interrogated?

F: Yes.

P: Do you have anything else to say?

F: No.

P: Is what you've said true?

F: Yes, all is true.

P: We've read the record of interrogation in English to you. Is it the same as what you've said?

F: Yes.

P: Please sign it.

F: OK.

警：刚才我说的英语你是否都能听明白？

外：能听明白。

警：这里是北京市公安局朝阳分局，先向你告知你因涉嫌违法犯罪，被北京警方依法传唤。

外：知道了。

警：现将以下文件向你送达，我们会用英语为你宣读，请你认真听。

警：（宣读《犯罪嫌疑人权利义务告知书》《涉外案件外国人权利告知书》《关于领事通报的声明书》和《关于领事探视的声明书》等文件之后）你听明白了吗？

外：是的，全都听明白了。

警：在这些文件后面签字。根据《中华人民共和国刑事诉讼法》的有关规定，你要如实回答我们的提问，对与本案无关的内容，你有拒绝回答的权利，你听清楚了吗？

外：听清楚了。

警：根据法律的有关规定，犯罪嫌疑人自愿如实供述自己的罪行，承认被指控的犯罪事实，愿意接受处罚的，可以依法从宽处理。

外：明白。

警：你的姓名和国籍？

外：我叫爱德华·怀特，来自新西兰。

警：请出示一下你的护照。

外：给你。

警：在中国的联系人是谁？

外：没有人。

警：从哪个口岸入境的？

外：北京首都国际机场。

警：你来中国干什么？

外：我来出差。

警：你认识这位女士吗？

外：不认识，从来没有见过她。

警：这位女士名叫杨宏，我们已经知道你俩之间的事情了，所以希望你能如实

Unit 17 Handling Cyber Crimes Involving Foreigners
涉外网络犯罪案件查处

交代。

外：好吧，不过我确实没有在现实中见过她。我们俩在一个婚介网上认识的，后来，她爱上我了。

警：你真的爱她吗？真想跟她结婚吗？

外：当然了。

警：据我们所知，你已经结婚了。你怎么可能再跟她结婚呢？杨宏反映：你告诉她你在世界500强的某公司任人事部经理，年薪10万美元，但你却先后向她要了7万美元；她多次要求同你见面，除了被抓这次，你都拒绝了。你怎么解释这一切？希望你不要再试图编造谎言，老老实实地把问题交代清楚。

外：好吧，我承认欺骗了她。我听说很多中国女孩都希望嫁给外国人，于是我就决定利用这点来赚点钱。我开始在网上物色合适的女孩，直到有一天，我遇见了杨宏。她自我介绍说她在一家外企工作，工资很高，她对西方文化比较感兴趣，而且希望将来能嫁到国外去。我告诉她我非常喜欢中国女孩，而且假装自己年薪也很高。后来，我想尽一切办法让她爱上我，并承诺今年就同她结婚。我跟她说结婚后就把她带到美国，并把她介绍到我们公司工作，并憧憬了婚后的美好生活。

警：她为什么给你转了那么多钱？

外：我发现她深深爱上我之后，感觉要钱的时机到了。最初，我跟她说我打算投资一个非常赚钱的项目，并希望她也能投点钱，这样我们就会赚更多的钱。她答应了并转给我2万美元。几个月之后，我告诉她打算在加州的洛杉矶买套房子作为我们的婚房，但手头还缺5万美元，她又给我转了5万美元。

警：我们接到另一位名叫陈晶的女士报案，是有关你的一起类似的案件。我们相信你一定认识她吧。

外：是的，她是第二个受害者，我运用类似的手段骗了她。我为自己的所作所为而感到非常后悔。

警：还有其他要补充的吗？

外：没有了。

警：讯问过程中，是否对你刑讯逼供了？

171

外：没有。

警：被讯问时，你是否神智清楚、思路清晰？

外：是的。

警：还有其他要补充的吗？

外：没有了。

警：以上回答是否属实？

外：属实。

警：以上讯问笔录刚才我们已经用英语读给你听了，记录的内容是否和你说的一致？

外：一致。

警：签个字。

外：好的。

| 情景 2 | Questioning a Victim of Bank Card Crime
           询问银行卡犯罪受害者

P：Hello, Madam. What can I do for you?

F：Hello, officer. My money in my bank account has been stolen.

P：How much money?

F：It's about 100,000 RMB.

P：Show me your passport, please.

F：Here you are.

P：OK, Miss Smith, why do you put so much money on one card?

F：It's the money I planned to use to buy stocks today but unfortunately, it was stolen last night.

P：We are really sorry to hear that. Please tell us what has happened in detail.

F：I received an email from the so-called bank yesterday afternoon. It said the bank was updating its system and I was expected to submit my personal information. There was a link in the email. After I clicked the link there appeared the website of the so-called bank. I logged in to my account

Unit 17　Handling Cyber Crimes Involving Foreigners
涉外网络犯罪案件查处

using the card number and password and submitted my personal information.

P: When did you find your money stolen?

F: This morning when I was going to buy stocks. I found no cent was left on my card.

P: The link you received in your email is illicit. After you clicked it, you were actually logging in to the phishing site, and they stole your card number, password and then your money so easily.

F: Yes, I guess so.

P: We will make a further investigation as soon as possible. Please leave your phone number and we'll contact you once there is any good news.

F: OK, thank you very much.

P: Do remember not to click any suspicious link. Besides, when you want to log in to your account, make sure to use the official site of the bank.

F: I will never forget the lesson learned this time. Thanks again.

P: You are welcome.

警：你好，女士，请问有什么可以帮忙的？

外：你好，警官，我银行账户中的钱被人转走了。

警：被转走多少钱？

外：大约10万人民币。

警：请出示一下你的护照。

外：给你。

警：史密斯女士，你为什么把那么多的钱放在一张卡上呢？

外：那是我准备今天上午用来买股票的钱，不幸的是，昨晚就被人转走了。

警：对此我们深表同情。请给我们具体讲一讲怎么回事。

外：昨天下午，我收到银行发来的一封电子邮件，声称他们银行正在升级系统，需要我提交一下个人信息，邮件中还附有一个链接。我点击链接之后，就出现了银行的网页，然后，我输入银行卡号和密码登录账号，提交了个人信息。

警：你什么时候发现银行卡内钱被转走了？

外：今天上午我准备买股票时，发现卡里一分钱都没有了。

警：邮件中的那个链接肯定有问题，你点击进入银行网页之后，实际上当时登录的就是一个钓鱼网站。他们得到你的银行卡号和密码之后，就能轻而易举地把卡内的钱转走。

外：是的，我猜是这样的。

警：我们会尽快做进一步的调查，请留下你的电话号码，有好消息后我们会第一时间通知你。

外：好的，非常感谢。

警：请切记以后不要随便点击任何不明链接，而且，如果登录银行账户的话，一定要通过银行官网进入。

外：我永远都不会忘记这次的深刻教训，再次谢谢你们。

警：不客气。

情景 3 Interrogating the Operator of an Online Gambling Platform
讯问网络赌博平台操控者

P: Can you understand my English?

F: Yes, I can.

P: This is Haidian branch of Beijing municipal public security bureau. First of all, we'd like to inform you of the fact that you've been summoned for questioning in accordance with law because you've been suspected of committing a crime.

F: I've got it.

P: I'll read the English translation of the following documents to you. Please listen carefully.

P: (After reading The Notification of Rights and Obligations of Criminal Suspects, Notification of Foreigners' Rights in Cases Involving Foreigners, Statement on Consular Notification, and Statement on Visit by Consular Officers.) Now, do you understand everything?

Unit 17　Handling Cyber Crimes Involving Foreigners
涉外网络犯罪案件查处

F: Yes, I do.

P: Then your signature, please. According to the Criminal Procedure Law of the People's Republic of China, you are expected to answer the questions honestly. You have the right not to answer questions irrelevant to the case. Are you clear?

F: Yes, I'm clear.

P: According to the relevant provisions of the law, criminal suspects can be treated with leniency by law if they voluntarily and truthfully confess their crimes, admit to the accused criminal facts, and are willing to be punished.

F: I see.

P: What's your name and nationality?

F: I am Harris Smith from the Philipines.

P: What did you do in your group?

F: I used to be a programmer, so I was in charge of the running and maintenance of the website. I just did what my boss told me to.

P: Who could gamble on your website?

F: Anyone could after they became a member. They could register as a member for free.

P: How many members were there on your website?

F: About 1000,000 members.

P: Approximately how many people gambled every day?

F: About 20,000 or 30,000.

P: How much money did they bet every day?

F: It depends, but on average, it's about 60,000 RMB.

P: Why did almost all lose money when they gambled on your website?

F: I don't know. Maybe it was just because they were unlucky.

P: It's not that easy and we've already got some evidence. We hope you can cooperate with us and tell us the truth.

F: OK. To some degree, I could decide their winning or losing by using some technical skills. I could see clearly all the information about the members including the money they bet. My boss told me to let the members win if it's their first time to gamble or if they bet a small sum of money. When they bet a large sum of money, I was told to make them lose and then the website would win the money.

P: You've done something really terrible. Many people lost all the money they had saved for almost all their lives and some even were forced to commit suicide because of the debt they owed to the website.

F: I feel sorry for them, but I think I have nothing to do with this because I just did my job. I had no choice but to do what I was told to.

P: Your explanation is ridiculous. It is illegal to organize gambling in China. What you had done violated Chinese law.

F: I didn't realize that and I really regret what I've done.

P: Are you tortured in the process of interrogation?

F: No.

P: Are your thoughts clear when being interrogated?

F: Yes.

P: Do you have anything else to say?

F: No.

P: Did you tell the truth?

F: Yes, everything is true.

P: We've read the record of interrogation in English to you. Is it the same as what you've said?

F: Yes.

P: Please sign it.

F: OK.

警：刚才我说的英语你是否都能听明白？

外：能听明白。

警：这里是北京市公安局海淀分局，先向你告知你因涉嫌违法犯罪，被北京警方依法传唤。

外：知道了。

警：现将以下文件向你送达，我们会用英语为你宣读，请你认真听。

Unit 17 Handling Cyber Crimes Involving Foreigners
涉外网络犯罪案件查处

警：(宣读《犯罪嫌疑人权利义务告知书》《涉外案件外国人权利告知书》《关于领事通报的声明书》和《关于领事探视的声明书》等文件之后) 你听明白了吗？

外：是的，全都听明白了。

警：在这些文件后面签字。根据《中华人民共和国刑事诉讼法》的有关规定，你要如实回答我们的提问，对与本案无关的内容，你有拒绝回答的权利，你听清楚了吗？

外：听清楚了。

警：根据法律的有关规定，犯罪嫌疑人自愿如实供述自己的罪行，承认被指控的犯罪事实，愿意接受处罚的，可以依法从宽处理。

外：明白。

警：你的姓名和国籍？

外：我叫哈里斯·史密斯，来自菲律宾。

警：你在这个团伙中主要负责什么？

外：我主要负责网站的操控与维护。我所做的一切都是为了完成老板的指示。

警：什么人可以在你们网站参赌？

外：任何人都可以免费在网站注册会员，成为会员之后就可以参赌。

警：你们网站共有多少注册会员？

外：大约有一百万名吧。

警：每天参赌人数多少？

外：二三万人。

警：每天的赌资大约多少？

外：不确定，但平均起来，每天大约有 60,000 元人民币。

警：为什么几乎所有在你们网站参赌的人都输得血本无归呢？

外：不知道。也许是因为他们太不走运了吧。

警：事情并不像你说的那样简单吧？目前我们已经掌握了很多关于你们网站的证据，希望你能如实交代，配合我们的调查工作。

外：好吧。从某种程度上来说，我可以运用技术手段控制参赌人员的输赢。我可以在后台看到所有人的信息，其中包括他们下注的赌资。对于那些第一次参赌或者下注数目小的参赌人员，老板都会要求我想办法让他们赢。对于那些下注数目大的参赌人员，我会按照老板指示，让他们输掉，这样网站就可以赢得那笔钱。
警：你的所作所为真是太过分了。很多人几乎输掉了毕生的积蓄，甚至有些人因为欠下巨额赌债无力偿还而被迫自杀。
外：我为他们的不幸感到遗憾，但我认为与我无关，我只不过做了自己的本职工作，因为我别无选择，只能按照指示去做。
警：你的这番解释简直就是荒诞至极。在中国，聚众赌博是违法的，你的行为已经触犯了我国法律。
外：我之前没有意识到这点，我现在感到非常后悔。
警：还有其他要补充的吗？
警：我们讯问时，是否对你刑讯逼供了？
外：没有。
警：被讯问时，你是否神智清楚？
外：清楚。
警：还有其他要补充的吗？
外：没有了。
警：以上回答是否属实？
外：属实。
警：以上讯问笔录刚才我们已经用英语读给你听了，记录的内容是否和你说的一致？
外：一致。
警：签个字。
外：好的。

| 情景 4 | Interrogating a Suspect Who Runs a Pornographic Website
讯问淫秽色情网站经营者

P: Can you understand my English?

F: Yes, I can.

P: This is Haidian branch of Beijing municipal public security bureau. First of all, we'd like to inform you of the fact that you've been summoned for

Unit 17 Handling Cyber Crimes Involving Foreigners
涉外网络犯罪案件查处

questioning in accordance with law because you've been suspected of committing a crime.

F: I've got it.

P: I'll read the English translation of the following documents to you. Please listen carefully.

P: (After reading The Notification of Rights and Obligations of Criminal Suspects, Notification of Foreigners' Rights in Cases Involving Foreigners, Statement on Consular Notification, and Statement on Visit by Consular Officers.) Now, do you understand everything?

F: Yes, I do.

P: Then your signature, please. According to the Criminal Procedure Law of the People's Republic of China, you are expected to answer the questions honestly. You have the right not to answer questions irrelevant to the case. Are you clear?

F: Yes, I'm clear.

P: According to the relevant provisions of the law, criminal suspects can be treated with leniency by law if they voluntarily and truthfully confess their crimes, acknowledge the accused criminal facts, and are willing to be punished.

F: I see.

P: What's your name and nationality?

F: I am Tom Smith from Canada.

P: Did you build the website—*www. * * *. com*?

F: Yes, I did.

P: What was your purpose in doing this?

F: I did it just for fun.

P: Really? As far as we know, you've made a lot of money running this website. We hope you can tell us the truth.

F: Well, I did build it just for fun at first. I uploaded some x-rated movies and pornographic pictures and visitors could watch them for free. Later I found

I could make a fortune because the website became so popular that many people visited it. I encrypted the movies uploaded later and only members could watch them.

P: How could people become a member?

F: Anyone could be a member after the membership fee was paid. They could contact me through my e-mail on the website.

P: How did they pay you?

F: They usually transferred the money to my bank account. After I received the fee, I would send a password to the member's mobile phone.

P: How much did you charge for the membership?

F: 300 RMB per year for an ordinary member and 700 RMB for a VIP. Those with different memberships have different rights. For example, ordinary members can watch 50 movies while VIP members can watch unlimited movies.

P: Where did you get these movies?

F: I downloaded them from the internet to my laptop in my country and brought them here.

P: It's illegal to spread pornographic materials in China and you've gone against the Chinese Criminal law.

F: I didn't realize that and I really regret what I've done.

P: Do you want to hire a lawyer?

F: Yes.

P: Who will take charge of this for you?

F: John. His phone number is…

P: Do you have anything else to say?

F: No.

P: Is what you've said true?

F: Yes, all is true.

P: We've read the record of interrogation in English to you. Is it the same as what you've said?

Unit 17 Handling Cyber Crimes Involving Foreigners
涉外网络犯罪案件查处

F: Yes.

P: Please sign it.

F: OK.

警: 刚才我说的英语你是否都能听明白?

外: 能听明白。

警: 这里是北京市公安局海淀分局,先向你告知你因涉嫌违法犯罪,被北京警方依法传唤。

外: 知道了。

警: 现将以下文件向你送达,我们会用英语为你宣读,请你认真听。

警: (宣读《犯罪嫌疑人权利义务告知书》《涉外案件外国人权利告知书》《关于领事通报的声明书》和《关于领事探视的声明书》等文件之后)你听明白了吗?

外: 是的,全都听明白了。

警: 在这些文件后面签字。根据《中华人民共和国刑事诉讼法》的有关规定,你要如实回答我们的提问,对与本案无关的内容,你有拒绝回答的权利,你听清楚了吗?

外: 听清楚了。

警: 根据法律的有关规定,犯罪嫌疑人自愿如实供述自己的罪行,承认被指控的犯罪事实,愿意接受处罚的,可以依法从宽处理。

外: 明白。

警: 你的姓名和国籍?

外: 我叫汤姆·史密斯,来自加拿大。

警: www.＊＊＊.com 这个网站是你创建的吗?

外: 是的。

警: 你创建该网站的目的是什么?

外: 只是想娱乐一下。

警: 真是这样吗?据我们调查,你已经利用该网站赚了不少钱。希望你能如实交代。

外: 好吧,一开始的时候,我创建这个网站的确是为了娱乐,上传了一些色情图片和影片,人们可以免费观看。后来,网站越来越受欢迎,访问量越来越多，我慢慢意识到我可以利用该网站大赚一笔，所以，我开始对后来上传的色情影片进行加密处理，只有成为网站会员才可以观看。

警：怎样才能成为会员呢？

外：只要缴纳会员费，任何人都可以成为会员。人们可以通过网站上留的电子邮箱跟我联系。

警：怎样给你支付会费呢？

外：通常都是银行转账。收到会费之后，我会给他们的手机发送一个密码，会员们可以利用他们的手机号和这个密码登录网站。

警：会费多少钱呢？

外：普通会员一年300元人民币，VIP会员一年700元人民币。不同级别的会员享有不同的权利，例如，普通会员一年只能观看50部影片，VIP会员可以无限量观看。

警：你是怎样弄到这些影片的？

外：我在加拿大时从其他网站上下载下来保存在笔记本电脑中，然后来中国时带过来的。

警：在中国，传播淫秽物品牟利是违法的，你已经违反了中国法律。

外：我不知道这是违法的，我为自己的所作所为感到后悔。

警：你是否需要聘请律师为你辩护？

外：需要。

警：通知谁为你办理这事？

外：约翰，他的电话是……

警：还有其他要补充的吗？

外：没有了。

警：以上回答是否属实？

外：属实。

警：以上讯问笔录刚才我们已经用英语读给你听了，记录的内容是否和你说的一致？

外：是的。

Unit 17　Handling Cyber Crimes Involving Foreigners
涉外网络犯罪案件查处

Part IV　Creative Work
创造性练习

Situation：讯问国际骗婚犯罪嫌疑人。

▶ 听录音，请在听到提示音后开始口译。

警：刚才我说的英语你是否都能听明白？

外：能听明白。

警：这里是北京市公安局西城分局，先向你告知你因涉嫌违法犯罪，被北京警方依法传唤。

外：知道了。

警：现将以下文件向你送达，我们会用英语为你宣读，请你认真听。

警：(宣读《犯罪嫌疑人权利义务告知书》《涉外案件外国人权利告知书》《关于领事通报的声明书》和《关于领事探视的声明书》等文件之后) 你听明白了吗？

外：是的，全都听明白了。

警：在这些文件后面签字。根据《中华人民共和国刑事诉讼法》的有关规定，你要如实回答我们的提问，对与本案无关的内容，你有拒绝回答的权利，你听清楚了吗？

外：听清楚了。

警：根据法律的有关规定，犯罪嫌疑人自愿如实供述自己的罪行，承认被指控的犯罪事实，愿意接受处罚的，可以依法从宽处理。

外：明白。

警：你的姓名和国籍？

外：我叫哈罗德·怀特，来自菲律宾。

警：你来中国干什么？

外：我来旅游。

警：你认识照片中的这位女士吗？(向其展示受害者的照片)

外：不认识，从来没有见过她。

警：根据我们调查，这位女士名叫刘梅，她已经跟我们说了发生在你俩之间的事情了，所以希望你能如实交代。

外：好吧，不过我确实没有在现实中见过她。我们俩在一个婚介网上认识的，后来，我们坠入了爱河。

警：你真的爱她吗？真想跟她结婚吗？

外：当然了。

警：据我们所知，你已经结婚了。你怎么可能再跟她结婚呢？刘梅反映：你告诉她你在美国硅谷一家著名公司任市场部经理，年薪10万美元，但你却先后以各种名义向她要了5万美元。希望你不要再试图编造谎言，老老实实地把问题交代清楚。

外：好吧，我承认欺骗了她。我听说很多中国女孩都希望嫁给外国人，于是我就决定利用这点来赚点钱。我开始在网上物色合适的女孩，直到有一天，我遇见了刘梅。她自我介绍说她在一家外企工作，工资很高，她对西方文化比较感兴趣，而且希望将来能嫁到国外去。我告诉她我非常喜欢中国女孩，而且假装自己年薪也很高。后来，我想尽一切办法让她爱上我，承诺今年就和她结婚。

警：她为什么给你那么多钱？

外：我发现她深深爱上我之后，感觉要钱的时机到了。最初，我告诉她我打算购买我们公司的股票，并希望她也能购买一些，这样我们就会赚更多的钱。她答应了并转给我1万美元。几个月之后，我告诉她打算在加州的洛杉矶买套房子作为我们的婚房，但手头还缺4万美元，然后她又给我转了4万美元。

警：我们接到另一位名叫陈华的女士报案，是有关你的一起类似的案件。我们相信你一定认识她吧。

外：是的，她是第二个受害者，我运用类似的手段骗了她。我为自己的所作所为而感到非常后悔。

警：你是否需要聘请律师为你辩护？

外：需要。

警：通知谁为你办理这事？

外：约翰，他的电话是……

警：还有其他要补充的吗？

外：没有了。

警：以上回答是否属实？

外：属实。

警：以上讯问笔录刚才我们已经用英语读给你听了，记录的内容是否和你说的一致？

外：是的。

警：签个字。

外：好的。

Unit 18
Handling Other Criminal Cases Involving Foreigners
其他涉外刑事案件处理

Besides those related to drugs and cybercrime, most of the criminal cases are involved in murder, rape, human trafficking, robbery, or jeopardizing national security. If foreigners commit crimes in China, almost all the cases are handled according to China's laws and judicial procedures. When police execute a search or an arrest warrant concerning a foreign criminal suspect, using correct and appropriate spoken English is critical. For example, imperative verbal commands can prevent suspects from resistance and help to avoid impulsive panic reactions from them out of misunderstanding. During the interrogation, kindly informing suspects of their rights and tactfully questioning them in fluent and idiomatic English can ensure and facilitate the procedures and help police officers obtain the truth from them. Below are some practical conversations for criminal police officers to learn and use on their tasks.

除了涉毒案件、网络案件，刑事案件还包括谋杀、强奸、贩卖人口、抢劫或危害国家安全等。外国人在中国境内的犯罪案件大都要按照中国的法律和司法程序处置。当警察搜查或逮捕外国犯罪嫌疑人时，使用正确、适当的英语至关重要。例如，对外国犯罪嫌疑人实施搜查、逮捕时，具有控制力的口头命令不仅会震慑嫌疑人使之不会反抗，而且会避免嫌疑人因误解而产生的冲动和惊慌。讯问犯罪嫌疑人时，使用流利地道的英语善意地告知其权利，机敏地提问，不仅能保证讯问顺利进行，还能使犯罪嫌疑人讲真话。以下是一些实用的对话，供一线民警学习并在执行任务时使用。

Part I　New Words and Expressions
生词与词组

private	英[ˈpraɪvɪt]；美[ˈpraɪvɪt]	adj. 私人的，私有的
residence	英[ˈrezɪd(ə)ns]；美[ˈrɛzɪdəns]	n. 住宅，住处
warrant	英[ˈwɒr(ə)nt]；美[ˈwɔrənt]	n. 委任状，（法院授权警方采取行动的）令状
subdue	英[səbˈdjuː]；美[səbˈduː]	vt. 征服、制服
handcuff	英[ˈhændkʌf]；美[ˈhændkʌf]	n. 手铐；v. 给……戴上手铐
innocent	英[ˈɪnəsnt]；美[ˈɪnəsnt]	adj. 无辜的；无罪的
resist	英[rɪˈzɪst]；美[rɪˈzɪst]	vt. 抵抗
ridiculous	英[rɪˈdɪkjələs]；美[rɪˈdɪkjələs]	adj. 可笑的；荒谬的
accidentally	英[ˌæksɪˈdentəli]；美[ˌæksɪˈdentəli]	adv. 意外地
blackmail	英[ˈblækmeɪl]；美[ˈblækmeɪl]	v. 勒索，敲诈
reaction	英[riˈækʃn]；美[riˈækʃn]	n. 反应
shameless	英[ˈʃeɪmləs]；美[ˈʃeɪmləs]	adj. 无耻的
disgusting	英[dɪsˈɡʌstɪŋ]；美[dɪsˈɡʌstɪŋ]	adj. 令人厌恶的

search warrant 搜查证

be subdued by force 武力制服

arrest warrant 逮捕证

be under arrest 被逮捕了

checked into the hotel 登记入住宾馆

how come 为什么

urged sb. to do sth. 敦促某人做某事

a large sum of money 大量的钱

swear at sb. 咒骂某人

Unit 18　Handling Other Criminal Cases Involving Foreigners
其他涉外刑事案件处理

Part II　Useful Sentence Patterns
常用句型

- This is the police officer from Haidian branch of Beijing municipal public security bureau. Open the door right now!
  我们是北京市公安局海淀分局的民警，现在立即将房门打开！

- We are notifying you that we need to search your house and we have a search warrant! Please cooperate immediately; otherwise, we'll do it by force.
  现向你告知，北京警方需对你的住所进行检查，请你立即予以配合。如拒绝配合，我们将强制实施！

- Now follow the officer's instructions, stand with your hands above your head, face the wall, feet apart!
  现在听从警官的指令，双手举过头顶，面对墙壁站立，双脚打开！

- Just follow the instructions of the officer, or you'll be subdued by force!
  服从警官的指令，否则我们将予以武力制服！

- We are notifying that all the ecstasy is confiscated by the police.
  现在向你告知，这些摇头丸被警方扣押。

- Turn around and stretch your hands. (*The suspect was handcuffed*) Come with us to the police station to be questioned.
  转过身来，伸出双手（上铐），跟我们到公安局接受调查。

- Don't move! This is the police from Beijing public security bureau!
  不许动！我们是北京市公安局的！

- This is the arrest warrant! You are under arrest.
  这是逮捕证。你被捕了。

- The police found the woman who checked into the hotel with you last night lying on the carpet of the room.
  警方调查发现昨晚同你一起入住宾馆的女士躺在宾馆地毯上。

■ Do you have anything else to say?

还有其他要补充的吗?

Part III　Situational Dialogues
情景对话

|情景 1|　Searching

　　　　　搜查

P: Open the door!

F: Who is it?

P: This is the police officer from Haidian branch of Beijing municipal public security bureau. Open the door right now!

F: Police? This is my private residence! Please leave me alone!

P: We are notifying you that we need to search your house and we have a search warrant! Please cooperate immediately; otherwise, we'll do it by force.

F: Wait a minute. I'm coming…

(The police officers found that the man is delaying on purpose maybe to destroy the evidence, so they broke in.)

P: (Showing him the search warrant) This is the legal document for the inspection of your house. Now follow the officer's instructions, stand with your hands above your head, face the wall, feet apart!

P: We will record the entire process of search on video. Are you clear?

F: Yes.

F: I have done nothing wrong!

P: Shut up! Just follow the instructions of the officer, or you'll be subdued by force!

F: …

P: Where is your passport?

Unit 18 Handling Other Criminal Cases Involving Foreigners
其他涉外刑事案件处理

F: In my bag on the desk.

P: What's your nationality?

F: I'm from Australia.

P: What's your name?

F: Andrew Jackson.

P: How to spell it?

F: A–N–D–R–E–W, J–A–C–K–S–O–N.

P: What is your date of birth?

F: May 1, 1989.

P: What is your job?

F: I'm a teacher at Beijing Language and Culture University.

P: Do you rent the house?

F: Yes.

(The police officer found some ecstasy under his pillow.)

P: What's this?

F: I don't know. It's not mine.

P: Why is it under your pillow if it isn't yours?

F: I'm innocent.

P: We are notifying that all the ecstasy is confiscated by the police.

F: I see.

P: Turn around and stretch your hands. (The suspect was handcuffed). Come with us to the police station to be questioned.

F: Please, officer. I'm innocent.

警：开门！

外：谁？

警：我们是北京市公安局海淀分局的民警，现在立即将房门打开！

外：警察？这是我的私人住宅！请不要打扰！

警：现向你告知，北京警方需对你的住所进行检查，请你立即予以配合。如拒绝配合，我们将强制实施！

外：等一等，我来……

(我民警发现对方故意拖延，有毁灭证据的可能，破门而入)

警：(向对方出示搜查证) 这是对你住所进行检查的法律文书。现在听从警官的指令，双手举过头顶，面对墙壁站立，双脚打开！

警：现向你告知，整个搜查行动我们都需要录像，你听清楚了吗？

外：我没干坏事！

警：闭嘴！服从警官的指令，否则我们将予以武力制服！

外：……

警：你的护照在哪里？

外：在我书桌的包里。

警：你的国籍？

外：澳大利亚。

警：你叫什么名字？

外：安德鲁·杰克逊。

警：怎么拼的？

外：A-N-D-R-E-W, J-A-C-K-S-O-N。

警：出生日期？

外：1989年5月1日。

警：你的职业？

外：我是北京语言大学的外教。

警：房子是你租的吗？

外：是的。

(我民警在外国人枕头底下发现摇头丸)

警：这是什么？

外：不知道。这不是我的。

警：不是你的，怎么会在你枕头底下？

外：我是无辜的。

警：现在向你告知，这些物品被警方扣押！

外：知道了。

警：转过身来，伸出双手（上铐），跟我们到公安局接受调查。

外：求你了警官，我是无辜的。

Unit 18　Handling Other Criminal Cases Involving Foreigners
其他涉外刑事案件处理

| 情景 2 |　Arresting
逮捕

P：Stop!

F：What's the matter?

P：Don't move! This is the police from Beijing public security bureau!

F：But…

P：What's your name?

F：Tomas Maier.

P：This is the arrest warrant! You are under arrest.

F：Why?

P：You are suspected of murder.

F：Oh no! Ridiculous! I'm innocent.

警：站住！

外：什么事？

警：不许动！我们是北京市公安局的！

外：这……

警：你叫什么名字？

外：托马斯·迈尔。

警：这是逮捕证。你被捕了。

外：为什么？

警：你涉嫌杀人。

外：不！胡说！我是清白的！

| 情景 3 |　Interrogating a Suspect Murderer
讯问杀人案嫌疑人

P：Do you understand my English?

F：Yes, I do.

P: This is Haidian branch of Beijing municipal public security bureau. First of all, we'd like to inform you of the fact that you've been summoned for questioning in accordance with law because you've been suspected of committing a crime.

F: I've got it.

P: I'll read the English translation of the following documents to you. Please listen carefully.

P: (After reading The Notification of Rights and Obligations of Criminal Suspects, Notification of Foreigners' Rights in Cases Involving Foreigners, Statement on Consular Notification, and Statement on Visit by Consular Officers.) Now, do you understand everything?

F: Yes, I do.

P: Then your signature, please. According to the Criminal Procedure Law of the People's Republic of China, you are expected to answer the questions honestly. You have the right not to answer questions irrelevant to the case. Are you clear?

F: Yes, I'm clear.

P: According to the relevant provisions of the law, suspects who voluntarily and truthfully confess their crimes, admit to the facts of the alleged crime and are willing to accept punishment may be dealt with leniently according to law.

F: I see.

P: What is your name and nationality?

F: I'm Charles Walter from the U. S.

P: How to spell?

F: C –H –A –R –L –E –S, W –A –L –T –E –R.

P: Who is your contact in China?

F: My wife.

P: How to contact her.

F: Her cellphone number is…

Unit 18 Handling Other Criminal Cases Involving Foreigners
其他涉外刑事案件处理

P: What's your job?

F: I'm a marketing manager with Dott Company.

P: Have you done anything illegal?

F: No.

P: The police found the woman who checked into the hotel with you last night lying on the carpet of the room. Who was she?

F: Wang Hong, my secretary.

P: How come she lay on the carpet?

F: I push her down accidentally.

P: Why did you push her?

F: She blackmailed me.

P: Why did she blackmail you?

F: She had sex with me and got pregnant. She urged me to marry her.

P: Did you agree?

F: No.

P: Why not?

F: I am married.

P: What was her reaction?

F: She asked for a large sum of money.

P: How much?

F: One hundred thousand dollars.

P: Did you agree to give her the money?

F: It was too much. So I said no to her.

P: What happened next?

F: She began to swear at me and scratch me.

P: Did you fight back?

F: Yes. She was so shameless and disgusting. I could no longer control myself.

P: How did you fight back?

F: I pushed her. She fell heavily against the edge of the wall and fainted.

P: Why didn't you send her to the hospital?

F: I was angry at that time, so I left.

P: Do you want to hire a lawyer?

F: Yes.

P: Who will represent you in this case?

F: Peter. His cellphone number is 13901991876.

P: Do you have anything else to say?

F: No.

P: Did you tell the truth?

F: Yes, everything is true.

P: We've read the record of interrogation in English to you. Is it the same as what you've said?

F: Yes.

P: Please sign it.

F: OK.

警：刚才我说的英语你是否都听明白了？

外：听明白了。

警：这里是北京市公安局海淀分局，先向你告知你因涉嫌违法犯罪，被北京警方依法传唤。

外：知道了。

警：现将以下文件向你送达，我们会用英语为你宣读，请你认真听。

警：(宣读《犯罪嫌疑人权利义务告知书》《涉外案件外国人权利告知书》《关于领事通报的声明书》和《关于领事探视的声明书》等文件之后) 你听明白了吗？

外：是的，全都听明白了。

警：在这些文件后面签字。根据《中华人民共和国刑事诉讼法》的有关规定，你要如实回答我们的提问，对与本案无关的内容，你有拒绝回答的权利，你听清楚了吗？

外：听清楚了。

警：根据法律的有关规定，犯罪嫌疑人自愿如实供述自己的罪行，承认被指控

Unit 18 Handling Other Criminal Cases Involving Foreigners
其他涉外刑事案件处理

的犯罪事实，愿意接受处罚的，可以依法从宽处理。

外：明白。

警：你的姓名、国籍？

外：我叫查尔斯·华特，美国人。

警：怎么拼的？

外：C-H-A-R-L-E-S, W-A-L-T-E-R.

警：你在中国的联系人是谁？

外：我妻子。

警：她的联系方式是什么？

外：她的手机号是……

警：你的职业？

外：我是多特公司市场部经理。

警：你有没有做过违法犯罪的事？

外：没有。

警：警方调查发现昨晚同你一起入住宾馆的女士躺在宾馆地毯上，她是谁？

外：我的秘书汪红。

警：她是怎么躺在地上的？

外：我不小心把她推倒的。

警：为什么推她？

外：她来敲诈我。

警：她为什么要敲诈你？

外：她和我发生过性关系并怀孕了。她逼我娶她。

警：你同意了吗？

外：没有。

警：为什么？

外：我已经结婚了。

警：她当时是什么反应？

外：她向我要一大笔钱。

警：多少钱？

外：10万美元。

警：你同意给她这笔钱了吗？

外：她要得太多了。我拒绝了她。

警：然后发生了什么？

外：她开始骂我，抓我。

警：你还手了吗？

外：还了。她太无耻、太令人厌恶了。我当时控制不住自己。

警：你是怎样还手的？

外：我推了她一下。她重重地撞到了墙角，然后就倒在地上了。

警：你为什么没有把她送到医院呢？

外：我当时很生气，所以就离开了。

警：你是否需要聘请律师为你辩护？

外：需要。

警：通知谁为你办理这事？

外：皮特，他的电话是13901991876。

警：还有其他要补充的吗？

外：没有了。

警：以上回答是否属实？

外：属实。

警：以上讯问笔录我们都用英语读给你听了，记录的内容是否和你说的一致？

外：是的。

Part IV Creative Work
创造性练习

Situation：讯问杀人案嫌疑人。

▶ 听录音，请在听到提示音后开始口译。

警：刚才我说的英语你是否都听明白了？

外：听明白了。

Unit 18　Handling Other Criminal Cases Involving Foreigners
其他涉外刑事案件处理

警：这里是北京市公安局海淀分局，先向你告知你因涉嫌违法犯罪，被北京警方依法传唤。

外：知道了。

警：现将以下文件向你送达，我们会用英语为你宣读，请你认真听。

警：(宣读《犯罪嫌疑人权利义务告知书》《涉外案件外国人权利告知书》《关于领事通报的声明书》和《关于领事探视的声明书》等文件之后) 你听明白了吗？

外：是的，全都听明白了。

警：在这些文件后面签字。根据《中华人民共和国刑事诉讼法》的有关规定，你要如实回答我们的提问，对与本案无关的内容，你有拒绝回答的权利，你听清楚了吗？

外：听清楚了。

警：根据法律的有关规定，犯罪嫌疑人自愿如实供述自己的罪行，承认被指控的犯罪事实，愿意接受处罚的，可以依法从宽处理。

外：明白。

警：你的姓名、出生日期和国籍？

外：我叫大卫·史密斯，出生于1993年6月5日，来自菲律宾。

警：民族宾馆监控视频显示，昨晚你和一名女士进入该宾馆206房间，那位女士是谁？

外：我的前女友安娜。

警：昨晚上发生了什么？详细说一下。

外：上个月我俩分手了，昨天她主动约我到酒店，说她怀孕了并逼我娶她。因为她性格暴躁，而且特别自私，我实在不想再同她在一起，我没答应，她便要我给她10万美元作为补偿。

警：你同意给她这笔钱了吗？

外：她要得太多了。我拒绝了她。她威胁说要去我们老板那里告我，我求她不要那样做，可她不听，拿起手机就要给我老板打电话，我把手机夺了过来。

警：然后发生了什么？

外：她开始骂我，抓我。我当时失去理智，便掐住她的脖子，大约三四分钟后她就晕了。

警：你当时为什么没有把她送到医院呢?
外：我以为她假装晕倒的,所以就离开了。
警：你是否需要聘请律师为你辩护?
外：需要。
警：通知谁为你办理这事?
外：爱德华,他的电话是……
警：还有其他要补充的吗?
外：没有了。
警：以上回答是否属实?
外：属实。
警：以上讯问笔录刚才我们已经用英语读给你听,记录的内容是否和你说的一致?
外：是的。
警：签个字。
外：好的。

Unit 19
Handling Terrorist Attack
应对恐怖袭击

As is well known, the U. S. launched a war against terrorism following the September 11, 2001 terrorist attack. And in China's Xinjiang Province, lots of terrorist attacks killed large numbers of innocent people and hundreds of police officers from 1990 to 2016 and caused incalculable damage to local communities. International and domestic violent extremists have been taking advantage of modern technology to enlarge their influence effectively and mobilize to evil activities quickly, posing a serious threat to peace and security of the world. Therefore, protecting our country from their attacks has become one of our priorities. At the end of 2015, China's top legislature adopted the country's first counterterrorism law to address terrorism at home and help maintain world security. It provides legal support to the country's counterterrorism campaigns as well as collaboration with international societies. Only when all countries cooperate with one another can terrorists be defeated completely. This unit offers an opportunity for police officers to learn about characteristics of terrorism, transnational experiences in combating terrorism in addition to some English expressions frequently used in international cooperation.

众所周知,遭受"9·11"恐怖袭击后,美国发动了反恐战争。自1990年至2016年,中国新疆地区发生了许多恐怖袭击,导致大量无辜平民和数百名警察伤亡,给当地造成了无法估量的损失。长期以来,国内外的暴力极端分子利用现代技术扩大影响,并组织发动恐怖袭击,对世界和平构成严重威胁。因此,保护我们国家不受恐怖袭击已成为我国首要任务之一。2015 年年底，为了防范和打击国内恐怖主义，帮助维护世界和平，我国最高立法机关通过了第一部反恐怖主义法，为我国的反恐行动及国际合作提供法律支持。只有各国通力合作，才能彻底击垮恐怖分子。通过本单元的学习，我国警务人员可以了解恐怖主义特点、跨国反恐经验，以及在国际反恐合作中经常使用的一些英语表达。

Part I   New Words and Expressions
生词与词组

terrorism 英[ˈterərɪzəm] 美[ˈterərɪzəm] n. 恐怖主义
hostage 英[ˈhɒstɪdʒ] 美[ˈhɑːstɪdʒ] n. 人质
deadly 英[ˈdedli] 美[ˈdedli] adj. 致命的
kidnap 英[ˈkɪdnæp] 美[ˈkɪdnæp] vt. 绑架
considerable 英[kənˈsɪdərəbl] 美[kənˈsɪdərəbl] adj. 相当大的
reinforce 英[ˌriːɪnˈfɔːs] 美[ˌriːɪnˈfɔːrs] vt. 加强
counter-terrorism 反恐
agency 英[ˈeɪdʒənsi] 美[ˈeɪdʒənsi] n. 机构
coordinate 英[kəʊˈɔːdɪneɪt] 美[koʊˈɔːrdɪneɪt] v. 调节，配合
intelligence 英[ɪnˈtelɪdʒəns] 美[ɪnˈtelɪdʒəns] n. 情报
execute 英[ˈeksɪkjuːt] 美[ˈeksɪkjuːt] vt. 实行；执行
surveillance 英[sɜːˈveɪləns] 美[sɜːrˈveɪləns] n. 监督；监视
analyze 英[ˈænəlaɪz] 美[ˈænəlaɪz] vt. 对……进行分析
combat 英[ˈkɒmbæt] 美[ˈkɑːmbæt] v. 与……战斗
enhance 英[ɪnˈhɑːns] 美[ɪnˈhæns] vt. 提高；加强
enormous 英[ɪˈnɔːməs] 美[ɪˈnɔːrməs] adj. 巨大的
internal 英[ɪnˈtɜːnl] 美[ɪnˈtɜːrnl] adj. 内部的
external 英[ɪkˈstɜːnl] 美[ɪkˈstɜːrnl] adj. 外部的
over-screening 过度检查
persecute 英[ˈpɜːsɪkjuːt] 美[ˈpɜːrsɪkjuːt] vt. 迫害

Unit 19 Handling Terrorist Attack 应对恐怖袭击

Afghanistan 英[æfˈgænɪstɑːn; æfˈgænɪstæn] 美[æfˈgænɪstæn] n. 阿富汗
Palestine 英[ˈpælistain] n. 巴勒斯坦
Bosnia 美[ˈbɑznɪə] n. 波斯尼亚
discriminate 英[dɪˈskrɪmɪneɪt] 美[dɪˈskrɪmɪneɪt] vt. 歧视
impact 英[ˈɪmpækt] 美[ˈɪmpækt] n. 影响
infringement 英[ɪnˈfrɪndʒmənt] 美[ɪnˈfrɪndʒmənt] n. 侵犯
disseminate 英[dɪˈsemɪneɪt] 美[dɪˈsemɪneɪt] vt. 宣传
contingency 英[kənˈtɪndʒənsi] 美[kənˈtɪndʒənsi] adj. 应变的
erase 英[ɪˈreɪz] 美[ɪˈreɪs] vt. 抹去
eliminate 英[ɪˈlɪmɪneɪt] 美[ɪˈlɪmɪneɪt] vt. 消除
speculation 英[ˌspekjuˈleɪʃn] 美[ˌspekjuˈleɪʃn] n. 猜测
leaflet 英[ˈliːflət] 美[ˈliːflət] n. 传单
distribution 英[ˌdɪstrɪˈbjuːʃn] 美[ˌdɪstrɪˈbjuːʃn] n. 分发
continuously 英[kənˈtɪnjuəsli] 美[kənˈtɪnjuəsli] adv. 连续不断地

Eastern Turkistan Islamic Movement 东伊运（恐怖组织）
human trafficking 人口贩卖
economic loss 经济损失
in charge of 负责
Department of Homeland Security 国土安全部
Department of State 国务院
Office of the Director of National Intelligence 国家情报总监办公室
Federal Bureau of Investigation 联邦调查局
Central Intelligence Agency 美国中央情报局
National Counter-terrorism Center 国家反恐中心
aim at 目的在于
in conjunction with 与……配合
are subjected to 受到……
be attributed to 归因于
at security check 安检站/口
ease tensions between...and... 缓解……和……之间的紧张关系

are liable to do sth. 很有可能做某事
at the eleventh hour 关键时刻
make a set of contingency plan 制订一套应急计划
prior to 在……之前
the status quo of 现状

Part II　Useful Sentence Patterns
常用句型

- Terrorists have done great harm to many countries by murdering, suicide bombing, hostage-taking, kidnapping and human trafficking.

  恐怖分子在全球范围内实施谋杀、自杀式爆炸袭击、劫持人质、绑架和贩卖人口等，给很多国家带来了极大的危害。

- Would you please introduce some successful measures taken to combat terrorism?

  请问您能介绍一些成功的反恐措施吗？

- And these pressures make positive police-community relations difficult to achieve.

  这些压力严重影响良好警民关系的建立。

- So whether discrimination against these communities is an objective reality or subjective feelings, law enforcement personnel as the main force of counterterrorism are most likely unwelcome.

  不管对这些社区的歧视客观存在还是他们的主观看法，作为反恐主力军的执法人员在这些社区极有可能不受欢迎。

- I think there's a need to take more active strategies in order to ease tensions between police and residents in these communities that are liable to be affected by extremism.

  我认为有必要在可能受到极端主义影响的这些社区采取积极的警务策略，以缓解比较紧张的警民关系。

Unit 19 Handling Terrorist Attack
应对恐怖袭击

- Terrorist attacks will cause fears and rumors, especially in these communities. And the media can help remove them.

  在这些社区，恐怖袭击极有可能在社区成员之间造成恐慌和谣言，而媒体宣传可以有效消除各种恐慌与谣言。

- Police agencies ought to make a set of contingency plans so that they can do publicizing at the eleventh hour by means of all available media and languages.

  警察机构应该制订一套媒体应急预案，关键时刻，利用一切可用的媒体和语言进行宣传。

- Conducting a series of open community forums to address fears and concerns.

  在社区举办一系列的讲座来消除居民的恐惧与担心。

- Continuously updating agency websites on the status quo of the on-going operations.

  警方网站应该及时更新事件进展情况。

- These measures must be very successful, I assume.

  我猜这些措施一定很有效吧？

Part III   Situational Dialogues
情景对话

情景 1 Learning Something about Terrorism
学习恐怖主义相关知识

P: Hello, Professor Eck. I am very happy to have the chance to learn something about terrorism.

F: My pleasure. Nowadays, terrorist crimes are transnational. Terrorist organizations take advantage of our modern technology to act through instant communication.

P: Yes, that's true.

F: Terrorists have done great harm to many countries by murdering, suicide bombing, hostage-taking, kidnapping and human trafficking.

P: Yes, they have had a bad influence on the whole society.

F: You are right. The September 11 attacks (also referred to as 9/11) was the deadliest terrorist attack on U.S. soil. The attack killed 2996 people, injured over 6000 others, and caused the U.S. at least $200 billion economic loss and the whole world about $1000 billion.

P: That's really terrible.

F: The American Government has spent a considerable amount of resources in establishing new counter-terrorism agencies and reinforcing existing ones since then.

P: Which agencies are in charge of counter-terrorism?

F: They are the Department of Homeland Security, Department of State, Office of the Director of National Intelligence, Federal Bureau of Investigation, Central Intelligence Agency, and National Counter-terrorism Center.

P: There are so many agencies involved. What roles do they play respectively?

F: Department of Homeland Security is the lead agency in charge of all domestic anti-terrorism and security activities. Department of State manages the development and implementation of all U.S. government policies and programs aimed at countering terrorism overseas. The Office of the Director of National Intelligence coordinates the gathering, analysis, and sharing of data among federal intelligence agencies such as the FBI and CIA. Federal Bureau of Investigation executes counter-terrorism actions such as surveillance and investigation in conjunction with other law-enforcement agents at the local, state, and federal level. Central Intelligence Agency collects, analyzes, and shares international intelligence and data to inform and carry out U.S. foreign policy, and National Counter-terrorism Center plans and coordinates counter-terrorism policies and programs among federal agen-

Unit 19　Handling Terrorist Attack
应对恐怖袭击

cies.

P: Would you please introduce some successful measures taken to combat terrorism?

F: OK. First it is very important to improve our ability to gather and analyse intelligence. Second, physical security and effective response should be enhanced. Third, it's necessary to increase community involvement.

P: I've learned a lot today. Thank you so much for the useful information.

F: You are welcome.

警：您好，艾克教授，很高兴能有机会向您请教恐怖主义相关问题。谢谢您！

外：很荣幸。当今恐怖犯罪的主要特点是跨国性，恐怖主义组织利用现代技术，通过即时通信实施恐怖袭击。

警：是的，的确是这样的。

外：恐怖分子在全球范围内实施谋杀、自杀式爆炸袭击、劫持人质、绑架和贩卖人口等，给很多国家带来了极大的危害。

警：是的，他们给整个社会造成了极其恶劣的影响。

外：你说得没错。发生在美国本土最为严重的恐怖袭击——"9·11"事件，造成高达2996人遇难，6000多人受伤，对美经济损失达2000亿美元，对全球经济所造成的损失达到1万亿美元左右。

警：那次恐怖袭击给美国和全球造成的人员、经济损失真是太惨重了。

外："9·11"事件之后，美国政府加大投入，新组建了一些反恐机构，并对现有机构进行加强与完善。

警：美国负责反恐的机构都有哪些呢？

外：目前，最为重要的一共有六家，分别是国土安全部、国务院、国家情报总监办公室、联邦调查局、中央情报局、国家反恐中心。

警：这么多家机构参与！他们的职责分别是什么呢？

外：国土安全部主要负责国内的反恐工作及安全问题；国务院主要负责美国国外反恐政策及计划的制订与实施；国家情报总监办公室主要负责协调情报的收集、分析、联邦调查局和中央情报局等联邦情报机构间的信息分享；联邦调查局联合地方、州、联邦等各级执法机构执行反恐行动；中央情报局主要负责国际情报的收集、分析、分享及执行美国的对外政策；国家反恐中心主要负责制订各种反恐政策及协调各联邦机构执行反恐计划。

警：请问您能介绍一些成功的反恐措施吗？

外：好的。为了有效打击恐怖主义，最重要的一点是提高相关机构收集和分析情报的能力，其次应该增强实体安全和政府各部门的应急能力，最后，应该提高社区居民的参与度。

警：今天我学了很多知识，谢谢您给我讲了这么多有用的信息。

外：不客气。

|情景2| Discussion on Strengthening Community Policing at the Age of Counter-terrorism
反恐时代加强社区警务的讨论

P: I quite agree with you that local police should double and redouble their outreach efforts in communities if they really want to win the war against terrorism.

F: Yes, but it's a pity that police officers as the main force of counterterrorism were unwelcome in some communities.

P: Why?

F: Residents feel discriminated against because of some negative media publicity. What's more, they regard some of the measures taken by law enforcement agencies as infringements on their civil liberties.

P: That's too bad. I think it'll be difficult to develop a positive police-community relationship.

F: You're right. A lot of actions should be taken to ease the tension between police and communities. For example, the police should pay close attention to the media sources the communities use, and to understand the residents' points of view regarding local and global events. What's more, the police should mobilize all possible channels to disseminate positive information to the communities.

P: That's great. Terrorist attacks will cause fears and rumors in communities

Unit 19 Handling Terrorist Attack 应对恐怖袭击

and the media can help to remove them.

P: Yes. Police agencies ought to make a set of contingency plans so that they can do publicizing at the eleventh hour through all available media and languages.

P: Could you be more specific?

F: Sure. For instance, if a doubt-eliminating plan is implemented before such actions as searching or arresting terrorists are taken within a community, much adverse influence can be erased.

P: What does such a plan usually include?

F: It usually includes the following: firstly, briefing community leaders on the situation before briefing the media, thus to reduce rumors and speculations; secondly, providing extra patrols in the area affected.

P: We do the same. And what's else?

F: Equipping police officers with information, including leaflets for distribution; and then, conducting a series of open community forums to address fears and concerns; finally, continuously updating agency websites on the status quo of the on-going operations.

P: These measures must be very successful, I assume.

F: Indeed. Many police agencies in the U.S. have used these tactics with great success.

警：我完全赞同您的观点，为有效应对恐怖主义，地方警察应努力加强社区警务服务。

外：的确。但遗憾的是，作为反恐主力军的警察在有些社区不太受欢迎。

警：为什么？

外：因为某些媒体的负面宣传，居民们感觉遭到了歧视，此外，他们认为警方采取的一些反恐措施侵犯了他们的自由。

警：太糟糕了。那样的话，将很难建立良好的警民关系。

外：是的。为了缓和紧张的警民关系，警察应积极采取各种措施。例如，应该关注社区使用的媒体来源，了解社区成员对当地和世界事件的看法。此外，警方应该利用各种渠道向社区传播积极的信息。

警：恐怖袭击极有可能在社区成员之间造成恐慌和各种谣言的传播，而媒体宣传则可以有效帮助人们缓解恐慌，澄清谣言。

外：是的。警察机构应该制定一套媒体应急预案，关键时刻，利用一切可用的媒体和语言进行宣传。

警：请您具体介绍一下好吗？

外：比如在社区抓捕恐怖分子或进行搜查时，如果实施社区疑虑消除计划，就可以避免很多负面影响。

警：请问这个计划包括哪些内容呢？

外：首先，向媒体通报情况之前，警方应该先向社区领导通报，以减少各种谣言和猜测，并在相关地区加强巡逻。

警：我们也经常这样做，还有其他措施吗？

外：其次，为警察们提供全面信息和各种传单，以便他们能够在社区中进行宣传；在社区举办一系列的讲座来消除居民的恐惧与担忧。最后，警方网站应该及时更新事件进展情况。

警：这些措施一定很有效吧？

外：是的。美国警方采取这些措施后，成效显著。

Part IV　Creative Work
创造性练习

Situation：中国特警队员向美国反恐专家约翰逊先生请教人质解救的成功经验。

▶ 听录音，请在听到提示音后开始口译。🎧

警：约翰逊先生，听说您是反恐专家，特别擅长人质解救，我拜读过您写的很多文章。

外：谢谢！

警：请问您能给我介绍一些人质解救方面的成功经验吗？

外：没问题。人质解救行动的主要目的就是救援队以最小代价成功解救所有人质。

Unit 19　Handling Terrorist Attack
应对恐怖袭击

警：是的，但要做到这一点，的确很难。

外：你说得没错。人质解救行动是最艰难的特种作战任务，通常分为三个步骤。

警：具体哪三个步骤呢？

外：第一步是制订方案、反复演习。挟持人质事件发生之后，救援力量应该在第一时间制订一个应急处置方案，如果劫持者开始杀害或转移人质，立即执行该方案。

警：还有其他方案吗？

外：有。在应急处置方案基础上，会根据不断收集到的情报信息制订一个更加完善的营救方案。除此之外，还要制订一个突发情况处置方案，当救援力量实施营救方案被恐怖分子发现时，作为营救方案的补充。

警：怎样才能保证营救方案顺利实施呢？

外：为了保证方案实施效果，参加营救任务的所有人员都要参与到方案制订、反复演习的过程。

警：第二个步骤是什么呢？

外：第二步就是靠近目标、发起突击。靠近目标的过程中，救援力量要随时准备实施突发情况处置方案。突击行动一旦开始，他们必须马上排除险情，控制人质。

警：这个步骤应该是最重要的吧？

外：是的，的确如此。第三步就是突击后处置。

警：这一步有哪些需要特别注意的吗？

外：当救援力量撤离时，不要遗漏任何人质或者让恐怖分子混入人质中。

警：今天我学到很多，谢谢您，约翰逊先生。

外：不客气。

警：希望将来有机会我们还能继续交流经验与合作。

外：我也希望如此。

Unit 20
International Police Exchange and Cooperation
国际警务交流与合作

With more and more international drug trafficking, money-laundering, human trafficking and terrorist attacks, it's critical for police from countries all over the world to cooperate with each other. International Criminal Police Organization—INTERPOL helps police all over the world to share criminal intelligence and facilitate international police cooperation such as cross-border investigations, hot pursuit, and arrests. It has played a very important role in preventing and combating all kinds of transnational crimes. English is widely used in the world, so it is one of the official languages of INTERPOL and an important language tool in international police interchange and cooperation. Police officers in our country should have a good command of English in order to communicate and cooperate with the police in the world. This unit will help police officers in our country to acquire some appropriate English often used in international interchange and cooperation.

随着毒品犯罪、非法洗钱、贩卖人口和恐怖袭击等有组织犯罪的不断国际化，世界各国警察间的合作显得尤其重要。国际刑警组织在世界范围内促进各国警察分享犯罪信息、协查犯罪事实证据的收集、缉捕犯罪分子，在预防和打击跨国犯罪方面发挥了重要作用。英语作为世界通用语言，成为国际刑警组织的官方语言，也是国际警务交流与合作中的重要语言工具。为了更好地参与国际交流与合作，我国警察必须具备较强的英语应用能力。本单元将帮助我国警察学习一些国际警务交流与合作常用的英语表达方式。

Unit 20 International Police Exchange and Cooperation
国际警务交流与合作

Part I New Words and Expressions
生词与词组

laundering	英[ˈlɔːndərɪŋ] 美 n. 洗（钱）
characteristic	英[ˌkærəktəˈrɪstɪk] 美[ˌkærəktəˈrɪstɪk] n. 特征
transnational	英[ˌtrænzˈnæʃnəl；ˌtrænsˈnæʃnəl]
	美[ˌtrænzˈnæʃnəl, ˌtrænsˈnæʃnəl] adj. 跨国的
trillion	英[ˈtrɪljən] 美[ˈtrɪljən] n. [数] 万亿
conduct	英[kənˈdʌkt] 美[kənˈdʌkt] v. 组织，实施，进行
authority	英[ɔːˈθɒrəti] 美[əˈθɔːrəti] n. 权力
derive	英[dɪˈraɪv] 美[dɪˈraɪv] vt. 获得
counterpart	英[ˈkaʊntəpɑːt] 美[ˈkaʊntərpɑːrt] n. 极相似的人或物
sector	英[ˈsektə(r)] 美[ˈsektər] n. 部门
financial	英[faɪˈnænʃl；fəˈnænʃl] 美[faɪˈnænʃl, fəˈnænʃl]
	adj. 金融的；财政的
authority	英[ɔːˈθɒrəti] 美[əˈθɔːrəti] n. 官方机构
relevant	英[ˈreləvənt] 美[ˈreləvənt] adj. 相关的
transaction	英[trænˈzækʃn] 美[trænˈzækʃn] n. 交易
identification	英[aɪˌdentɪfɪˈkeɪʃn] 美[aɪˌdentɪfɪˈkeɪʃn] n. 鉴定，识别
multinational	英[ˌmʌltiˈnæʃnəl] 美[ˌmʌltiˈnæʃnəl] adj. 多国的

anti-money laundering 反洗钱

taken advantage of 利用

Department of Treasury 财政部

Department of Justice 司法部

Federal Reserve 美国联邦储备委员会

Internal Revenue Service 国家税务总局

cooperate with one another 与……合作

fight against 打击

permit...to do sth. 允许……做某事

financial regulatory authority 金融监管部门

play a role in dealing with... 在处理……方面发挥作用

customer identification 客户身份识别
financial transaction reporting system 货币交易报告制度

Part II   Useful Sentence Patterns
常用句型

- I'm so happy that you can give me an introduction to anti-money laundering in the U. S. I really appreciate it.
  很高兴您能介绍美国打击洗钱犯罪行为的具体情况,我不胜感激。

- Could you please introduce some measures taken to fight against money laundering in the U. S. ?
  请您介绍一下美国在打击洗钱犯罪方面的具体措施好吗?

- Money laundering has become a global crime, so it needs multinational cooperation to win the battle.
  洗钱已经成为全球化犯罪,因此,世界各国必须密切合作,才能对这一犯罪行为进行有效打击。

- I hope we can share information and cooperate with each other on this issue.
  希望今后我们能够继续相互交流与合作。

- Without your help, we wouldn't have solved the case so easily
  如果没有贵方的鼎力相助,我们不会这么容易破案的。

Part III   Situational Dialogues
情景对话

|情景 1| An Introduction to Anti-money Laundering in the U. S.
         美国反洗钱的经验介绍

Situation: Steven Hendershot is an officer from FBI of the United States. He

Unit 20

International Police Exchange and Cooperation
国际警务交流与合作

makes an introduction to anti-money laundering in the U. S. to a Chinese officer.

P: Mr. Hendershot, I'm so happy that you can give me an introduction to anti-money laundering in the U. S.. I really appreciate it.

F: My pleasure.

P: What is the main characteristic of money laundering in the U. S. ?

F: Its basic characteristic is transnational and flexible. The Money launderers often use the latest technical means. Besides, it has expanded into new areas.

P: How much money is laundered every year in the U. S. ?

F: Each year, between \$1.5 trillion and \$3 trillion is laundered in the world. It is estimated that half of this laundered money is conducted through banks in the USA. How about in China?

P: About 200 billion RMB is laundered each year in China. Criminals usually launder money through the purchase of stocks and gold by using online banks or phone banks. Money laundering has become a very serious problem.

F: It sure is. Money laundering will encourage the development of such criminal activities like drug trafficking and online gambling. What's worse is that terrorists can take advantage of it.

P: That is really terrible. Which agency is in charge of anti-money laundering in your country?

F: Many agencies are responsible for this, such as, Department of Treasury, Department of Justice, Federal Reserve and Internal Revenue Service, etc. They cooperate with one another.

P: Could you please introduce some measures taken to fight against money laundering in the U. S. ?

F: Sure. The U. S. government gives investigative agencies the authority to trace, seize and ultimately confiscate criminally derived assets, and builds the necessary framework for permitting the agencies involved to exchange information among themselves and also with counterparts in other countries.

P: I really like that part.

F: It is critically important for the government to include all relevant voices in developing a national anti-money laundering program.

P: Can you give me some details?

F: It should, for example, bring law enforcement and financial regulatory authorities together with the private sector to enable financial institutions to play a role in dealing with the problem. This means, among other things, involving the relevant authorities in establishing financial transaction reporting systems, customer identification, and record-keeping standards.

P: Money laundering has become a global crime, so it needs multinational cooperation to win the battle.

F: Yes, I totally agree with you. I hope we can share information and cooperate with each other on this issue.

P: Sure. I do hope we can have close cooperation. Thank you for so much useful information.

F: You are welcome.

警：亨德肖特先生，很高兴您能介绍美国打击洗钱犯罪行为的具体情况，我不胜感激。

外：深感荣幸。

警：请问美国的洗钱犯罪活动有哪些特点呢？

外：我国洗钱活动的基本特征是国际性和灵活性，犯罪分子运用最新的技术手段。此外，这一犯罪活动已经扩展到其他很多领域。

警：请问美国每年洗钱的数额是多少？

外：每年全球非法洗钱的数额在1.5万亿至3万亿美元之间。据估计，大约一半的钱是在美国银行完成的。中国的情况怎么样呢？

警：中国每年的洗钱数额大约是2000亿元人民币。犯罪分子运用网上银行、电话银行等，通过购买股票、黄金等手段进行洗钱。洗钱犯罪已经成为一个非常严重的问题。

Unit 20　International Police Exchange and Cooperation
国际警务交流与合作

外：的确如此。洗钱将会助长贩毒、网络赌博等一系列的犯罪行为。更为糟糕的是，它可能会被恐怖分子利用。

警：这样后果真的很严重。请问在美国哪些机构负责反洗钱呢？

外：我国反洗钱监管机构主要包括财政部、司法部、美联储、国家税务总局等，各机构之间密切合作。

警：亨德肖特先生，请您介绍一下美国在打击洗钱犯罪方面的具体措施好吗？

外：没问题。为了有效打击洗钱，美国政府赋权予相关机构调查、追踪、没收所有的犯罪所得。并且，建立了一套工作机制，负责打击洗钱犯罪的相关机构除了可以在国内相互交流信息外，还可以同其他国家的机构交流合作。

警：我特别赞同这一点。

外：特别重要的一点是，美国政府组织各相关负责机构，制订了一个全国反洗钱计划。

警：您能具体介绍一下吗？

外：该计划将执法部门、金融监管部门和私营金融机构有效联合在一起，共同制订货币交易报告制度、客户身份识别和交易记录保存标准等，保证金融机构在打击洗钱方面发挥应有的作用。

警：非法洗钱已经成为全球化犯罪，因此，世界各国必须密切合作，才能对这一犯罪行为进行有效打击。

外：是的，我完全赞同您的观点。希望今后我们能够继续相互交流与合作。

警：没问题，我也特别希望我们能够密切合作。谢谢您给我介绍了这么多有用信息。

外：不客气。

情景2　Show Thanks to INTERPOL National Central Bureau Canada
向国际刑警组织加拿大国家中心局表达感谢

Situation: Wangqiang, an officer from INTERPOL National Central Bureau, China met Mr. White from INTERPOL National Central Bureau, Canada on a forum. He showed thanks to Mr. White for the help that Canadian police *offered*.

P: Hello, Mr. White. I'm Wangqiang from INTERPOL National Central Bureau, China. Nice to meet you.

F: Hello, Mr. Wang. Nice to meet you too.

P: Mr. White, I would like to show thanks to you for helping us to investigate a transnational drug trafficking case at the beginning of this year.

F: Our pleasure. How is the case now?

P: The criminals involved have been arrested and sentenced. Those major drug dealers were sentenced to death or life imprisonment.

F: That's great.

P: Without your help, we wouldn't have solved the case so easily. Your cooperation in the investigation was really a great help to us.

F: I'm glad we can help. International police cooperation has become more and more important nowadays.

P: I can't agree with you more. There are so many transnational crimes and it's impossible for one country to win the battle against them.

F: It's true.

P: Hope we can cooperate more with each other in the future.

F: Sure.

警：您好，怀特先生。我是国际刑警组织中国国家中心局的王强，很高兴见到您。

外：您好，王先生。很高兴见到您。

警：怀特先生，今年年初，贵中心局协助我国警方调查一个跨国毒品大案，我们深表感谢。

外：很荣幸为贵国提供帮助。那个案子现在怎么样了？

警：所有涉案人员全部到案，并接受了审判。几名主犯被判死刑或无期徒刑。

外：太好了。

警：如果没有贵方的鼎力相助，我们不会这么容易破案的。贵国警方的协助调查确实帮了我们很大的忙。

Unit 20　　International Police Exchange and Cooperation
　　　　　　国际警务交流与合作

外：很高兴我们能帮上忙。如今，国际警务合作变得越来越重要了。
警：我完全赞同您的说法。现在跨国犯罪如此猖獗，单靠一个国家的努力，不可能成功赢得打击跨国犯罪这场战役的。
外：的确如此。
警：希望我们将来继续保持合作。
外：没问题。

Part IV　Creative Work
创造性练习

Situation：中国警察向美国警察威尔逊先生请教美国黑帮犯罪的预防和打击等问题。

听录音，请在听到提示音后开始口译。

警：威尔逊先生，您能介绍一下美国的黑帮犯罪问题吗?
外：好的。美国黑帮暴力犯罪发展迅速，到目前为止，已经蔓延到全国50个州和哥伦比亚特区。
警：这已经成为一个非常严重的社会问题了。
外：的确如此。更糟糕的是，很多青年人加入了黑帮。对11个城市中近6000名八年级学生所做的调查结果显示，17%的学生曾经加入过黑帮。
警：他们为什么喜欢加入黑帮呢?
外：年轻人加入黑帮的原因主要有以下几点：寻求黑帮保护、感觉好玩、赢得尊重和金钱。
警：如何解决青少年黑帮犯罪问题呢?
外：执法机构、社区、学校和家庭需要密切合作来预防和打击黑帮犯罪。而且，青少年司法和犯罪预防办公室提供了很多干预计划。
警：您能介绍一下这些计划吗?
外：没问题，我来重点介绍其中的一个项目——攻击行为替代训练。
警：谢谢。

外：那是一个专门为多次违法犯罪的暴力青年而设计的预防计划，分组为青少年提供为期10周、共30小时的认知行为训练，每组有8至12名青少年。在这10周中，每人每周参加3次1小时的课程，内容包括技能训练、愤怒情绪控制和道德理性训练。

警：这个计划一定很有效吧？

外：是的，该计划在纽约布鲁克林加入黑帮的青年人身上，表现出积极的效果。

警：在中国，黑帮犯罪也是一个非常严重的社会问题，希望今后我们能够继续就这个问题保持相互交流与合作。

外：没问题。

警：谢谢您给我介绍了这么多有用信息。

外：不客气。

创造性练习参考答案

Unit 1

Interpreter: Good afternoon, Mr. Satterfield and Mr. Muller. Let me introduce Mr. Sun, police chief of Beijing Public Security Bureau. (To Mr. Sun) Mr. Sun, this is Sgt. John Satterfield, and this is Sgt. Brian Muller. They are from Los Angeles Sheriff's Department, USA.

Sun: How do you do?

Foreigners: How do you do?

Sun: Welcome to Beijing. Your participation will add much to this forum.

F: Thank you. We're very glad to have this chance to come to visit your university.

Sun: And the forum provides an opportunity for us to share our experience.

F: It sure does.

Sun: I hope you'll have a pleasant stay here.

F: Thank you. I'm sure we will.

Sun: We'd like to invite you to dinner this evening.

F: Oh, that's very kind of you.

Sun: You must be tired after your long journey. Have a good rest. See you this evening.

F: See you.

Unit 2

F: Hello.

P: Hello. Is that Mr. Smith speaking?

F: Yes. Who is that calling?

P: Hi, Mr. Smith, this is officer Li Yang from Yuetan Police Station.

F: Hi, officer Li.

P: Mr. Smith, in order to provide better service, We'll call on foreign residents in our neighborhood to conduct a survey and gather some suggestions on our work. When will be convenient for you?

F: I've had an appointment today. How about two o'clock tomorrow afternoon?

P: OK. See you two tomorrow afternoon then.

F: See you.

Unit 3

1.

F: Excuse me, officer. Could you please tell me how to get to Quanjude Restaurant in Qianmen?

P: Sure. It's quite far from here. You'd better take a taxi or a bus.

F: How much will it take if I go there by taxi?

P: It's about 40 RMB.

F: I see, thank you. If I take a bus, Which bus should I take?

P: Bus Number 1.

F: Where can I take it?

P: There is a bus stop just across the street.

F: How long does it take to get there?

P: It's about a 30-minute ride.

F: Thank you.

P: Don't mention it.

2.

W: Excuse me. Could you please tell me how to get to the Blue Ash campus?

F: Sure. You can take the shuttle bus. It leaves for Blue Ash every 2 hours.

W: When will the next one leave?

F: In about ten minutes.

W: Where can I take the bus?

F: Just outside the gate.

W: How to get back?

F: Take the same shuttle bus. It returns from the same place as it arrives there. There is a return bus also every 2 hours.

W: Thank you very much.

F: You're welcome.

Unit 4

Mr. Harding: Help! Help!

Police: What's wrong?

Mr. Harding: I've injured my leg.

Police: Does this hurt?

Mr. Harding: Yes.

Police: Don't worry. We'll take you to the hospital.

Mr. Harding: I can't move.

Police: Let us help you.

(In the car)

Police: Your name and nationality, please?

Mr. Harding: Jack Harding from Singapore.

Police: The phone number of your family?

Mr. Harding: Call my wife. Her phone number is…

Police: (To his cell phone) Hello! Mrs. Harding?

Mrs. Harding: Yes. Who is it speaking?

Police: The police. Your husband has been injured. Come to… Hospital at once, please.

Mrs. Harding: OK. Is it serious?

Police: No.

(Mrs. Harding arrives)

Mrs. Harding: What did the doctor say?

Police: A fracture. (To Harding) Feeling better now?

Mr. Harding: Yes, much better.

Police: I must go now. Take care.

Mr. and Mrs. Harding: Thank you very much.

Police: My pleasure. Bye-bye.

Mr. and Mrs. Harding: Bye-bye.

Unit 5

P: Hello, this is Beijing 110. Can I help you?

F: Hello, I have been robbed just now.

P: Please stay calm and tell me what happened in detail.

F: I drew 10,000 RMB from bank at about 10:00 this morning. After I walked out of the gate and about 100 meters away from the bank, a man ran up to me, beat me, kicked me and grabbed the bag containing all the money drawn from the bank.

P: Which bank? What's the exact address?

F: At Baiyun Road Branch of Industrial and Commercial Bank of China. It's about 500 meters north of Baiyun Bridge.

P: Where did the man run after the robbery?

F: He ran to the north along Baiyun Road.

P: All right, sir, the police officer will arrive in five minutes. We will keep in contact with you, and please tell me your phone number.

F: 18810453878.

P: All right. Please stay where you are and wait for a moment.

F: OK, thank you very much.

P: You are welcome.

Unit 6

P: Hello, sir. Can I help you?

F: Hello, officer. I've lost my wallet.

P: Let me write down the detailed information.

F: OK.

P: Your name?

F: Robert Wade.

P: How do you spell that?

F: R – O – B – E – R – T, W – A – D – E.

P: Nationality?

F: America.

P: Where are you staying now?

F: Room 321, Friendship Hotel.

P: Phone number?

F: 13712374177.

P: When did you lose it?

F: Between 10 and 11 this morning.

P: Where?

F: Friendship Store.

P: What kind of wallet?

F: A leather one.

P: Color?

F: Black.

P: What's in it?

F: 120 dollars in cash, 2000 dollars in traveler's check.

P: Traveler's check? From which bank?

F: Yes, Bank of America.

P: Please report this to the bank.

F: Yes, I will.

P: Anything else?

F: A credit card.

P: Please report this to the credit card company.

F: Yes, I will.

P: Is that all?

F: That's all.

P: We'll contact you when we find it.

F: Thank you.

P: Not at all.

Unit 7

P: Good morning, sir. What's your name and nationality, please?

F: Good morning. My name is Chris Smith and I come from the U.S.

P: Mr. Smith, could you show me your passport, please?

F: Here it is.

P: OK, thank you. Is this gun yours?

F: Yes, it's a toy gun. I bought it as a gift for my son who is crazy about collecting all kinds of guns.

P: This gun is restricted in China and can't be carried along with you. It should be confiscated.

F: No, you can't do that. It's a gift for my son. Besides, it's legal to carry a gun in our country.

P: Sorry, our law is different from yours. According to Article 32 of Public Security Administration Punishments Law of the People's Republic of China, Anyone who illicitly carries any gun, ammunition, crossbow, dagger or any other tool controlled by the state shall be detained for not more than 5 days, and maybe concurrently fined 500 yuan. If the circumstances are lenient, he (she) shall be given a warning or be fined not more than 200 yuan. Anyone who illicitly carries any gun, ammunition, crossbow, dagger or any other tool controlled by the state into a public place or public transport tool shall be detained for not less than 5 days but not less than 10 days and maybe concurrently fined 500 yuan.

F: Sorry, officer. I don't mean to break the law, and I don't know the law before for this is my first time to China.

P: All right. But I have to confiscate the gun by law. What's more, please go to the police station with us for further investigation.

F: OK.

P: Thank you for your cooperation.

Unit 8

P: Hello, sir.

F: Hello, officer. What's up?

P: This is a routine check. Please show me your driver's license.

F: Here you are.

P: Your driver's license has expired.

F: Really?

P: Yes, it expired three months ago.

F: Oh, I'm really sorry but I haven't realized that.

P: Please show me the vehicle license of this car.

F: Here you are.

P: The plate number indicated in the license is different from that on the car. Why?

F: I don't know. I borrowed this car from one of my friends.

P: What's his name and how to contact him?

F: His name is Tony Flynn and his phone number is 13301344851.

P: OK. Please go with us to the traffic police station for further investigation.

F: I really have no idea and have nothing to do with it.

P: Turn off the engine and get out of the car.

F: OK.

Unit 9

F: Hello, officer. What's the matter?

P: Hello, sir. The road is temporarily closed to traffic.

F: Why?

P: A group of cars carrying members of a foreign delegation will go across this street.

F: How long will it be closed?

P: About half an hour.

F: Oh, no. I am hurrying to catch a movie in Xidan Joy City and it's about the time.

P: If you are in a hurry, you'd better make a detour and take another road.

F: How?

P: Turn right here. Go along this street and turn left at the first crossing. Walk straight ahead for about 500 meters and you will get there.

F: Thank you.

P: You're welcome.

2.

P: Hello, sir. Please don't park here.

F: Why? There isn't a "NO PARKING" sign here.

P: The traffic is too heavy here at this moment. Any parking or stopping would cause a traffic jam.

F: I will park here for just several minutes and then leave.

P: You can't do that even for one minute. If you illegally park here, your car will be towed away and you'll have to pay for the ticket.

F: OK. Is there any parking lot nearby?

P: Yes, there is one not far away from here.

F: How to get there?

P: Drive forward for about 500 meters and turn right. You'll see a sign for the parking lot. It's on your right side.

Unit 10

P: Hello, young man! Are you students of the International School of this community?

F: Yes, we are.

P: Which country are you from?

F: Canada.

P: I'm a guest counselor at your school. Your battery driven bicycles have been refitted, right?

F: Yes.

P: The speed limit for battery-driven bicycles is 20 kilometers per hour. You were racing against each other, and exceeded the speed limit. It's noisy and dangerous.

F: But it's OK in my country. It's a lot of fun.

P: It's not allowed in China, you know. It's against the law.

F: Oh, I didn't know that before. I will never do it again.

P: Good! Thank you for your cooperation, young man!

Unit 11

P: Hello! Sir. Can I help you?

F: Hello, officer. I came from San Francisco to visit my brother. I arrived yesterday and stayed in his house. I've heard that I'm supposed to report to the local police station for accommodation registration. Is that right?

P: Yes. According to the law, you have to do it within 24 hours of your arrival. What's your name, nationality and birth date?

F: I'm Jacob Brown from the U.S. I was born on September 5, 1990.

P: Please show me your passport.

F: Here you are.

P: What's your job and workplace?

F: I'm a teacher at Stanford University.

P: What's your purpose for coming to China?

F: On business.

P: Did you begin to stay in your brother's house yesterday? What's the specific address?

F: Yes. The address is Building 3 Room 1306 in Baiyun Road.

P: When will you leave?

F: In three days.

P: What is your phone number?

F: My phone number is... and his is...

P: All right, Mr. Brown. The registration is done.

F: Thank you. Good-bye.

P: You are welcome. Good-bye.

Unit 12

P: Hello, sir. We are police officers from Haidian branch of Beijing municipal public security bureau. Do you work here?

F: Yes, I teach English at this school.

P: How did you get the job?

F: A friend of mine helped me.

P: How long have you been working here?

F: Almost two months.

P: Have you signed a contract with the school?

F: No.

P: Show me your passport, please.

F: Here you are.

P: The type of your visa is X1. Are you an overseas student?

F: Yes.

P: Which university are you studying in?

F: Beijing Language and Culture University.

P: Show me your residence permit, please.

F: Wait a moment. Let me find it.

P: There is no indication of work-study or intern on your residence permit. Therefore, you are not allowed to work out of school.

F: I'm sorry. I didn't know this before.

P: According to Article 22 of Exit-Entry Administration Law of the People's

Republic of China, you are suspected of working illegally, so please come to the police station with us to be questioned.

F: OK.

Unit 13

P: We are police officers from Chaoyang branch of Beijing municipal public security bureau. We are going to ask you a few questions in accordance with the law. Please tell the truth and you have a legal responsibility for what you say.

F: I see.

P: What's your name and nationality?

F: I'm Edward Smith from Canada.

P: Show me your passport, please.

F: Here you are.

P: When did you come to China? What for?

F: I came here to work this August.

P: Where are you working now?

F: I teach English at University of Science and Technology of China.

P: Where are you staying?

F: Room 203 of the dormitory building for foreign teachers at that University.

P: Do you know why you have been brought here?

F: Yes. And I'm very sorry. I shouldn't have hit the cashier.

P: Tell us in detail what happened.

F: I just broke up with my girlfriend a few days ago and I was in a low mood. In order to cheer me up, I went to the bar to have some drinks this afternoon.

P: How much did you drink?

F: I drank 2 bottles of wine.

P: Were you drunk?

F: Yeah. I knocked a wine glass off the table and broke it into pieces. When I paid my bill, the cashier charged me an additional 50 yuan for the broken glass. I thought it was too much and refused. I wanted to leave but she dragged me. At that moment, I lost my temper and punched her.

P: How many times did you punch her?

F: One on the mouth and the other two on the face.

P: Did she fight back?

F: No.

P: After investigation, we learned that your punches bruised her face and dislodged one of her teeth.

F: I drank too much and couldn't control myself.

P: Is there anything else you want to say?

F: No.

P: This is the record of this interrogation. I will read it to you in English and please sign your name if there is nothing wrong.

F: OK.

Unit 14

P: We are police officers from Chaoyang division of Beijing traffic police bureau. Who called the police just now?

F: It was me, officer.

P: Who was injured? How was the injury?

F: The driver of the motor car was seriously injured on the head. He's been sent to hospital in an ambulance.

P: Show us your driver's license, motor vehicle driving permit, car insurance and passport, please.

F: OK.

P: What happened?

F: I was driving to the east. When I came to the middle of the intersection, the motor car crashed into my car from the right.

P: Did you brake?

F: Yes, I tried. But it's too late when I saw him.

P: Was the traffic light red or green before you entered the intersection?

F: It's green.

P: What was your speed in the intersection?

F: About 50 kilometers per hour.

P: We've photographed and recorded the damage to the cars. Now let's get them out of the way. Is your car movable?

F: I think so.

P: Move your car to the right side of the road.

F: OK.

P: Please come along with us to the traffic police station for further investigation.

F: OK.

Unit 15

P: Excuse me, sir. What are you doing here?

F: I'm chatting with them.

P: What's your name and nationality?

F: I'm Evan White from Canada.

P: What's your purpose for coming to China?

F: I'm a resident journalist.

P: Show me your passport, please.

F: Here it is.

P: You are gathering news here, aren't you?

F: Oh, yeah, you could say that.

P: Show me your press card, please.

F: Sorry, I've left it at home.

P: According to the Chinese law concerned, you've broken the law if you conduct interviews without a press card.

F: I'm terribly sorry about it. I was in such a hurry when I left home this morning.

P: Please delete all the photos and recordings you've got in this interview.

F: OK.

Unit 16

P: Can you understand my English?

F: Yes, I can.

P: This is Haidian branch of Beijing municipal public security bureau. First of all, we'd like to inform you of the fact that you've been summoned for questioning in accordance with law because you've been suspected of committing a crime.

F: I've got it.

P: I'll read the English translation of the following documents to you. Please listen carefully.

P: (After reading The Notification of Rights and Obligations of Criminal Suspects, Notification of Foreigners' Rights in Cases Involving Foreigners, Statement on Consular Notification, and Statement on Visit by Consular Officers.) Now, do you understand everything?

F: Yes, I do.

P: Then your signature, please. According to the Criminal Procedure Law of the People's Republic of China, you are expected to answer the questions honestly. You have the right not to answer questions irrelevant to the case. Are you clear?

F: Yes, I'm clear.

P: According to the relevant provisions of the law, criminal suspects can be treated with leniency by law if they voluntarily and truthfully confess their crimes, admit to the accused criminal facts, and are willing to be punished.

F: I see.

P: Please tell us your name, nationality and date of birth.

练习参考答案

F: My name is…. I'm a Pakistani, born on August 8, 1988.

P: What is your address in your home country?

F: Green Road, Islamabad.

P: What is your occupation?

F: I'm a worker in… Chemicals Company, Pakistan.

P: Do you have any previous convictions?

F: No, I haven't.

P: Have you ever been investigated by the police for any offense?

F: No. I've never been investigated either in Pakistan or China.

P: You excreted 50 heroin pills weighing 300 grams, and we found another 200 grams of heroin in your sandals. From whom did you get the drug?

F: From my boss.

P: What is his name?

F: His name is…

P: Did you buy the drug from him?

F: No. He asked me to bring the drug into China.

P: Did you get money from your boss for smuggling the drug?

F: Yes. He paid me 5000 dollars.

P: Drug smuggling is a serious crime in China. Do you know that?

F: I know. I feel very sorry for what I have done. I hope you will let me go with a lenient punishment.

P: We may be able to help you, but only if you cooperate with us, by confessing your crime and telling us everything you know about this case.

F: All right. As far as I know, my boss will send another one to bring in some more heroin.

P: Who?

F: My boss will send…

P: At what time?

F: He will take the same flight from Islamabad the day after tomorrow.

P: To whom are you supposed to deliver the drug after you come to China?

233

F: My boss asked me to deliver it to a Nigerian named…

P: Where will you deliver the drug to him?

F: In Guangzhou.

P: The exact time and place of the delivery?

F: …will tell me by phone.

P: Could you go with us to Guangzhou to track down Emeka?

F: Sure.

P: So much for today. Are you tortured in the process of interrogation?

F: No.

P: Are your thoughts clear when being interrogated?

F: Yes.

P: Do you have anything else to say?

F: No.

P: Is what you've said true?

F: Yes, all is true.

P: We've read the record of interrogation in English to you. Is it the same as what you've said?

F: Yes.

P: Please sign it.

F: OK.

Unit 17

P: Can you understand my English?

F: Yes, I can.

P: This is Xicheng branch of Beijing municipal public security bureau. First of all, we'd like to inform you of the fact that you've been summoned for questioning in accordance with law because you've been suspected of committing a crime.

F: I've got it.

P: I'll read the English translation of the following documents to you. Please listen carefully.

P: (After reading The Notification of Rights and Obligations of Criminal Suspects, Notification of Foreigners' Rights in Cases Involving Foreigners, Statement on Consular Notification, and Statement on Visit by Consular Officers.) Now, do you understand everything?

F: Yes, I do.

P: Then your signature, please. According to the Criminal Procedure Law of the People's Republic of China, you are expected to answer the questions honestly. You have the right not to answer questions irrelevant to the case. Are you clear?

F: Yes, I'm clear.

P: According to the relevant provisions of the law, criminal suspects can be treated with leniency by law if they voluntarily and truthfully confess their crimes, admit to the accused criminal facts, and are willing to be punished.

F: I see.

P: What's your name, nationality?

F: I am Harold White from the Philippines.

P: What did you do in China?

F: I'm on a vacation trip.

P: Do you know the lady in the picture? (show him the picture of the victim)

F: No, I have never seen her.

P: The young lady is Liumei. She has told us things happened between you and her. We hope you can tell us the truth.

F: Well, it's true that we've never met each other in real life. We got to know each other on a match-maker website. With time passing by, we fell in love with each other.

P: Do you really love her? Do you really want to marry her?

F: Sure.

P: As far as we know, you are married. How can you marry her? According to

Liumei, you told her that you were a marketing manager with a yearly payment of $100,000 at a famous company in Silicon Valley, but you've asked her to give you $50,000. We do hope you can stop telling lies.

F: OK, I admit I've cheated her. I heard that many Chinese women like to marry foreigners, so I decided to take advantage of this to make some money. I began to hunt for a suitable woman online and I chatted with Liumei one day. She told me that she was working in a foreign enterprise with a high salary. She said she was interested in foreign cultures and hope to marry a foreigner. I told her I liked Chinese woman and pretended to be a man with a high salary. I managed to make her fall in love with me and promised to marry her this year.

P: Why did she give you so much money?

F: I found she had a crush on me and thought it's time to ask money from her. At first, I told her I was going to buy some stocks from my company and asked her to buy some too in order to make more money for us. She gave me $10,000. Several months later, I told her I wanted to buy an apartment for our marriage in San Francisco California but I was $40,000 short. Then she gave me the money to buy the apartment.

P: Another lady named Chenhua reported a similar case in which you got involved. We are pretty sure that you know her.

F: Yes, she is the second lady I cheated in a similar way. I really regret what I've done.

P: Do you want to employ a lawyer?

F: Yes.

P: Who will take charge of this for you?

F: John. His phone number is…

P: Do you have anything else to say?

F: No.

P: Is what you've said true?

F: Yes, all is true.

P: We've read the record of interrogation in English to you. Is it the same as what you've said?

F: Yes.

P: Please sign it.

F: OK.

Unit 18

P: Can you understand my English?

F: Yes, I can.

P: This is Haidian branch of Beijing municipal public security bureau. First of all, we'd like to inform you of the fact that you've been summoned for questioning in accordance with law because you've been suspected of committing a crime.

F: I've got it.

P: I'll read the English translation of the following documents to you. Please listen carefully.

P: (After reading The Notification of Rights and Obligations of Criminal Suspects, Notification of Foreigners' Rights in Cases Involving Foreigners, Statement on Consular Notification, and Statement on Visit by Consular Officers.) Now, do you understand everything?

F: Yes, I do.

P: Then your signature, please. According to the Criminal Procedure Law of the People's Republic of China, you are expected to answer the questions honestly. You have the right not to answer questions irrelevant to the case. Are you clear?

F: Yes, I'm clear.

P: According to the relevant provisions of the law, criminal suspects can be treated with leniency by law if they voluntarily and truthfully confess their crimes, admit to the accused criminal facts, and are willing to be punished.

F: I see.

P: Tell us your name, date of birth and nationality, please.

F: I'm David Smith, born on June 5th, 1993. I'm from the Philippines.

P: According to the surveillance video of Minzu hotel, you and a lady went into room 206 last night. Who was she?

F: She was Anna, my ex-girlfriend.

P: What happened that night? Tell us the details.

F: We broke up last month. She invited me to the hotel last night telling me she was pregnant and urged me to marry her. She was so bad-tempered and selfish that I didn't want to be together with her any longer, so I refused her. She asked for 100,000 dollars as compensation.

P: Did you agree to give her the money?

F: It was too much. So I said no to her. She threatened to tell my boss and I begged her not to do that. However, she picked up the phone going to dial the number but I grabbed her phone.

P: What happened next?

F: She began to swear at me and scratch me. I lost control and grabbed her neck. After about three or four minutes, she passed out.

P: Why didn't you send her to the hospital?

F: I had thought she just pretended, so I left.

P: Do you want to hire a lawyer?

F: Yes.

P: Who will take charge of this for you?

F: Edward. His phone number is…

P: Do you have anything else to say?

F: No.

P: Did you tell the truth?

F: Yes, all is true.

P: We've read the record of interrogation in English to you. Is it the same as what you've said?

F: Yes.

P: Please sign it.

F: OK.

Unit 19

P: Mr. Johnson, I've heard that you're an expert in counter-terrorism and especially good at hostage rescue.

F: Thank you.

P: Could you please tell me some experience in hostage rescue?

F: Sure. The purpose of a hostage rescue operation is the safe rescue of all hostages alive with minimal damage to the rescue force's personnel or equipment.

P: Yes, but it's really difficult to do so.

F: You are right. Hostage rescue operations are the most difficult type of special operation missions. It can be broken down into three major phases.

P: What are they?

F: The first phase is planning and rehearsals. At the onset of the hostage-taking, the rescue force must develop an emergency plan. This plan is utilized if the hostage-takers decide to start killing and moving the hostages.

P: Is there any other plan?

F: Yes. From the initial plan, a furthermore refined deliberate plan is developed and conducted if the negotiations fail. Besides, there should be an emergency-deliberate plan. It is a contingency plan when the rescue force is detected by the terrorist while conducting the deliberate plan.

P: How to conduct the three plans successfully?

F: It's important for all the participants of the rescue team to get involved in the planning and rehearsal process.

P: What's the second phase?

F: It is approach and assault. During the approach, the rescue force must be ready to execute all contingency plans rehearsed as part of their emergency-deliberate plan in case they become compromised. Once the assault begins, they must immediately neutralize the threat and control the hostage.

P: This phase is the most important, I think.

F: Yes, it sure is. The third phase is post-assault.

P: Is there something important in this phase?

F: The rescue force must pay particular attention not to leave any of the hostages behind during the exfiltration, or take a terrorist with them instead.

P: I've learned a lot today. Thank you, Mr. Johnson.

F: My pleasure.

P: I hope we can have more chances to communicate and cooperate in the future.

F: I also hope so.

Unit 20

P: Mr. Wilson, would you please talk about gang crime in the U. S. ?

F: OK. Gang violence in the U. S. has become widespread—all 50 states and the District of Columbia report gang crimes.

P: It's been a very serious social problem.

F: Yes. What's worse, so many youths join gangs. A survey of nearly 6,000 eighth-graders conducted in 11 cities with known gang problems found that 17 percent had belonged to a gang at some point in their lives.

P: Why do they like to be a gang member?

F: Youth reported the following reasons for joining a gang, that is, for protection, for fun, for respect, and for money.

P: How to deal with this problem?

F: Law enforcement agencies, communities, schools and families have to work together for gang prevention, intervention and suppression. Office of Juvenile Justice and Delinquency Prevention has offered some good programs.

P: Could you please introduce some of them?

F: Sure. I would like to introduce one of the programs—Aggression Replacement Training.

P: Thank you.

F: It's a prevention program for highly aggressive and delinquent youth. It consists of a 10-week, 30-hour cognitive-behavioral program administered to groups of 8 to 12 adolescents. During these 10 weeks, youth typically attend three 1-hour sessions per week on skill streaming, anger control, and moral reasoning training.

P: I'm sure it must be very effective.

F: Yes. It showed positive results when tested with gang-involved youth in Brooklyn, NY.

P: Gang crime is also a very serious problem in China, so I hope we can share more information and cooperate with each other on this issue in the future.

F: Sure.

P: Thank you for so much useful information.

F: You are welcome.

附录 I 常用警务英语词汇

1. 常用缉毒英语词汇

A. 可用作毒品或可用来加工毒品的化学品

depressant 镇抑（郁）剂

sedative/ tranquilizer 镇静剂

excitant /stimulant/dope 兴奋剂

narcotics 麻醉剂

hallucinogens 迷幻剂

cough medicine 咳药

organic solvents 有机溶剂

precursors/precursor chemicals 易制毒化学品

B. 常见毒品名称

amphetamine 安非他明

methamphetamine/meth/crank/crystal/crystal meth/chrome/ice 脱氧麻黄碱；冰毒

methylephedrine 甲基麻黄碱

opium 鸦片

opioid 类鸦片

morphine 吗啡

heroin/China white/ brown/ smack/ hammer/ skag/ junk 海洛因

cocaine/coke/powder/nose candy/Charlie/marching powder/snort

white dragon 可卡因

caffeine 咖啡因

cannabis/marijuana/pot/dope/joint/sativa/hash/gania Mary Jane/reefer/skunk/spliff/smoko/weed 大麻

Ketamine/ khat 氯胺酮/K 粉

triazolam/midazolam/zopiclone 三唑仑/咪达唑仑/佐匹克隆

nimetazepam 硝甲西泮

diazepam/valium 安定

physeptone/methadone 菲仕通/美沙酮

buprenorphine 盐酸叔丁啡

naltrexone 环丙甲羟二羟吗啡酮

ecstasy/E/MDMA/disco biscuits/mitsubishi 快乐丸/摇头丸

PCP/angel dust 盐酸苯环已哌啶/兴奋剂

glue 强力胶

LSD 迷幻药

dolantin 杜冷丁

methaqualone 甲喹酮/甲苯喹唑酮/安眠酮/（俗称佛得）

magu (a Thai word for a stimulant drug that is a combination of methamphetamine and caffeine) 麻古

C. 毒品犯罪行为、地点及手段

producing drugs 生产毒品

processing drugs 加工毒品

an illegal drug processing plant 毒品加工厂

small-scale meth labs 小型冰毒加工点

a meth kitchen/ a crystal meth laboratory 冰毒加工点

possessing drugs 持有毒品

carrying drugs 携带毒品

to smuggle drug hidden in the courier's body 人体藏毒

to smuggle drug with the courier and the drug separated 人毒分离

using an unwitting passenger to carry hidden drug into another country unknowingly 利用不知情游客秘密携带毒品入境

drug trafficking 毒品买卖

to form a production, sale, transport and smuggling chain 形成生产、销售、运输和走私一条龙

cross-border drug crime 跨境毒品犯罪

covert means/ secretive means 隐蔽手段

dividing the contraband into smaller parts and exploiting the security loopholes to traffic them through road and water transport or even postal services 将违禁毒品化整为零，利用安全漏洞，通过陆路、水路交通甚至邮递手段进行贩运

hiding drugs deep inside or underneath legal carg 将毒品深藏于合法货物之下

wrapping drugs in aluminium foil to hinder detection by X-ray machines 将毒品包裹于铝箔内以妨碍 X 光机检查

hiding drugs in false bottoms and other hidden compartments in baggage, cargo containers, trains, boats, and motor vehicles 将毒品藏于包裹、货物箱、火车、船只和机动车的伪造的底部或隐蔽的夹层

to swallow heroin and other drugs in condoms or small plastic bags to smuggle 体内藏毒——将装有毒品的安全套或小塑料袋吞入体内偷运

to insert drug into the rectum or vagina to smuggle 将毒品塞入直肠或阴道偷运

using pregnant women to carry drugs 利用怀孕妇女运送毒品

drug abuse/abusing drugs/ taking drugs 滥用毒品/吸毒

to take drugs orally 口服毒品

to inject drugs 注射毒品

to abuse drug by intravenous injection 静脉注射毒品

to share needles/syringes 共用针头/注射器

to smoke drugs 以香烟或烟管吸入毒品

to inhale or breathe in drugs 烟雾吸入毒品

to sniff drugs 鼻孔吸入毒品

to put heroin on tinfoil, burn it, and breathe in the smoke 将海洛因放在锡纸上，用火烧，将烟吸入

DUI (driving under the influence) 吸毒后驾车

D. 毒品罪犯名称

drug processor 制毒者
meth cook 冰毒制造加工者
drug kingpin / major drug lord 毒枭
drug dealer / drug trafficker 毒贩子
drug mule 人体贩毒者
human mule 体内携毒者
trafficking gang 贩毒团伙
drug abuser 滥用毒品者
drug addict 吸毒成瘾者
intravenous drug user/IDU 静脉使用毒品者

E. 毒品源头

the Golden Crescent (the mountainous regions of Afghanistan, Pakistan and Iran) 金新月（阿富汗、巴基斯坦、伊朗交界处的山区）
the Golden Triangle (the area where Laos, Myanmar and Thailand meet) 金三角（老挝、缅甸、泰国接壤地区）

F. 毒品危害

dependence 依赖性
drug addiction 赌瘾
to get addicted to heroin 海洛因成瘾
bloodborne viruses 由血液传播的病毒
hepatitis B/C 乙/丙型肝炎
HIV (human immunodeficiency virus) 人体免疫缺损病毒/艾滋病病毒
Aids (acquired immunodeficiency syndrome) 艾滋病

G. 禁毒缉毒戒毒

drug law enforcement/drug control 禁毒

to obstruct the sources and intercept on the route 堵源截流

interception 截获

to crack down on... 打击……

detoxification 戒毒；脱毒瘾

Methadone is used to help addicts detoxify 美沙酮被用来帮助瘾君子戒毒

withdrawal 戒毒或脱瘾

to withdraw from heroin 戒绝海洛因

to wean sb.（away）from drugs/drinking/gambling）使某人渐渐戒毒/戒酒/戒赌

a detox ward 戒毒病房

detox 戒毒诊所/戒毒病房

rehabilitation clinic/center 康复诊所/中心

compulsory drug rehabilitation center 强制戒毒中心

voluntary drug rehabilitation center 自愿戒毒中心

the International Day against Drug Abuse and Illicit Trafficking（June 26）国际禁毒日

2. 违法犯罪行为英文名称

A. 常见违反出入境管理法律法规行为

illegal entry 非法入境

illegal residency 非法居留

illegal employment 非法就业

illegal overstay 非法滞留

violating residence administration 违反居留管理

violating accommodation administration 违反住宿管理

illegal traveling 非法旅行

B. 常见违反治安管理法律法规行为

disturbing public order 扰乱公共秩序

impairing the administration of social order 妨害社会秩序管理

carrying weapons or forbidden cutting tools and explosives 携带武器、管制刀具、炸药

gang-fighting 结伙斗殴

infringement upon citizen's rights 侵犯他人人身权利

encroaching upon public or private property 侵犯公私财物

prostitution 卖淫

whoring 嫖娼

gambling 赌博

coercing, including or using any person to go begging 胁迫、诱骗或利用他人乞讨

forcing any other person to work by violence, menace or by any other means 以暴力、威胁或者其他手段强迫他人劳动

illegally restricting the personal freedom of any other person, intruding the house of any other person or searching the body of any other person 非法限制他人人身自由,非法侵入他人住宅或者非法搜查他人身体

insulting any other person openly or making up stories to defame any other person 公然侮辱他人或者捏造事实诽谤他人

attempting to make any other person subject to criminal punishment or public security administration punishment by making up stories and bringing a false charge against any other person 捏造事实诬告陷害他人,企图使他人受到刑事追究或者受到治安管理处罚

peeping into, sneaking photos, wiretapping or spreading the privacy of any other person 偷窥、偷拍、窃听、散布他人隐私

threatening the personal safety of any other person by writing threat letters or by any other means 写恐吓信或者以其他方法威胁他人人身安全

interfering with the normal life of any other person by sending any obscene, insulting, threatening or other information time after time 多次发送淫秽、侮辱、恐吓或者其他信息,干扰他人

threatening, insulting, beating or revenging upon the witness and his (her) close relatives 对证人及其近亲属进行威胁、侮辱、殴打或者打击报复

blowing any person or intentionally injuring the body of any person 殴打他人或者故意伤害他人身体

acting indecently towards any person or deliberately exposing his body at a public place 猥亵他人或者在公共场所故意裸露身体

abandoning any person who hasn't the abilities to live by himself 遗弃没有独立生活能力的被抚养人

forcibly buying and selling any goods or forcing any person to provide services or accept services 强买强卖商品，强迫他人提供服务或者强迫他人接受服务

stealing, swindling, plundering, pillaging, extorting or intentionally damaging or destroying any public or private property 盗窃、诈骗、哄抢、抢夺、敲诈勒索或者故意损毁公私财务

refusing to execute the decision or order lawfully issued by the people's government in an emergent situation 拒不执行人民政府在紧急状态情况下依法发布的决定、命令

hindering any fire engine, ambulance, engineering emergency-relief vehicle or police car from passing 阻碍执行紧急任务的消防车、救护车、工程抢险车、警车等车辆通行

forcibly rushing into the warning area or warning zone delimited by the public organ 强行冲闯公安机关设置的警戒带、警戒区

obstructing and functionaries of the state organ from performing their duties 阻碍国家机关工作人员依法执行职务

instigating, inducing or cheating any other person to take or inject any drug 教唆、引诱、欺骗他人吸食、注射毒品

coercing or cheating any medical worker to prescribe any narcotic or psychotropic drug 胁迫、欺骗医务人员开具麻醉药品、精神药品

taking or injecting any drug 吸食、注射毒品

illegally holding less than 200 grams of opium, heroin or methyl amphetamine, or a small quantity of other drugs 非法持有鸦片不满二百克、海洛因或者甲基苯丙胺不满十克或者其他少量毒品

organizing or making any obscene performance 组织或者进行淫秽表演

joining people in licentious activities 参与聚众淫乱活动

C. 常见违反交通法规行为

driving without a license 无证驾车
drunk driving 酒后/醉酒开车
speeding/exceeding the speed limit 超速
failure to obey a traffic signal 违反信号灯
running a red light 闯红灯
illegal parking 违章泊车
illegal turn 违章转弯
illegal passing 违章超车
illegal lane changing 违章变线
going a wrong way on a one-way street 单线逆行
overload/having too many people in one's car 超载
driving where prohibited 禁区行使
hit and run 肇事逃逸
not having one's seat belt fastened 没系安全带
not wearing a helmet 没戴安全头盔
jaywalking 擅自穿越马路

D. 其他常见违法犯罪名称

predicate offence 上游犯罪
crime/offence/perpetration 犯罪
minor crimes/misdemeanor 轻罪
delinquency 违法行为；过失
juvenile delinquency 青少年犯罪
major crimes/felony 重罪
recidivism 重新犯罪；累犯
a calculated crime 预谋犯罪
arson 纵火

organized crime 有组织犯罪

transnational crime 跨国犯罪

transborder crime 跨境犯罪

white-collar crime 白领犯罪

computer crime 计算机犯罪

cybercrime 网络犯罪

economic crime 经济犯罪

crimes against property 侵犯财产罪

dereliction of duty/negligence of duty 玩忽职守；职务犯罪

environmental crime 破坏环境罪

treason 叛国罪

crimes against persons 侵犯他人人身权利

homicide 杀人

murder 谋杀

serial murder 系列谋杀

manslaughter 过失杀人

vehicular manslaughter 车辆过失杀人

poisoning 投毒

assault 伤害

physical assault 人身伤害

serious assault 严重伤害

bigamy 重婚罪

hooliganism 流氓行为

sexual assault 性伤害

to solicit a prostitute 召妓

rape 强奸

gang-rape/to gang rape 轮奸

traffic in children and women 贩卖妇女儿童

offenses against children 伤害儿童罪

lewdness with a minor/molestation/to molest a child 猥亵儿童罪

to visit a pornographic website (a porn website) 访问淫秽网站
to distribute pornographic materials 传播淫秽内容
to organize a cyber strip show 组织网上脱衣（裸体）表演
kidnapping 绑架
abduction 诱拐
hostage-taking 劫持人质
hijacking 劫持
aircraft hijacking 劫持飞机
people smuggling /to smuggle oneself abroad 偷渡
theft/larceny 盗窃
burglary 入室盗窃
snatch 抢夺
robbery 抢劫
armed robbery 武装抢劫
smuggling 走私
fraud 诈骗
extortion/blackmail 敲诈
piracy 盗版
identity theft 盗窃个人身份信息
libel 诽谤（文字）
embezzlement /corruption 盗用公款；侵吞财物；贪污
tax evasion 逃税
money laundering 洗钱
bribery/graft 贿赂
ask for bribery 索贿
to bribe；to pay/offer/give bribes 行贿
to accept or take a bribe from... 受……贿赂
forgery 冒他人签名
insider trading 内幕交易
vandalism 蓄意破坏

sedition/running riot 煽动闹事

graffiti 涂鸦

security vehicle (banknote vehicle) hold-ups/robbery of cash vans 抢劫运钞车

traffic in stolen motor vehicles 贩卖被盗机动车辆

theft of vehicles carrying freight 盗窃货运车辆

traffic in drugs, weapons and explosives 贩卖毒品、武器、爆炸物

traffic in precious substance (gold, diamonds or currency) 贵重物非法交易（黄金、钻石、货币等）

possession and sale of firearms 非法拥有或贩卖武器

transnational or trans-border drug trafficking 跨国或跨境贩卖毒品

sabotage of production and construction facilities 破坏生产建设设施

the production or peddling of pornography 制黄贩黄

pornography, gambling and drug abuse 黄赌毒

pornographic publications and illegal publishing practices 黄色出版物和非法出版活动

E. 常见案件类型名称

executive cases 行政案件

public order cases 治安案件

civil cases 民事案件

criminal cases 刑事案件

serious cases 大案要案

drug-related cases 涉毒案

gun-related cases 涉枪案

bombing case 爆炸案

a case of armed kidnapping 武力绑架案

robbery and rape cases 抢劫强奸案

a series of coordinated bombings 连环爆炸案

3. 常用罪犯英文名称

offender/criminal/culprit/perpetrator 罪犯

a first offender 初犯

juvenile delinquent 青少年犯

an old or a hardened criminal 惯犯

felon 重犯

principals of a crime 主犯，首犯

the main culprit 主要案犯

accomplice/accessory 共犯/同谋犯

accomplice/accessory under duress 胁从犯

convict 已决犯

prisoner 囚犯

detainee 被拘留者

wanted criminal 通缉犯

a terrorist 恐怖主义分子

absconder 潜逃者

fugitive/escaped convict 逃犯

escaped prisoner 越狱犯

a convict on the run/at large 在逃犯

recidivist 重犯；累犯

remandee 还押犯；还押候审者；保释候审者

arsonist 纵火犯

bomber 爆炸案犯

serial bomber 系列爆炸案犯

human trafficker 人贩子

murderer 谋杀犯

serial killer 系列杀人犯

sex offender 性罪犯

bigamist 重婚罪犯

rapist 强奸犯

robber 抢劫犯

burglar 入室抢劫者

mugger 行凶抢劫者

fraud/fraudster 诈骗犯

road bandit 车匪路霸

mafia-style gang 黑社会性质的团伙

triadic elements and local despots 黑恶势力

local kingpin 恶霸

triadic groups 黑社会性质组织

gang/ring/mafia/criminal group/criminal syndicate/criminal enterprise 犯罪团伙

gang leader/ringleader/mafia boss 团伙头目

cult 邪教组织

4. 常见物证英文名称

physical evidence 实物证据；物证

material evidence 对定案有决定影响的证据

evidentiary items 证据物

direct or prima facie evidence 初步证据（指如对方反证驳不倒即证明事实为真实的证据）

circumstantial evidence 情况证据；间接证据；旁证

corpus delicti 构成犯罪的主要证据或主要事实

associative evidence 关联证据（证明嫌疑人与犯罪有联系的证据）

voiceprint 声纹；声印

fingerprint 指纹

lip print 唇纹

auricle mark 耳廓痕迹

skin ridge characteristics 肤纹特征

impression by tooth 牙齿痕迹

footprint 足迹

bare-footprint 赤足迹

shoe impression 鞋印

wearing shoe footprint 穿鞋足迹

three-dimensional footprint 立体足迹

foot type characteristics 足型特征

walking characteristics 步伐特征

falling step mark 踏痕

raising foot tread mark 蹬痕

trace evidence 微量物证

trace scent 微量气味

biological traces 生物痕迹

DNA profile DNA 分型

the visual indication of a body fluid 可见体液痕迹

bloodstain 血迹

saliva 唾液

dried saliva 干唾液

semen 精液

sperm 精子

fluid of the eye 眼液

urine 尿液

bile 胆汁

gastric juice 胃液

hairs 毛发

pulled head hair 揪下的头发

pubic hair 阴毛

tissue embolism 组织栓塞

fingernail cutting or scraping 剪/刮下的指甲碎屑

explosive trace 爆炸痕迹

point of burst 炸点

crater 弹坑

debris 废墟

fragmentation 爆炸碎片

residues of explosive 炸药残留物

cap/detonator 火帽；雷管

fuse 导火索

shrapnel（填充在爆炸装置里的铁钉、金属碎片等）杀伤物

timer 定时装置

wrapping 爆炸装置外包装

battery 电池

glass crack mark 玻璃破碎痕

radiation-shaped crackle 放射裂纹

dent 凹痕

indent mark 凹陷痕迹

lined mark 线条痕迹

scratch 划痕

skid mark 刹车痕迹

tire impression 轮胎压痕

pry-marks 撬压痕迹

fabric print 纺织物痕迹

laundry and dry-cleaning marks 水洗和干洗痕迹

objects unrelated or foreign to the scene 不属于现场的或外来的物品

objects unusual in location or number 位置或数量反常的物品

objects damaged or broken 被损毁或打破的物品

cord 绳子

ligature 带子

sharp instrument 锐器

blunt instrument 钝器

weapons 武器

ammunition 弹药

bullet 子弹；弹头；弹丸

shell castings 弹壳

empty cartridge case 空子弹壳

stolen property 赃物

mud/soil 泥/土

cigarette butts 烟蒂

licked envelope 舔过的信封

used stamp 使用过的邮票

drug paraphernalia 吸毒用具

smear 油污；污点

paint evidence 油漆证据

gun grips 枪柄

light switches 电灯开关

doorknobs 门扭

handheld electronic devices 带手柄的电器

cell phone 手机

telephone receiver 电话听筒

automobile steering wheels 汽车方向盘

firearm mark 枪弹痕迹

tool marks 工具痕迹

impress 压印

imprint 痕迹

cutting mark 割削痕迹

separation mark from combination body 整体分离痕迹

throwing action mark 抛掷作用痕迹

mark by breaking lock 开锁痕迹配钥匙痕迹

mark of pliers and scissors 钳剪痕迹

wear 磨损

throttling mark 扼痕

bite mark 咬痕

grazes /brush trace 擦痕
stabbing and cutting mark 刺切痕迹
striated mark 擦划痕迹
striking mark 打击痕迹
abrasion 表皮脱落
contused wound/bruise 挫伤
broken skin 皮肤破裂
destroyed tissue 软组织破坏
lacerated wound 裂伤
fracture 骨折
wound 伤口
stab wound 刺伤
incised wound 割伤
cut wound 砍伤
wound by blunt weapon 钝器致伤
wound by sharp weapon 锐器致伤
bullet wound 枪伤
suggillation 瘀斑
hemorrhage 大出血
death spots 死斑
impact wave acting mark 冲击波作用痕迹
electric mark 电流斑
scar 伤疤
tattoo 纹身
document evidence 书证
documentary evidence 证明文件
written evidence 字据；书面证据
testimony 口供；证言
handwriting 笔迹
inked prints 油墨或墨水痕迹

digital (electronic) evidence 数字/电子物证

telephone intercept evidence 电话截获证据

video camera footage 监控录像

5. 法庭常用语

A. 庭审涉及的人员称谓

procurator 检察官

prosecutor 公诉人；原告；起诉人

judge 法官

the presiding judge 主审法官；审判长

complainant/ plaintiff 原告

defendant/the accused 被告

respondent 离婚案被告

jury 陪审团

jurors 陪审员

witness 证人

eye-witness 目击证人

material eye-witnesses 对定案有决定影响的目击证人

prosecution ［美］公诉人/起诉人及其律师（总称）

lawyer counsel /attorney ［美］律师

the counsel for one's defense 某人的辩护律师

defense attorney 辩护律师

the counsel for the prosecution 控方律师

leading counsel for the prosecution 主控律师

criminal lawyer 刑事律师

prosecuting lawyer 代表原告的律师

barrister ［英］出庭律师

solicitor ［英］诉状律师

B. 指控、起诉、作证与申辩

to open a court session 开庭

to hold a hearing 开庭审理

to adjourn（法庭）暂时休庭

to indict...for/on... 指控某人犯某罪

He was indicted for murder/on three counts of murder. 他被控杀人/三项谋杀罪。

to accuse...of... 指控/指责某人犯某罪

He was falsely accused of stealing. 他被诬告犯有偷窃罪。

They indignantly accused the police of brutality. 他们愤慨地指责警察行为野蛮。

to charge...with... 指控某人犯某罪

The driver was charged with speeding. 司机被控超速驾车。

He was charged with negligence of duty. 他被指控失职。

to sue...for.../to sue sb. for damages 控告某人要求赔偿损失

to sue a newspaper for libel 控告某家报纸登诽谤性文章

to sue for a divorce 诉请离婚

to start proceedings (against sb.) for divorce 提出与某人离婚

to bring... to court 对……提出起诉；将……送上法庭

She decided to take him to court. 她决定对他起诉。

The suspect was brought to court for trial. 嫌疑人被送上法庭受审。

to bring... to justice 依法惩处

The burglar was brought to justice. 那个入室盗窃案犯被送交法庭审判。

to prosecute...for.../to prosecute sb. for fraud 告发某人犯欺诈罪

He was prosecuted for bigamy. 他因犯重婚罪而受到起诉。

to bring an action against 起诉

He brought an action against her. 他起诉了她。

to allege（often used in passive voice or the form of past participle）无充分根据地指控

They were alleged to have brought goods into the country illegally. 他们被指控非法携带货物入境。

to litigate 诉讼

litigation/action 诉讼

proceedings 诉讼程序

to try 审理；审判

to be tried for arson 以纵火罪受审

trial 审判；审理

to be on trial for... 因……而受审

to be on trial for murder 因谋杀罪而受审

to stand trial for... 因……而受审

to be a witness at the trial 在审判时出庭作证

to testify to/against/on behind of...作不利于/有利于……的证词

to testify falsely against/on behalf of... 作不利于/有利于……的伪证

to testify to one's innocence 证明某人无罪

Witnesses testified to his attempts at rape. 证人就他的强奸企图作证。

to testified that... 作证说……

perjured evidence 伪证

to perjure/to commite perjury 作伪证

to perjure oneself to pin an offence on... 作伪证栽赃于……

to enter a plea of guilty 表示认罪

to plead guilty 认罪；（对控告）表示服罪

to plead not guilty （对控告）表示不服罪

to plead innocent 申辩自己是清白的

C. 判决与量刑

verdict （陪审团的）裁决

judgment （法庭的）判决

to pass judgment on a prisoner （法庭）对犯人作出宣判

to give a verdict of guilty/not guilty （培审团）作出有罪/无罪的裁定

a verdict for/against the plaintiff （陪审团作出的）原告胜诉/败诉的裁定

to acquit 宣告无罪；无罪释放

acquittal 宣告无罪；无罪释放

to be found guilty 被证明有罪

to be found not guilty 被证明无罪

to be found innocent 被证明是清白的

to plea-bargain 达成认罪辩诉协议；通过达成认罪辩诉协议谋求较轻处罚等

The jury acquitted him of (the charge of) murder. 陪审团宣告他谋杀罪（的罪名）不成立。

to convict 定罪

He has twice been convicted of fraud. 他已有两次被判诈骗罪。

He was a convicted murder. 他是已定罪的谋杀犯。

to sentence… to… years of imprisonment/life imprisonment/death penalty (capital punishment) 判处某人……年监禁/终身监禁/死刑

to be jailed for… 被判处监禁……年

The gang boss/mafia boss was jailed for 20 years. 团伙头目被判20年徒刑。

to receive a jail term of 20 years 被判监禁20年

to hand down sentences ranging from…to…to… 判处某人……年到……年徒刑

Beijing municipal higher people's court handed down sentences ranging from 3 and a half years to 20 years to the gangsters. 北京市高级人民法院判处这些团伙成员3年半到20年有期徒刑。

probation（监禁）缓刑

to be sentenced to three years' probation under suspended sentence of one year's imprisonment 被判一年徒刑缓刑3年

reprieve/ stay of execution 死刑缓期执行

to be sentenced to death with a two-year reprieve 被判死刑，缓期两年执行

to receive a two-year stay of execution 获得死刑缓期两年执行

6. 常见爆炸物、易燃品、自制炸弹主要零部件名称

A. 常见爆炸物、易燃品

explosives 炸药（统称）

TNT 梯恩梯

dynamite 达纳炸药

C-4 塑四炸药

RDX 黑索金；旋风炸药

HMX 奥克托金；奥克多

PETN 季戊炸药

ANFO 铵油炸药

AN-TNT 铵梯炸药

emulsion 乳胶炸药

slurry 浆状炸药

water gels 水胶状炸药

PLX 液体炸药

contact explosive 触摸炸药

black powder 黑色火药

bomb 炸弹

plastic bomb 可塑炸弹

mail bomb 邮件炸弹

grenade 手榴弹

fire-bomb/incendiary bomb 燃烧弹

petrol bomb 汽油弹

Molotov cocktail 燃烧瓶

IED (improvised explosive device) 自制炸弹

mechanical IED 机械原理起爆自制爆炸装置

electrical IED 电起爆自制爆炸装置

beeper-ignited bomb 寻呼机引爆炸弹

body bomb 人体炸弹

car bomb 汽车炸弹

detonator/blasting cap 雷管

firecracker 爆竹

hairspray/hair gel 发胶

banana oil (used as a paint solvent) 香蕉水

petrol/gasoline/gas 汽油

kerosene 煤油
ethyl alcohol/alcohol 酒精

B. 自制炸弹主要零部件名称

detonator/blasting cap 雷管
electrical detonator 电雷管
prime explosive 主爆药
booster 助爆药
shrapnel（填充在爆炸物里的铁钉等）杀伤物
fuse 导火索
wire 导线
leg wire of the detonator 电雷管脚线
igniter 引爆装置
inductance 感应器
catapult 弹射器
initiator 起爆器
battery 电池
collapse circuit initiator 继电器起爆器
timer 定时器
resistor/capacitor timer 电阻/电容定时器
switch 开关
mercury switch 水银开关
toggle switch 拨动式开关
pressure release switch 压缩反弹开关
tension release switch 张力释放开关
rocker switch 簧压摇杆开关
lever switch 拉杆开关
slide switch 滑动开关
magneto-electric switch 电磁开关
tape（固定用）胶带
wrapping 外包装

附录 II 公安机关各级领导职务英文名称

Minister of Public Security 公安部部长

Executive Vice Minister of Public Security 公安部常务副部长

Vice Minister of Public Security 公安部副部长

Secretary of Commission of Disciplinary Inspection, Inspector General, MPS 公安部纪律检查委员会书记、督察长

Director General of Political Department, MPS 公安部政治部主任

Assistant Minister of Public Security 公安部部长助理

Director of… Provincial Public Security Department 省公安厅厅长

Director of… Autonomous Region's Public Security Department 自治区公安厅厅长

Director/Chief of… Municipal Public Security Bureau 直辖市公安局局长

Director/Chief of…Municipal (Prefecture's) Public Security Bureau 市（地、自治州、盟）公安局局长

Director/Chief of…Sub-Bureau of…Public Security Bureau 市辖区公安分局局长

Director/Chief of… County (City, Banner) Public Security Bureau 县（市、旗）公安局局长

Deputy Director/Chief 副局长

Director of Police Sub-Station 公安派出所所长

附录 III　涉外机构名称

Embassy 大使馆

Consulate General 总领事馆

Consulate 领事馆

the Public Security Ministry 公安部

Agencies Directly Under the Public Security Ministry 公安部直属机构

General Office 办公厅

Supervision Department 警务督察局

Personnel & Training Department 人事训练局

Public Relations Department 宣传局

National Immigration Administration 国家移民管理局

Food and Drug Crime Investigation Bureau 食品药品犯罪侦查局

Economic Crime Investigation Department 经济犯罪侦查局

Public Order Administration Department 治安管理局

Criminal Investigation Department 刑事侦查局

Public Information Network Security Supervision Department 公共信息网络安全监察局

Penitentiary Administration Department 监所管理局

Traffic Control Department 交通管理局

Legal Affairs Department 法制局

International Cooperation Department 国际合作局

Logistics and Finance Department 装备财务局

Drug Control Department 禁毒局

Science & Technology Department 科技局

Counter-Terrorism Department 反恐局

Info-communications Department 信息通信局

the Provincial Public Security Department 省公安厅

the Municipal Public Security Bureau 市公安局

the County Public Security Bureau 县公安局

Public Security Sub-Bureau 公安分局

Traffic Police Station 交警队

Police Station/Police Sub-Station 派出所

Police Box 治安岗亭

Detention House 拘留所

the Division of Alien Administration 外国人管理处

the Administration Division of Exit and Entry 出入境管理处

Port Visa Office 口岸签证办公室

Frontier Inspection Post 边防检查站

the Quarantine Office 检疫站

Health and Quarantine Office 卫生检疫局

the Customs 海关

Foreign Affairs Office 外事办公室

附录 IV 服务设施名称

reception room/reception desk 接待处

inquiry desk/information room/information desk 问讯处

checkroom/left-luggage office/depository 行李寄存处

currency exchange 货币兑换处

the lost and found 报失及拾物招领处

parking lot 停车处

bicycle park 自行车存车处

guest room 客房

gymnasium 健身房

swimming pool 游泳池

billiard room 台球室

dining room 餐厅

cafeteria 自助餐厅

restaurant 饭店

bar 酒吧

restroom/bathroom 洗手间

W. C. (water closet)/toilets 厕所

附录 V 中国警衔名称

General Commissioner 总警监
Deputy General Commissioner 副总警监
Commissioner First Class 一级警监
Commissioner Second Class 二级警监
Commissioner Third Class 三级警监
Supervisor First Class 一级警督
Supervisor Second Class 二级警督
Supervisor Third Class 三级警督
Superintendent First Class 一级警司
Superintendent Second Class 二级警司
Superintendent Third Class 三级警司
Constable First Class 一级警员
Constable Second Class 二级警员

附录 VI 应急电话

Emergency Police Service：110
报警电话：110
Telephone Directory Inquiry：114
查号台：114
Fire Alarm Service：119
火警电话：119
First Aid Service：120
急救电话：120
Traffic Accident Alarm Service：122
交通事故报警台：122

附录 VII 证件名称

passport 护照

ordinary passport 普通护照

diplomatic passport 外交护照

service passport/passport for public affairs/business passport 公务护照

special passport 特殊护照

visa 签证

ordinary visa 普通签证

on-the-spot visa 口岸签证

diplomatic visa 外交签证

service visa 公务签证

courtesy visa 礼遇签证

business visa 商务签证

one, two, or multiple entry visa 一次二次或多次入境签证

re-entry visa 返回签证

visa D 定居签证（D 字签证）

visa Z 工作签证（Z 字签证）

visa X 学生签证（X 字签证）

visa F 访问签证（F 字签证）

visa L/tourist visa/visit visa 旅游、探亲签证（L 字签证）

visa G/transit visa 过境签证（G 字签证）

visa C 乘务签证（C 字签证）

visa J-1 常住记者签证（J-1 字签证）

visa J-2 短期记者签证（J-2 字签证）

health certificate 健康证明书
vaccination certificate/inoculation certificate 预防接种证书
foreign expert certificate 外国专家证
business license 营业执照
residence certificate/residence card 居留证
temporary residence card 临时居留证
resident representative card 常住代表证
press card 记者证
accreditation card 委派证
letter of admission/admission notice 入学通知书
letter of invitation 邀请信
the official letter from the Chinese host institution 中方接待单位出具的公函
ticket/admission ticket 入场券
travel permit for aliens 外国人旅行证
employment certificate/work permit/working card 劳动就业许可证
confirmation of reporting the loss of property 财物报失证明
birth certificate 出生证
death certificate 死亡证明
the cremation certificate 火化证明
the preservation certificate 防腐证书
coffin exit permit 棺柩出境许可
vehicle registration 车辆登记证
automobile insurance card 机动车保险证
vehicle safety check paper 车检证
driver's license 驾驶证
international driver's license 国际驾驶证

附录 VIII 常用涉外法律法规名称

the Nationality Law of China 中国国籍法

Exit and Entry Administration Law of the People's Republic of China 中华人民共和国出境入境管理法

Regulation of the People's Republic of China on the Administration of the Entry and Exit of Foreign Nationals 中华人民共和国外国人入境出境管理条例

Law of the People's Republic of China on Penalties for Administration of Public Security 中华人民共和国治安管理处罚法

Provisions on the Administration of Religious Activities of Aliens within the Territory of the People's Republic of China 中华人民共和国境内外国人宗教活动管理规定

Regulations Concerning Foreign Journalists and Permanent Offices of Foreign News Agencies 中华人民共和国外国记者和外国新闻机构管理条例

Law of the People's Republic of China on Assemblies, Processions and Demonstrations (2009 Amendment) 中华人民共和国集会游行示威法（2009修正）

Road Traffic Safety Law of the People's Republic of China (2011 Amendment) 中华人民共和国道路交通安全法（2011修正）

Regulation on the Implementation of the Road Traffic Safety Law of the People's Republic of China (2017 Revision) 中华人民共和国道路交通安全法实施条例（2017修订）

Regulations of the People's Republic of China Concerning Diplomatic Privileges

and Immunities 中华人民共和国外交特权与豁免条例
Regulations of the People's Republic of China Concerning Consular Privileges and Immunities [Effective] 中华人民共和国领事特权与豁免条例
Vienna Convention on Diplomatic Relations 维也纳外交关系条约
Vienna Convention on Consular Relations 维也纳领事关系条约

附录 IX 常见涉外处罚名称

warning 警告

to suspense a licence 吊扣执照

to revoke a licence 吊销执照

forfeiture/confiscation 没收

restitution 赔偿，归还

fine 罚款

detention 拘留

to shorten one's period of stay in China 缩短在华停留期限

order to leave the country within a specified time 限期出境

deportation 驱逐出境

expatriation 遣返

fixed-term imprisonment 有期徒刑

life imprisonment 无期徒刑

附录 X　各国警察常用武器装备

protective equipment 防护装置

shield 盾牌

helmet 头盔

protective mask 防护面具

goggles 护目镜

body armor 防弹服

first aid packet 急救包

restraining devices 控制器具

handcuffs 手铐

flex cuffs 收缩手铐

capture net 捕捉网

portable vehicle arresting barrier 便携式机动车路障

sticky foam 粘合泡沫

non-lethal weapons/less-lethal weapons 非致命武器

baton 警棍

water cannon 水炮；高压水枪

stun gun 电击枪

Taser 泰瑟枪（两个弹着点分别为正负两极的电击枪）

shock belt 电击带

bean bag（用以驱散人群的内装鸟枪子弹或砂粒的）豆弹小袋

pellet 橡皮子弹

stun-grenade 眩晕弹

flashbang 闪光震爆弹

laser dazzler 激光耀眼器
long range acoustical device 长波听觉烦扰器
incapacitant 失能剂，晕昏剂
aerosol 喷雾器
pepper spray/CN/CS/OC 胡椒气喷雾器
gas grenade 气弹
canister 气雾罐
tear-gas 催泪弹
mace 梅斯催泪毒气
hand-held aerosol tear-gas projector 手提式喷雾催泪瓦斯发射器
lethal weapons 致命武器
pistol 手枪
revolver 左轮手枪
semiautomatic pistol 半自动手枪
rifle 步枪
automatic rifle 自动步枪
shotgun 散弹枪
submachine gun 冲锋枪
special surveillance equipment 特殊检测设备
stethoscope 电子偷听器
metal detector 金属探测器
explosive detector 爆炸物探测器
night-vision sights 夜视仪
voice monitoring equipment 噪音监测仪
SWAT mirror 特警观察镜
breaching tools 突破工具
glass cutter 玻璃切割器
circular saw 圆形锯
chain saw 链锯
bolt cutter 门闩/窗闩剪断器

sledgehammer 破门锤

hydraulics 液压器

whisper mike 微声耳麦（耳语麦克风）

handheld radio 无线电对讲机

walkie-talkie 步话机

laptop 手提式电脑

mobile fingerprint scanner 手提式指纹扫描器

附录 XI　国际刑警组织通报

Red Notice: To seek the location and arrest of wanted persons wanted for prosecution or to serve a sentence.

红色通报：为逮捕或临时拘捕并引渡在逃犯而发出的通报。

Yellow Notice: To help locate missing persons, often minors, or to help identify persons who are unable to identify themselves.

黄色通报：通报查找失踪人员（通常是未成年人），或帮助身份不明人识别身份。

Blue Notice: To collect additional information about a person's identity, location, or activities in relation to a crime.

蓝色通报：通报收集某一犯罪活动相关人员的身份、位置或行为活动的信息。

Black Notice: To seek information on unidentified bodies.

黑色通报：通报收集无名尸的信息情况。

Green Notice: To provide a warning about a person's criminal activities, where the person is considered to be a possible threat to public safety.

绿色通报：通报发布犯罪分子的犯罪活动及公共安全可能受到威胁的区域等相关预警信息。

Orange Notice: To warn of an event, a person, an object, or a process representing a serious and imminent threat to public safety.

橙色通报：预警通报严重威胁公共安全的犯罪行为、犯罪分子、危险物品或犯罪过程。

Purple Notice: To seek or provide information on modus operandi, objects, devices and concealment methods used by criminals.

紫色通报：收集或发布犯罪分子使用的作案手段、涉案危险品、作案工具和藏匿犯罪事实所用方法等相关信息而发出的通报。

INTERPOL-United Nations Security Council Special Notice: Issued for groups and individuals who are the targets of UN Security Council Sanctions Committees.

国际刑警——联合国安理会特别通报：专门发布联合国安理会制裁委员会制裁的犯罪团伙或个人的信息。

参 考 文 献

1. 刘振江. 警官实用英语口语 [M]. 北京：机械工业出版社，2010.
2. 吕杨. 涉外警务英语口语 [M]. 武汉：武汉大学出版社，2015.
3. 岳洪锦. 实用警务英语 [M]. 北京：对外经济贸易大学出版，2014.
4. 曹冬月，孟志敏，张璐. 实战警务英语 [M]. 北京：民族出版社，2015.
5. 张慧德，沈一波. 公安外国人管理 [M]. 北京：中国人民大学出版社，2015.
6. 卫芳菊，袁明忠. 反恐怖行动与恐怖案例分析 [M]. 北京：中国书籍出版社，2015.